What Others Are Saying About Dr. Dale Fife and *The Light Giver*…

As I finished reading *The Light Giver*, a resounding "Wow!" came out of my mouth. The revelation that broke open in my spirit filled me with expectant hope for future encounters in that "secret place"! Dr. Fife is truly a twenty-first-century "son of Issachar." With anointing flowing through his pen, he opens portals that transcend time and space. I found myself walking with wonder and awe in the middle of his God visions. My heart was ignited with a burning to run through the walls of distraction and spend time with the Lover of my soul. The understanding of time, light, and history that Dr. Fife shares will inspire you to transcend this world into the dimensions of kingdom living. The God-given illuminations serve as a clarion call to emerge from the shadows and live in the glorious presence of our Lord.

—Rev. Janet Shell
Worship to the Nations, Bradenton, Florida

Every once in a while, you find a book that goes beyond fascinating to inspiring. It makes you want to put the book down, not because it loses your attention but because you can no longer refrain from doing the very thing the author is describing. This is such a book. The visions and wisdom shared by Dr. Fife in *The Light Giver* will captivate you. More important, you will find yourself wanting to run to the "secret place" to enjoy Jesus for yourself! From the beginning of the book, describing the excitement of serving as a temple priest, to the final pages, in which Dr. Fife shares keys to resting in God's presence and hearing Him speak, I realized how easily I get distracted from the main thing. All I want to do is run to the "secret place," again and again!

—Weston Brooks
Senior Pastor, River of Life Christian Fellowship, Tolland, Connecticut

I often dream of finding the perfect getaway weekend, during which I can reconnect with God and become still long enough to hear Him speak to my heart. But such times are hard to find. *The Light Giver* is truly that kind of experience—a spiritual vacation, right in your hand! If you need an encounter with your Papa and a fresh perspective on your life, you will want to go on this adventure with Dr. Fife. Whether you are looking for solid biblical teaching or a Holy Spirit-led confirmation of what God is stirring within your heart, you will find it in these pages!

—*Elizabeth Enlow*
Senior Pastor, Daystar Church, Atlanta, Georgia

I so enjoyed *The Light Giver* that I have been rereading parts of it again. It is both timely and necessary, and the body of Christ is richer for Dale's work. My wife and I were deeply impacted by his first book, *The Secret Place*. Now, once again, he has written a compelling and needful book for the church. In a broad and multifaceted approach, Dale deals with the issue of how God reveals Himself to us as individuals today. This modern-day mystic unlocks the experience for which each one of us was redeemed—namely, intimacy with God and revelation for life's situations. Dale's deep and powerful assessment of this vital topic will enable you, regardless of your level of understanding of this subject, to be challenged spiritually and intellectually.

—*Dale Schlafer*
President, Center for World Revival & Awakening, Bradenton, Florida
Author, *Revival 101*

A central ethos of the human spirit is to seek the basis of reality. The Christian worldview boldly states that there is but one true reality. *The Light Giver* reveals how intimacy with the Creator can be achieved by revelation, vision, and discernment through the light of Christ. It is a prescription for those who struggle to draw nearer to the true source of light. Rather than just another volume on polemic theology, *The Light Giver* is a captivating unveiling of Dr. Fife's journey toward a closer relationship with the Author of true reality, a journey that God intends for all of us to embark upon.

—*Thomas Warren, M.D.*
Charlotte, North Carolina

In *The Light Giver*, Dr. Fife skillfully helps us to see light as foundational to godly revelation, time, and wisdom. As an artisan, he frames Scriptures and accents their light to guide us progressively to see more and more from God's point of view. Artfully, he woos us to our own "secret place" and coaches us in how to spend time in intimacy with God—the secret to fruitful relationship and service with our Creator.

—*Keith E. Yoder, Ed.D.*
Founder and President, Teaching the Word Ministries

Dr. Fife doesn't write from secondhand information. The passion you experience when you read one of his books comes directly from his personal and intimate encounters with God. He has done it again in *The Light Giver*. As you read this book, you will see characters from the Bible come alive; you will be made to feel as if you are actually in the tabernacle; and each chapter will draw you deeper into the presence of God. If you are desperate to know God in a new and living way, you will be absolutely captivated by *The Light Giver*.

—*Mark Gidley*
Pastor, Faith Worship Center, Glencoe, Alabama

The Light Giver is another spiritual gem being given to the body of Christ! When I read it, my passion for greater intimacy with God was ignited. *The Light Giver* has absolutely energized the flame in my soul for God's presence. Dr. Fife has a genuine gift for bringing Scripture to life in such a way that you feel as though you are present as it unfolds. In this book, he takes you on a fascinating journey through time—from eternity past to eternity present and into eternity future—bringing you face-to-face with the wisdom of the ages. This is a must-read for anyone who wants his light to shine brightly in the midst of darkness.

—*Apostle Edward J. Kurdziel*
Pure Heart Church, Grand Rapids, Michigan

As I began to read *The Light Giver*, I was immediately drawn into the atmosphere of God's house. As Dr. Fife shared his personal account of "Neglecting the Light," I began to weep and cry out, "Yes, Lord—this is where I am! This is why I am here!" From that point on, I was transfixed by the pages of this book. In Dr. Fife's teachings on the tribe of Issachar and the history of time, we see the importance of seeking God in a more intimate way. This book will bring you to that place.

—*Timothy Whitton*
Senior Pastor, New Life Fellowship, Plainville, Connecticut

As you read this book, you will discover a vivid journey through history, travel through time, and encounter hidden treasures of wisdom that will guide you to the presence of Him who is Light. This book is a must-read for those who are passionate for God's presence.

—*Jim D. Price*
Senior Pastor, Heritage Fellowship, Jefferson City, Tennessee

Dr. Fife's book is an interesting account of his journey into the realm of the Holy Spirit and fellowship with the Father. It is a well-researched account of his experience and the lessons that he learned. Beyond his own experience, Dr. Fife encourages all of us to enter our own "secret place" and to come forth as lights in a darkened world. His descriptions of the tabernacle and the nature of light are more than worth the price of the book.

—*Charles Simpson*
Author and Bible teacher, Charles Simpson Ministries, Mobile, Alabama

From the first page of *The Light Giver*, I was gripped by the Holy Spirit! What tremendous insight God has given to Dale as he unfolds each encounter and experience with God through the pages of this book. Be prepared to have your world shaken. You will be ignited as you read this book!

—*Dr. Brian Simmons*
Founder, Stairway Ministries, Wichita, Kansas

If you love God's presence, you will be fascinated by *The Light Giver*, another pearl in the collection of revelatory works by Dr. Dale Fife. These pearls always return to their core message: the "secret place" of encounter with God. Here, you will discover how history, time, and science all give witness to the Light Giver Himself. It will take you on an adventure that feels like fiction, informs like a textbook, and inspires like the Holy Spirit. When the book is over, the adventure is not, because *The Light Giver* serves as a catalyst, propelling readers to embark on their own adventures with Him. This is a book for the hungry heart and the scholar alike that will teach, challenge, and excite the desire for more of Him.

—*Mandy Adendorff*
Artist, evangelist, teacher, and writer

This book quickly pulls the reader into the adventurous domain of knowing and experiencing God. Dale uses the power of story to kindle within us a vision for what intimacy with God could really be like. Open the curtain and step inside.

—*Bob Sorge*
Author, *Exploring Worship*

The Light Giver is a book desperately needed by God's people today. Like a multi-faceted diamond, it contains numerous glistening, light-reflecting elements. It's a supernatural revelation, but it's more than that. It's an incredibly insightful Bible study, but it's more than that, too. It's a spiritual memoir of Dale's own spiritual journey. I can safely say that you've never read a book like this one. In addition to learning things about the pathway to the heart of God and His biblical pattern in the wilderness tabernacle, you'll glean remarkable insights from the realms of history, science, and philosophy. Through this book, *The Light Giver* Himself issues a powerful, personal invitation for you to come deeper into His presence than you've ever gone before. Accept His invitation, and your life will never be the same!

—*Jim Buchan*
Pastor and Founder, Crosslink Ministries, Charlotte, North Carolina

This book will take you to a spiritual place of intimacy with God that all of us thirst for. Dale's view, and the information he reveals, will astound you. This is more than intuition; it is the revelation of a seer whose discernment is clearly anointed by the Holy Spirit. Read and be blessed!

—Dr. Ron MacDonald
Trinity Ministry Institute, Pinellas Park, Florida

When I received a copy of *The Light Giver*, I anticipated taking only a few short days to read it in its entirety. Within the first few pages, however, I quickly discovered that the valuable content of this book required my full attention. I relished the opportunity to digest and meditate upon the information therein. To put it simply, Dr. Fife has undoubtedly struck gold. This book is not merely the gathering of information; rather, it brings precious truths of revelation to the surface.

Not only is the content of *The Light Giver* rich and unearthing, but its challenge to the reader to be a carrier of God's light is written in a distinct, refreshing voice, as well. If nothing else, we must shine in the midst of a wicked and perverse generation for all to see the glories of the gospel. The Creator who said, "Let there be light!" has provided the way for *all* to partake of His glory.

I highly recommend Dr. Dale Fife's *Light Giver*. I am confident that readers will be equipped, enriched, and empowered.

—Dr. Leon van Rooyen
Founder and President, Global Ministries and Relief

Dr. Dale Fife once again has taken us to a deeper place in the realm of the kingdom. Reading *The Light Giver* is like taking a journey with the Holy Spirit. The words and images take us into a deeper place in the spiritual realm. This book will lead you to a supernatural encounter with the One who is Light.

I know Dale is an authentic man of prayer whose passion is intimacy with God. If you want to be motivated and need some practical help in your spiritual communion with Jesus, this book is a treasure that you will read over and over.

—Rev. Barbara G. Lachance
Founder and Director, Spirit Wind Healing Center, Stonington, Connecticut

Dr. Fife, I have greatly enjoyed reading your first three books. They are all truly inspiring. When I heard you were writing a new book, I waited with great anticipation for its printing. *The Light Giver* is on a whole new level—we are timekeepers! My understanding of light and time has risen to a new dimension. I want to thank you for the thoughts you have put to paper and encourage you to continue writing. *The Light Giver* is a challenging and inspiring light that shines, releasing revelation into the army of God for the His kingdom.

—*Reuben Beachy*
Director, Christian Leadership Institute, Sarasota, Florida

I love this book! I can sit and get caught up in a story told by Dr. Fife any day. Dr. Dale Fife is one of the two best storytellers I've ever encountered. Adding to the story's equation, the fact that this revelatory story was experienced with Jesus gives the term *storyteller* a whole new meaning. This book, like the others authored by Dr. Fife, is as down-to-earth as it is heavenly. Biblical principles such as our calling to be "light carriers" are depicted in such a way that anyone can understand them. Read this book, and you will be strengthened and transformed through encounters with the Light Giver.

—*Priscilla Zananiri*
Cofounder, Abana Ministries

The Light Giver by Dr. Dale Fife extends an invitation for us to join the author's sacred moments of solitary times with God and experience firsthand the intimate feelings and precise instructions that are found there. It responds to the apostle Paul's prayer for us in Ephesians 1:17, "*That the God of our Lord Jesus Christ, the Father of glory, may give unto you the spirit of wisdom and revelation in the knowledge of Him,*" and it gives us a glimpse into the mysteries and secrets of God's heart. More than just information and insight, Dale's writing opens a spiritual doorway to experience the atmosphere of God's presence through a rich tapestry of living drama, validated by the Word of God, and bringing spiritual transformation.

I was introduced to Dr. Fife through his earlier book *The Secret Place*. His passion for God's presence and his father's heart resonated in my spirit. *The Light Giver* continues the journey and will ignite your hungry heart to awaken from slumber and seek a more intimate relationship with God. In these perilous times, the church needs prophetic insight and strategy with demonstration of the fire of God. As you read this book, allow the Light Giver, Christ Himself, to ignite the wick of your lampstand and refresh the oil of His Holy Spirit in order to make your flame burn bright again.

—*Phil Derstine*
Pastor, Christian Retreat Family Church
Bradenton, Florida

While reading the first portion of Dr Fife's *Light Giver*, I thought it would be much in the same vein as the other books he has written. I have loved all of his books. They have been very beneficial for me personally, not to mention a joy to read. I love the way he writes. However, in *The Light Giver*, I discovered a new dimension. Dale gives us a depth of intellect wonderfully combined with the mystical dynamics of a seer. This combination is extraordinary! At the end of each segment, I could not put the book down. I wanted to see what he was going to say in the next revelation.

I know that many will be blessed by God as they receive the truth and be encouraged in their own life to dwell with Him the secret place when they see the fruit and receive this challenge to experience the secret place.

It is with great joy that I recommend this book to every Christian. Thank you, Dale, for this amazing read. I look forward to what God has for us next, through you.

—*Dr. Don Richter*
President, Harvest Preparation International Ministries
Sarasota, Florida

The
LIGHT
GIVER

The
LIGHT
GIVER

Dr. Dale A. Fife

WHITAKER
HOUSE

Author Photograph by: Lisa Price ♦ www.lisapricephotography.com

THE LIGHT GIVER:
Discovering God's Uncommon Wisdom

Mountain Top Global Ministries
12631 30th Street Circle East
Parrish, Florida 34219
E-mail: MnTopMin@aol.com; PastorDF@aol.com
Web site: www.SonPointeChurch.org

ISBN: 978-1-60374-576-5
Printed in the United States of America
© 2013 by Dr. Dale Arthur Fife

Whitaker House
1030 Hunt Valley Circle
New Kensington, PA 15068
www.whitakerhouse.com

Library of Congress Cataloging-in-Publication Data (Pending)

1 2 3 4 5 6 7 8 9 10 11 ⩔ 20 19 18 17 16 15 14 13

This book is dedicated to Brandon, Aaron, Brianne, Anthony, Joanna, and Asa.

You are a source of abundant joy in our lives
and the delight of a proud grandma and grandpa.

You are greatly loved.

Always seek the Light Giver!

CONTENTS

FOREWORD

Several years ago, I was given a copy of Dr. Dale Fife's book *The Secret Place*. As a pastor, I am often given books to read, but this one was different from most. This one so impacted me that I encouraged our entire church to read it. Since then, I have led small group discussions about the ways in which readers have been prodded by the writing into the very presence of God. Dr. Fife's books are gifts from our "Papa" to our generation, calling us into encounters with His heart in ways we must learn to access if we are going to fulfill our unique place in advancing the kingdom of God.

The Light Giver is another walk with this prophetic scribe on a well-traveled path into God's presence. To read his picturesque descriptions of what he has found is to know the peace, joy, and rest that he personally carries, because he has learned to prioritize *his* secret place. I would like to share some things with you that began to stir in me as I read this most recent adventure. I hope they will help to prepare you for your introduction to *The Light Giver*.

Imagine you had a father who loved you perfectly all the days of your life and had only good intentions toward you—a father who loved knowing you and gave you full access to him so that you could know him, too. Imagine that your father had an enemy who loathed him so deeply that this enemy would do whatever it took to inflict pain on him. Enraged by the reality that he couldn't actually harm your father, this enemy, like any worthy villain, switched to "Plan B": harm that which is most valuable to the heart of this good father—his sons and daughters. If this enemy couldn't touch the father, he would at least ruin the father's reputation among the ones he loved by destroying his good name and convincing the objects of his affection that he wasn't who he seemed to be and that he definitely shouldn't be trusted. If this enemy was persistent enough, he might even be capable of convincing a good many of the sons and daughters that this perfect father didn't exist—or that, *if* he existed, he didn't really care about them, leaving them to figure out life as orphans until he felt like coming to get them.

You don't have to imagine this scenario. It is our current reality. We do, in fact, have a perfect Father. And there is an enemy who knows that the Father's one desire is for His children to know Him. That is all the Father has ever wanted— to be known. The battle has always been over intimacy in its purest state, between the One who *is* love and the ones who were created to *receive* love. This battle had its front lines in the garden of Eden, where we walked and talked face-to-face with this Father and knew Him as He knows us—there was no separation. We knew our value, and the proof of that value was our assignment: to be like Him, being partnered with Him and having dominion over all of His creation. One bite of the supernatural fruit from the tree of the knowledge of good and evil set into motion questions that would echo in every human from Adam and Eve forward: "Is He good or is He evil?" and "Can He be trusted?" Nothing undermines true intimacy like doubt inspired by the mind of reason that makes calculations based on man's limited perspective of his circumstances.

Generations later, the battle continues to rage as God's children, young and old, wonder if they are loved and valued. We, the sons and daughters who couldn't be more loved or valued, live as orphans with rejection complexes that cause us to look at every circumstance as proof of whether our Father loves us rather than going straight to Him to experience His love for ourselves. The strongest of these orphans take the lead in every area of culture and offer up their best solutions to the problems at hand. They strategize and learn to figure it out alone, making the best of whatever life means to them, hoping to find love and some proof of their value.

Recently, I heard that the majority of the world's most well-known leaders throughout history were orphans. Our world and the cultures of every nation have been greatly impacted by men and women who grew up facing the knowledge that they were not cared for and, therefore, had to take care of themselves.

Entire nations are governed and influenced by an "orphan mentality," which urges people to figure out life by themselves. Even nations like the United States of America, founded by those who believed there is indeed a God, show evidence in every area of culture that we have done it our own way. We haven't looked to the Father who loves us and who, out of a desire for intimacy with us, has given us access to all of His supernatural solutions for our problems. So, we live out of a false reality that tells us that if God exists, He doesn't really care about every area of life. If He exists, He watches from a distance to see how we'll do without Him.

Nothing could be further from the truth. The truth is seen only by the Spirit in the spirit realm, which, by the way, is more real than this earthly realm. But you won't know that until you go there for yourself! You won't know that God can be known and experienced until you dare to believe that He *wants* to be known.

Intimacy is a choice. It requires time and desire. Intimacy with the Father produces the knowledge of God, in which you know that He is good and can be trusted. We can live evaluating the circumstances of our lives and riding the waves of doubt and debate like a little girl holding a flower, plucking the petals to discover if "he loves me" or "he loves me not." Or, we can insist on going straight to the Source. The heart of this Father provides the healing and provision for every ache and craving humanity has ever had—every longing *you* have ever had.

The book you are about to read will escort you to the most enticing door you have ever seen: the entrance into the very heart of your Father. I think God handpicked Dr. Fife—a man who prefers to be called "Dad" by those who know him—to deliver this personal invitation for you to come into the Father's heart, where the love and value you were created to receive await you. God chose Dale, not only to teach you how to win the battle for intimacy, but also to lead the way by example. Like every good teacher, this dad will be teaching you without your even realizing it!

Have you ever known someone who had such a depth of character and a walk with God that you wished you could just sit with him and learn how he got there? Well, God is about to fill that very desire of your heart. Dale Fife is one of those rare spiritual dads who has taken the time to invite you into the places it took him a lifetime to discover, not to impress or awe you but to inspire you and teach you how to get there yourself.

Habakkuk chapter 2 tells us that the *"nations weary themselves in vain"* (verse 13) but that *"the earth will be filled with the knowledge of the glory of the*

Lord" (verse 14). Remember when Moses asked to see God's glory, and God hid him in the rock so that His goodness might pass before Moses? One aspect of the glory of the Lord is His goodness. One day, the nations will no longer strive as orphans, doing things their own way—in vain. We are receiving an unshakable kingdom that will reflect the fact that we have a Father whose ways are motivated by love, and love alone.

The knowledge of this good Father and His glory cannot be displayed to the world if we don't first see it and taste of it ourselves. Do you yearn to find a love and discover an assignment that will fill your need for value, once and for all? Do you desire to be so thoroughly convinced of your value that you have enough to give away? Determine right now that the book you hold is the beginning of the encounter you always hoped to have with the Father. Determine to win the battle for intimacy. And may He bless you abundantly as you read *The Light Giver*.

—Johnny Enlow
Senior Pastor, Daystar Church, Atlanta, Georgia
Author, *The Seven Mountain Prophecy* and *The Seven Mountain Mantle*

INTRODUCTION

The Dream

I receive so many e-mails that I can't possibly read them all. The delete button on my computer keyboard is worn smooth from my attempts to eliminate spam and focus on what is important. But one message stood out among the myriad kind remarks, encouraging words, and questions from God-seekers. It arrived on January 15, 2008, with the familiar greeting, "You've got mail." The sender, after expressing how much my books had helped her, informed me that she'd had a dream about me. She explained, "I dreamt that you wrote another book. I saw the cover lit up with blazing light. The title was The Secret of the Golden Fire."

Although her message is long gone from my computer memory, I could not delete it from my thoughts and my heart. It had lodged itself within my spirit. Every now and then, it would resurface in my conscious mind. *That's interesting, but it will never happen,* I always thought, and I'd dismiss the notion as quickly as it had come to mind. I continued to disregard both the message and the messenger as just another one of those well-intentioned modern-day prophets who missed it. Then, the vision came!

The Vision

Prophetic visions are not planned or scheduled like an appointment. They come according to God's timing and at His discretion. They are initiated by the Holy Spirit, and, when they arrive, the revelation that ensues is eye-opening and life-changing. Revelation brings wisdom and understanding.

People often ask me why God speaks to me the way He does, with such scope and depth. It's true that not everyone receives prophetic visions that require an entire book to describe. The only answer I can offer is that it is not because I have attained some great level of spiritual maturity. I am no different from you. Besides, spiritual maturity is not based on gifting; it is based upon our degree of obedience. I can't speak for you, but I have a long way to go in this arena. Neither can I point to my spiritual passion and faith to exercise the prophetic ministry as the reason. The apostle Paul encouraged all of us to do that. I am also sure that it isn't because of my lifelong study of the Bible. While all of these things are important, they do not qualify us to receive revelation.

I really believe the reason God speaks to me as He does is simply because I make myself available to Him. It is my obedience to Jesus' directive:

When you pray, you shall not be like the hypocrites. For they love to pray standing in the synagogues and on the corners of the streets, that they may be seen by men. Assuredly, I say to you, they have their reward. But you, when you pray, go into your room, and when you have shut your door, pray to your Father who is in the secret place; and your Father who sees in secret will reward you openly. (Matthew 6:5–6)

The secret is *"the secret place."* Make yourself available, and the resulting blessing will be evident to others.

And so it was that, one day, I entered into my secret place, not really knowing what the Father had to say to me. One thing I was certain of, though: He *was* waiting for me there. He always is! The vision appeared instantly, and I was transported in the Spirit to a time and a place thousands of years in the past for what was to become a journey of revelation. God wanted to introduce me to an ancient priest who had discovered the secret of the golden fire. This was not just a casual meeting but an in-depth encounter with a man who, from firsthand experience, understood prophetic revelation and the wisdom it brings. My life has been forever changed. The account of this prophetic journey, and the revelation it brought, begins in chapter one. The consequence of this insightful vision set me on a search to understand the significance of light and its power and influence in our lives.

Fire and Light

Who could forget the amazing scene from the movie *Castaway* in which Tom Hanks, his hands raw and bleeding from an exhausting all-day attempt to ignite a few twigs with friction from a spinning stick, finally creates a spark and the resulting wisp of smoke? The carefully husbanded ember grows into a blazing bonfire that lights up the beach and sends smoke swirling into the night sky. Hanks dances and twirls around the flames in his loincloth like David before the ark, his hands raised to the heavens. "Fire! I made fire!" he boasts, pounding his chest with glee as he jubilantly gazes up at the ascending storm of sparks. If God had been watching, I think He would have laughed in amusement at the exaltation over human effort.

In comparison, can you imagine the explosive scene when God said, *"Let there be light"* (Genesis 1:3) and the entire cosmos went nuclear? Hanks would have knelt on the beach wonderstruck when God set the lights in the heavens—the moon to rule the night and the sun to rule the day. (See Genesis 1:17–18.) To this day, firestorms on the surface of the sun still emit such power and solar energy that their influence interrupts our electrical and communication systems on earth, while the UV rays burn our skin. That's what I call making fire!

Fire and light are inseparable. They capture our imagination and never cease to amaze and astound us. Tell children not to play with fire, and they will ignore you. They are fascinated! Light itself remains an enigma hidden in the mind of God, its Creator. God is both a light and a consuming fire. He is the Light Giver. We cannot understand the secret of the golden fire without going to Him who is the ultimate Source of light.

Think the Unthinkable

Moses encountered God in fire and light at the burning bush. (See Exodus 3.) The priests of God ministered behind the closed curtain of the tabernacle, where only the chosen could bear the penetrating rays of the light emanating from the golden lampstand, as a column of fire-born energy swirled and whistled above their heads throughout the night. The prophets and seers understood the secret of the golden fire, and the sons of Issachar walked in its enlightenment. God wants you and me to walk in this same supernatural revelation! He wants us to transcend human limitations in order to access the supernatural realm of the Spirit. He invites us into His marvelous, blazing light.

Paul's passionate desire for Christians of all eras is that we might comprehend the incomprehensible. He wrote,

> *For this reason, because I have heard of your faith in the Lord Jesus and your love toward all the saints (the people of God), I do not cease to give thanks for you, making mention of you in my prayers. [For I always pray to] the God of our Lord Jesus Christ, the Father of glory, that He may grant you a spirit of wisdom and revelation [of insight into mysteries and secrets] in the [deep and intimate] knowledge of Him, by having the eyes of your heart flooded with light, so that you can know and understand the hope to which He has called you, and how rich is His glorious inheritance in the saints (His set-apart ones).* (Ephesians 1:15–18 AMP)

A Kingdom Scribe

Jesus said, *"Every scribe instructed concerning the kingdom of heaven is like a householder who brings out of his treasure things new and old"* (Matthew 13:52). I can identify with this Scripture. This has been my task. *The Light Giver* is filled with excerpts taken from the treasure chest of my personal journal, as I scribed them in His presence. Many times, I found myself frantically sketching the visions as they appeared in the Spirit before they vanished into eternity. There is fresh prophetic revelation and insight in the secret place.

You will also find wisdom from the past—lessons learned by former generations who discovered the secret of the golden fire. They were spiritual trailblazers who pioneered a pathway of illumination for us. And, of utmost importance, you will read countless signposts from Scripture, confirming that the pathway is correct. It is my prayer that you will not only be informed but also transformed as you experience His marvelous light. I have fulfilled my assignment. The scroll is complete. The results are in your hands.

Calling All God Seekers

The last days are upon us. We desperately need to discern the times we are living in and interpret history in the light of Him who is light. Only through His wisdom can we mark time and understand the meaning of the past, the significance of the present, and the potential of the future. We must have insights from the kingdom of heaven! God says that He will speak to us through dreams and visions.

> *And it shall come to pass in the last days, says God, that I will pour out of My Spirit on all flesh; your sons and your daughters shall prophecy, your young men shall see visions, your old men shall dream dreams.* (Acts 2:17)

It is time for us to listen carefully to what God is revealing in the Spirit. As His disciples, we need to make this a first priority. We must see beyond our human limitations.

Saint Anselm, the Archbishop of Canterbury, in his pursuit of an absolute verification that God exists, based his final proof on the paradoxical capacity of the mind to see beyond its own limits—to think the unthinkable. He wrote,

> Come now, insignificant man, fly for a moment from your affairs, escape for a little while from the tumult of your thoughts. Put aside now your weighty cares, and leave your wearisome toils. Abandon yourself for a little to God, and rest for a little while in Him. Enter into the inner chamber of your soul, shut out everything save God and what can be of help in your quest for Him, and having locked the door, seek Him out. Speak now, my whole heart, speak now to God: I seek Your countenance, O Lord, Your countenance I seek.[1]

Are you a God seeker? Then join me in the secret place. Open your spirit to receive fresh illumination. You are about to encounter the Light Giver and the secret of the golden fire.

PART ONE

THE SECRET OF
THE GOLDEN FIRE

"In Your light we see light."
—Psalm 36:9

1

NIGHT SHIFT IN GOD'S HOUSE

Without any advance notice of the Holy Spirit's approach, God invaded my space! Sudden and spontaneous prophetic revelation swirled in my head as if someone had thrown a switch and turned on a light inside of me. The vision flowed so freely, my fingertips raced across the keyboard to keep up with the information downloading into my spirit. The words tumbled out of my mind like a freshly uncapped spring of pure, crystal clear water cascading onto the page of the computer screen. I was no longer sitting dutifully in the sanctified atmosphere of my secret place. God was speaking!

Seer on Assignment

The world around me grew faint and distant. *I am seeing this*, I acknowledged with guarded caution and gratitude for God's presence. *But I shouldn't be surprised*, I reminded myself. *That's what seers do! We see by the Spirit.*

The vivid scene surrounded me as though I was sitting in an IMAX movie theater. "This is amazing!" I uttered, immersing myself in the unfolding panorama.

The distant noise of a bleating sheep drifted into the camp from somewhere behind me. The delightful sounds of children at play and the voices of women chatting over a charcoal fire in front of a nearby tent suggested that it was late afternoon. One of the women cautiously turned the spit over the fire pit. Supersized chunks of meat sizzled and crackled as their juices dripped and sputtered upon the white-hot coals. The woman rubbed her bloodshot eyes and squinted through the cloud of rising smoke. The pungent scents of roast lamb and garlic incensed the air with an unmistakable odor. It was so real that I licked my dry lips in anticipation.

I felt like a movie director searching for the stage-setting instructions on the first page of a screenplay. *This is not my study*, I reminded myself. *Where am I?* The time frame seemed like three thousand years ago. *This must be the wilderness encampment of Israel*, I concluded. *Of course*, I realized. *I can even feel the dry desert air on my skin.* But one primary concern overruled the amazing scene unfolding around me: *The Spirit must have brought me here for a specific reason.*

"Lord," I prayed, "what is it You want to say to me?"

"Watch carefully, My son," the Spirit replied. "I want you to learn what it means to serve Me in the light of the golden fire. You are about to experience life through the eyes of one of Israel's chosen servants. His name is Simeon, and for this one night, I have granted you the privilege of understanding life from his point of view. You were summoned here to witness a sacred event. You have much to learn about the Light Giver. The Father wants to reveal the secret of the golden fire. It is time for His people to embrace a greater depth of wisdom and revelation for the final days ahead."

The Spirit's directive was very precise. I felt like a character in the old TV series *Mission Impossible*. At the opening of every episode, the secret agent, Jim, was given a dossier with photographs and a description of the person he was to find, along with a tape recording that explained the mission. But he was always given another option: "Jim, this is your assignment, if you choose to accept it." The scene always ended with a final statement: "This tape will self-destruct in sixty seconds."

My thoughts came at hyper speed. *The secret of the golden fire? The Light Giver? What did He mean by "a greater depth of revelation and wisdom"? Are these really the final days?* The enigma of God's secret drew me in. This was more than just an assignment; it was an invitation to revelation. I felt an overwhelming sense of humility and, at the same time, intense excitement and anticipation for the adventure ahead.

"Lord, I am ready to obey You," I prayed. "Please don't let the vision end until You have fulfilled all that is in Your heart to reveal."

"Watch and observe carefully," the Spirit replied. "Open your spirit to receive insight and understanding. Vision is the threshold of communication."

Lights, Camera, Action

When the curtain was fully raised, the vision proceeded with a clarity that can come only from abandonment to the Holy Spirit and absolute spiritual focus. I centered all of my concentration on Simeon.

I feel like I already know this man, I thought. *It's as if I have read his autobiography. Maybe he's a distant relative or cousin.* It's amazing how much you can know about someone by the Spirit, just as Jesus knew things about Nathanael before the two of them ever met in person. (See John 1:43–51.)

It was immediately obvious that Simeon moved with a sense of knowing. His eyes glistened with an unusual sparkle of perception. They peered right through you. His carefully tailored priestly robe gave a distinct, set-apart notion of holiness to his demeanor. I wondered what could possibly have endowed this young man with such insight and knowledge. Some might have called it intuition; others may have attributed it to his father. "Good genes!" they would have commented. "He's a true son of Aaron." But this kind of wisdom could not be inherited. The real reason for his keen discernment was that it had come to him as a direct result of his priestly duties. Simeon worked the night shift in the tabernacle. His assignment was to tend to the lampstand in the secret place.

Simeon made his way through the crowded passageways between the tents of Israel's encampment. His agility and nimbleness betrayed his youthfulness, even though his weathered face bore wrinkles from years of wilderness wandering beneath the desert sun. But what captured my attention was his eyes. With a heightened sensitivity in my spirit, I observed his conduct carefully and listened to all that was said. He was to become my eyes and ears.

Simeon stopped at the doorway of the tent of his dear friend Abijah, located near the front wall of the tabernacle. Moses, Aaron, and the other priests always camped here. From this position, they could oversee the entryway to the outer court and had unhindered access to the tabernacle, where they could perform their duties without distraction from the rest of the camp. Theirs was a privileged allotment. The homes of the priests were closest to God's presence.

Duty Calls

The rose-yellow blush of the late afternoon sun slowly faded. "I love this time of day!" Simeon remarked to Abijah with youthful enthusiasm. "The transition from day to night doesn't mean darkness and weariness to me, as it does to most folks. I get excited just thinking that soon it will be time to go to work. Everything within me comes to life. I tell you, Abijah, since I have been ministering at the lampstand, I am never without light. My spirit is on fire, just like the lampstand itself."[1]

"It's true, Simeon," Abijah replied, with the seasoned tone of an older colleague. "Darkness makes the light more profound. As priests, we must always keep in mind that God is veiled in the darkness and shadow of divine mystery. (See 1 Kings 8:12; Psalm 18:11, 97:2.) His greatest truth is discovered in the midst of obscurity. When things appear the darkest, God's light shines brightest." (See John 1:3–4; Isaiah 9:2.)

Simeon lifted his forefinger, pressing it vertically against his forehead, and pointed heavenward in order to focus all his mental energy in concentrated thought. Pondering Abijah's words, he concluded, "His light ignites and transforms us."

Simeon's response prompted Abijah to recall the joy of eating the bread of His presence with his priestly companions the day before in the Holy Place, encompassed in the golden glow of the lampstand.[2]

Simeon turned an inquisitive eye toward the massive cloud resting above the tabernacle as if it were a celestial timepiece. (See Exodus 13:21–22; 40:33–38; Numbers 9:15–23.) Then, he quickly returned his attention to Abijah, his mentor, not wanting to show any disrespect. But he could not hide his eagerness.

Abijah was not offended. He understood and identified with Simeon's zeal. They were equally consumed by a passion for God's presence. This constant longing explained the very reason for their existence. Like all of mankind, they had been created for intimacy with God.

"And to think we are among the privileged ones," Abijah said. "We actually get to serve in the tabernacle under the cloud of His glory and in the light of His presence. You'd better get going, Simeon," he warned. "It's almost dark. You don't want to be late for work. The last thing you need is for the lampstand to be unlit on your watch. It could result in judgment and terrible darkness for the entire nation."

Simeon turned instantly toward the tabernacle entrance. "See you in the morning, Abijah." He waved over his shoulder in farewell and then disappeared into the throng of priests near the entrance to the outer court. As he walked toward the tabernacle and prepared for his privileged responsibilities, the young priest quoted from memory the instructions God gave to Moses:

> *Command the children of Israel that they bring to you pure oil of pressed olives for the light, to make the lamps burn continually. Outside the veil of the Testimony, in the tabernacle of meeting, Aaron shall be in charge of it from evening until morning before the LORD continually; it shall be a statute forever in your generations. He shall be in charge of the lamps on the pure gold lampstand before the LORD continually.* (Leviticus 24:1–4)

A cadre of priests lingered outside the wide entrance of the tabernacle, exchanging friendly greetings with their colleagues. The enthusiasm of their fellowship was genuine. It was always like this when the shifts changed.

"I cherish these moments of connection with my fellow workers," Simeon sighed with satisfaction. Those who were finishing their day in the presence of God always had some bit of inspiration to share. His ears were especially tuned to detect any word of a God encounter.

Fresh Oil

"Simeon, wait! Simeon!" John shouted, pushing his way through the crowd toward the beautifully woven curtain that marks the entrance to the outer court. "I've brought you some fresh oil for the lamps tonight."

Simeon reached out, not for the oil, but to embrace his brother-in-law. John's earthen-brown robe was aged from years of journeying in the wilderness, but John wore it like a suit of honor. Grinning through his jet-black beard with the joy of giving, John flung his hairy, muscular arms around Simeon with unabashed affection and then planted a kiss on his left cheek. The priest in his holy garments and the pilgrim in his traveling clothes, embracing in the center of the crowd, constituted a prophetic picture of God's purpose for His chosen people. (See Exodus 19:6; 1 Peter 2:9–10.)

"Mary and I pressed it this morning," John said, relaxing his bearlike embrace. "It's fresh—the purest virgin olive oil in the camp. Praise be to the Lord that I arrived in time for you to use it for this evening's sacrifice." (See Exodus 30:8; 1 Samuel 3:3; 2 Chronicles 13:11.)

Simeon accepted the precious flask of olive-green liquid with both hands. "Thank you, John. Your faithfulness and sacrifice will not go unnoticed. Throughout these thirty-nine years of our pilgrimage, God's people have not failed to contribute their best oil for the lamps." Simeon then placed his right hand on John's shoulder. Looking directly into his eyes, he discerned the man's soul. "You're a faithful man," he said. "May God's favor continue to be upon you, and upon Mary and the children, as well. I will pray for you tonight before the altar of incense. Tell Mary I send my love and blessing. Peace be with you!"

"God's favor and peace be with you, too, Simeon. Perhaps God will lead us into the Land of Promise soon."

"It will be soon, John," Simeon said with a tone of assurance. "I know it will be soon!"

John's smile returned, and he disappeared into the rows of tents bordering the tabernacle. His thoughts about the future were more hopeful as he retraced his steps back to his own tent among his kinsmen from the tribe of Judah. Like Simeon, he also lived near the front wall of the tabernacle.

The Atmosphere of God's House

The crowd had dwindled to only a few priests. Simeon felt a tingling excitement in his chest as he approached the thirty-five-foot-wide doorway to God's house. "I love my life," he whispered with heartfelt gratitude.

Looking up into the twilight canopy of desert sky, he imagined that the twinkling stars bursting into view were the diamonds on his wife's necklace, and he fondly pictured Sarah's regal beauty. Quickly, he conceded that no one—not even Sarah—compared to God's splendor. Breathing deeply, he filled his lungs with cool night air. "I'm a blessed man," he said.

Directly in front of him, the curtain of the entrance shimmered in the evening breeze, displaying the richness of its fabric and the royal blend of prophetic colors. Blue, purple, and scarlet threads had been skillfully woven into the white linen cloth. "Beyond this curtain," Simeon whispered in reverence, "everything is different. Here, in the very heart of the camp, enclosed within the walls of the tabernacle, there is an environment like no other on earth. The atmosphere is holy and pure. Stepping through this entrance is like passing into another realm, separate from this world. It's truly heaven on earth." (See Hebrews 8:5.)

Simeon's priestly training had prepared him well. He knew that the atmosphere of God's house must be guarded and protected. It was his duty to ensure its protection—at the cost of his life, if need be. This holy atmosphere required purity in his performance as a priest. "I must offer my service of worship with clean hands and a pure heart," he reminded himself, just as he always did each and every night before his shift began. (See Psalm 24:3–5.)

Simeon hesitated before the door of the tabernacle. While others in the camp were preparing for sleep, he was fully awake. It was time for him to report for duty. Adrenaline surged through his body, supercharging his senses. The anticipated moment had arrived. His entire being trembled at the immensity of his actions.

The God-Dimension

With a single step, Simeon passed through the doorway and entered into the God-dimension. Instantly, he was engulfed in supernatural light. The cloud of glory had dissipated, and, in its place, a swirling column of liquid fire towered over him, extending above the roof of the Holy of Holies. Surging and twirling with incredible power, the fire rose far into the early night sky, its vortex forming a portal between heaven and earth. He stared breathlessly at the sight, slowly tracing its ascent until his neck bent completely back. The reflection of the unquenchable flames danced over the surface of his eyes.

"That sound," he said in awe, "it's like no other on earth. It's compelling, persuasive, and captivating—pure energy." The column throbbed and surged with an intonating resonance from beyond this world. A constant droning hum filled the atmosphere with pulsating power. It charged the air inside the tabernacle enclosure with such energy that it made Simeon's flesh tingle and the hairs on his arms bristle and stand up. *Could this ethereal sound be the strains of angelic worship filtering through the fiery vortex from the heavenly realms?* Simeon wondered.

Every now and then, molten sparks separated from the column and showered down on the tabernacle roof like droplets of white-hot lava—a crackling reminder of God's awesome holiness and power for those who ministered beneath the covering in the Holy Place.

Simeon resisted the overwhelming desire to fall to his knees and worship the Holy One. The weight of God's glory pressed down on him, reminding him of his humanness. But he knew that if he stopped, he would be unable to go any further. And there was priestly work to be done. His duty was to tend the lampstand. "I will enter Your gates with thanksgiving, and Your courts with praise" (see Psalm 100:4), he said in awed reverence, as he forced himself to move deeper into the tabernacle.

Blood, Fire, and Holy Smoke

Billows of thick, pungent smoke rose from the brass altar of sacrifice as Simeon passed by it on his way to wash in the laver. (See Exodus 27:1–8; 38:1–7; 40:6 KJV) The sprinkled blood of the sacrifice was still liquid fresh. The priest had just anointed the horns of the altar. Blood trickled down the sides of the sacred altar, forming scarlet rivulets that stained the ground crimson red around its base. To Simeon's right, a reluctant, bleating lamb cried out as it was being prepared for the evening sacrifice.

"Were it not for this blood, none of us could approach the Almighty," Simeon said with a shudder. "Without the shedding of blood, there can be no forgiveness. Sacrifice is never easy. It costs everything, even life itself, to approach God and worship Him adequately."

He nodded to the priest, a distant relative, who had just skewered a large chunk of meat with his long fork. He flipped it over on the red-hot grate above the crackling fire and quickly squinted back at Simeon, partly in acknowledgment and partly to keep the smoke out of his eyes. Fat from the roasting sacrifice fell onto the glowing coals, discharging a thick plume of smoke that rose from the altar like a cloud, infusing the air with an aroma that made Simeon salivate.

"No wonder God takes pleasure in this odor," he said. "So do I." The enticing smell of charbroiling meat not only made him think about food; it also connected his thoughts, as smell so often does, with associated memories. He instantly recalled his school days, when he had studied for the priesthood.

He quoted from memory the instructions for priestly ministry given by Moses and Aaron:

The sons of Aaron the priest shall put fire on the altar, and lay the wood in order on the fire. Then the priests, Aaron's sons, shall lay the parts, the head, and the fat in order on the wood that is on the fire upon the altar; but he shall wash its entrails and its legs with water. And the priest shall burn all on the altar as a burnt sacrifice, an offering made by fire, a sweet aroma to the LORD.
(Leviticus 1:7–9)

Inner Session

Simeon approached the laver circumspectly. Like his fellow priests, he knew that this was not a ritual cleansing to be performed perfunctorily or a duty merely to be dispensed in order to get on to more important things. Without the proper cleansing of his soul, he could not proceed any further into God's presence.[3] He set down the precious cruse of lamp oil and focused on the crucial task at hand. (See Exodus 29:4; 30:17–21; 38:8; 40:7.)

"Nothing is hidden that cannot be seen by God," Simeon acknowledged. Leaning over the pool, he began to wash his hands in the sacred water. He was not in a hurry. Rubbing his hands together in the cool liquid, he gazed down into the sacred basin of water. The reflection of his heart seemed to lie exposed in the mirrored depths of the supernatural pool. His soul was laid bare before God. His sustained silence revealed the depth of his soul-searching. Then, softly, honestly, a confession poured from his lips. "My thoughts are so impure, Lord." He paused. "Greed motivates my desires, and I'm so jealous and envious of others— You know who I mean, Father." The images of several individuals came to his mind. There was another, longer pause, as he waited for the Spirit to take him deeper. Then, he cried, "I'm so driven by ambition and pride."

Finally, after several more excruciating minutes, he painfully forced the words from his mouth, choking on their shamefulness. "I'm a priest, Lord. How can I live like this?" he agonized. From deep within his soul, the wretchedness spewed forth. "It is lust, Father. Lust consumes me. I can't stand it any longer. I can't find victory over my thoughts. My eyes wander constantly. I am so unclean. How can I ever come before Your holy presence?" He felt as if his very words were polluting the crystal-clean pool of water. "Forgive me, Lord. Cleanse me of this disgraceful sin."

It was finished! His confession brought cleansing. The hidden emotional pain of his sin and hypocrisy was gone. Peace flooded his soul. As best he knew, his heart was pure. He could stand before the Lord and minister in the Holy Place once more. (See 1 John 1:5–10.)

One final requirement remained. Bowing down to the lower pool of water at the base of the laver, he washed first his right foot and then his left. The defilement of the dusty encampment, as well as his own life's journey, now lay dissolved at the bottom of the pool of God's mercy.

"Guide my steps, Lord," Simeon prayed. (See Psalm 37:23–24.) He grasped the flask of oil and stood erect. Fixing his eyes straight ahead toward the Holy Place, he stepped away from the laver and moved deeper into God's presence.

2

THE LIGHT KEEPER

The vision left me breathless with anticipation. "This is overwhelming, Lord," I gasped, overcome by the vividness of the events that had been unfolding before me. "I feel as though I am Simeon. I can discern his thoughts and emotions."

"This is why I have summoned you here," the Spirit replied. "You must see as he sees and think as he thinks."

I prepared myself for what was about to happen. *The Holy Place*, I thought with a sense of awe and godly fear. *No one dares enter here without the proper credentials and appropriate spiritual preparation. It is by invitation only. I am about to go beyond the veil with Simeon into this sacred space, thanks to the Holy Spirit.*

"Guide my steps, Lord," I prayed, repeating Simeon's request. "Take me deeper into Your presence."

The Vision Continues

The last vestige of twilight disappeared beyond the stark desert horizon in the west, and a cold blanket of darkness crept across the encampment. Simeon picked up his pace. He needed to tend to the lamps immediately. "Just a few more paces to the outer veil," he said, to encourage himself. A single white, glowing spark fell at his feet. He glanced up hurriedly at the towering pillar of fire swirling above his head. "You *are* a holy God," he confessed with genuine fear.

Simeon reached up to open the linen screen separating the Outer Court from the Holy Place. Five gold-overlaid pillars held it securely in place. It hung suspended on hooks of pure gold. (See Exodus 26:36–37.) Simeon's father had known the craftsman who had woven the curtain, long before Simeon was born. "He was a fine man. Father told me so. He was meticulous in his work. But they're both gone now," Simeon said with sadness. "They're buried in the desert, along the trail of our endless wandering. So many people have died on this journey."

A familiar sadness crept over him like the encroaching desert night. From his early childhood, he had been haunted by thoughts of opportunity lost. He felt like he had been sentenced to prison for a crime he did not commit. Nightmares often awakened him. Scenes of countless graves, a trail of tears, had littered the landscape of his lifelong journey in the wilderness. *How many more before it's over?* he agonized, but the recollection of his conversation with John soothed his pain. "It won't be long now!" he reiterated. His words were a confession of the faith in his heart.

Sacred Space

The change of atmosphere was instantaneous and dramatic. The curtain protecting the Holy Place closed behind him, leaving him within a rarified space so holy that he feared he would be consumed alive. The tangible glory of God surrounded him. Gleaming gold glistened and shimmered into the incensed air. His flesh felt like it was on fire. White-hot tears formed in the corners of his eyes. Only God's grace kept him standing upright.

Simeon breathed in short gasps. Holding the air in his lungs as long as possible, he concentrated every ounce of his mental discernment and sensual acuity on his surroundings. Standing in this timeless space, he felt as if he was suspended between earth and heaven. Everything around him took on eternal significance. In this moment, he was closer to God's presence than anyone else in the entire encampment. One careless move—an act of presumption, a mere hint of arrogance—and his priestly privilege would have been forfeited.

He moved cautiously toward the far end of the room, stopping momentarily to obtain some incense and the gold-handled lighting wick lying next to the table of showbread. Then, he proceeded deeper into the sacred chamber.

A single curtain was the only barrier separating him from certain death. The awe-inspiring cherubim woven onto its surface served as a warning for him to approach with the utmost reverence. The cherubim's assignment was to guard the presence and glory of God beyond the veil in the Most Holy Place. (See Exodus 26:31–37; Mark 15:37–38; Hebrews 9–10.) No one except Moses and the high priest could pass beyond this partition.

Incensing God

Taking a generous amount of incense from the vessel, Simeon sprinkled it across the hot embers on the golden altar. Its rich, extravagant fragrance burst forth. A mysterious, mystical vapor filled the air with a scent so precious and sacred that its use was forbidden beyond this holy place. "The value of the altar is this incense," Simeon acknowledged. "You love the smell of this enticing fragrance, Jehovah. It's reserved for You alone. It is formulated to awaken Your passion and mercy! Almighty God, may this incense provoke You to action."

The smoke curled upward and perfumed the room with the unmistakable aroma of sweet spices. The odor of the consecrated recipe of stacte, onycha, galbanum, and frankincense hung above him like an ethereal mantle near the roof of the enclosure. Its essence infused everything in the room, including Simeon. "God is so close," Simeon uttered. The saturated atmosphere provoked him to pray. His words mingled with the incense and penetrated through the veil, into the presence of God in the Holy of Holies.

"God of our fathers Abraham, Isaac, and Jacob," Simeon said, "Your name be praised forever. May Your wisdom and justice always rule over us. Grant to Your people Your continuing provision on this wilderness journey. Holy God, may the blood of our sacrifice insure Your mercy. Keep us from the tendency to destroy ourselves, and give us victory over our enemies. Grant to us a compassionate and merciful heart like Your own."

Keeping his promise, Simeon continued, "I lift to You my sister and brother-in-law, Mary and John, tonight. Let Your favor and blessing be upon them." Not wanting to be self-serving, he added, "And also upon all of Your children throughout the encampment."

For a long time, Simeon, wrapped in the supernatural cloud of incense and cloaked in a transparent prayer shawl, continued to intercede for his nation. His impassioned plea penetrated the barrier between him and God. "Almighty God, please fulfill Your promise. Bring us into the land of Your blessing and favor beyond the river."

Simeon bent to retrieve the gold-handled wick from the base of the altar, where he had placed it. Thrusting the linen wick into the glowing coals, he uttered a final request: "Let my prayers ascend to You as the evening sacrifice. Gather them, like this holy incense, before Your throne." He turned from the altar of incense before the veil and hastened toward the golden lampstand.

Like the points of a compass, each piece of furniture in this sacred space kept him oriented. The altar of incense was positioned on the west side, before the veil, just outside the Holy of Holies. The table of showbread stood on the north wall.[1] The golden lampstand stood along the south wall. The entrance was always on the easternmost side of the tabernacle. Its placement, toward the rising sun, served as a timepiece for Simeon. The first rays of dawn signaled him that his duties had been fulfilled. "Daylight is still hours away," he realized. "My shift has only just begun."

God's Lampstand

The seven lamps were lifeless as Simeon approached and stood before the lampstand. He gazed at the glistening, pure-gold object with reverence. *These lamps are the eyes of God*, he reminded himself. (See Zechariah 3:9; 4:2, 6, 10; Revelation 5:6.) *He sees me; His light penetrates my being; His presence and nature emanate from each lamp.*

The skilled priest scanned the hundred-twenty-five-pound lampstand, searching for any flaw, scratch, or imperfection that might hinder its function. "I need to perform my job with excellence. The light of God must be perfectly cared for," he said in a cautious tone.

Simeon's right hand traced the circumference of the center shaft, which supported the entire weight of the lamps. He applied a gentle rocking pressure, but the lamp did not move. *It's standing solid and secure on the tabernacle floor*, he assured himself.

Following along the hammered gold center stem, he carefully examined the four expertly crafted, cup-shaped almond blossoms with their calyxes[2] and petals. With a jeweler's eye for detail, he scrutinized the juncture of all six lamp branches to the central trunk, alternating between the almonds, looking for any hints of cracking or weakness. Then, on either side of the lamp, he studied each of the six branches with their three almond blossoms, calyxes, and petals. He took in each detail with the passion of an ancient scribe eager to decipher an encrypted message. (See Exodus 25:31–40; 37:17–24; 39:37; Daniel 5:2–5.)

The Hidden Secret

Satisfied that he had not missed a single detail, Simeon began carefully transferring fire from the altar of incense to the lampstand. Slowly, with just a wisp of smoke, each oil-soaked wick began to glow before springing to life with a wavering flame. Simeon waited to be sure that each flame remained ablaze before he moved on to the next one.

After carefully lighting each lamp in the appropriate order, Simeon stepped back to view the entire lampstand in its shimmering, regal glory. Peering up at the splendor of the lamp, he took it all in: the trunk with its branches; the almonds; the petals and calyxes; the oil lamps. Suddenly, something transpired that superseded his natural ability to comprehend. In a burst of revelation, he saw the lampstand through God's eyes. Simeon gasped in amazement, instantly aware of the revealed secret. "This is far more than a lampstand," he stammered. "It's a tree—a supernatural almond tree!"

He quickly connected the lampstand to the rod of Aaron, which rested securely within the ark of the covenant beyond the veil in the adjoining room. "The rod that budded," he whispered. He realized the incredible significance of his discovery. The almond tree was always the first to bud and blossom in springtime. For this reason, it was often referred to as the "awakening tree" or the "vigilant tree."

"This is a supernatural instrument of revelation!" Simeon declared. "It is far more than a perfunctory lamp serving to illuminate this darkened holy chamber. It is also designed to awaken my spirit."

His eyes darted to and fro, rapidly tracing the almonds on each branch, connecting each successive cup in descending order, like a connect-the-dots puzzle. The resulting lines, like the radii of a semicircle originating from the single, prominent, topmost almond on the main trunk, spread out like a fan, descending toward him. Simeon was standing in the supernatural radiance of God's illumination. He was encompassed in seven distinct rays of divine light, the full orb of God's supernatural wisdom and provision. It was a perfect rainbow of color.

Every cell of Simeon's body began to quiver with supernatural energy. Standing before the lampstand, the young priest was being divinely prepared to receive impartation. He was fully awake, hypersensitive, a human receiver tuned in to God for supernatural revelation.

The seven flickering lamps danced over him, their flames imparting something beyond the light itself. In his spirit, he heard the voice of God summoning him to rise above the limited perceptions of his flesh and to transcend the inadequate intellectual abilities of his own mind. He was being lifted up to the God-realm of perception and understanding, where things are discerned with inward eyes and spiritual ears. He welcomed this irresistible invitation from the Holy One to draw close and receive instruction. Simeon inched forward, pressing closer to the "awakening tree."

The Gift of Light

"Light is God's gift to mankind," Simeon said. "*Darkness was on the face of the deep. And the Spirit of God was hovering over the face of the waters. Then God said, "Let there be light"; and there was light. And God saw the light, that it was good'* (Genesis 1:2–4)."

"We take so much for granted," Simeon added, though no one but God was listening. "Without light, we could not exist. It dispels the darkness and reveals the world to us. Our days and nights, even the years of our lives, are measured by it." He smiled, realizing that most of the camp was asleep at this very moment.

"Oh, no," he said with alarm, as the center wick began to sputter. "It's the most important one. What have I done? How could I have missed it? I was sure that it was fine. I know I checked it. Maybe there's a flaw in the wick itself." In desperation, he realized what needed to be done. "I'll have to trim the lighted wick; I have no choice." He grabbed the wick trimmer from the gold tray next to the lampstand.[3]

3

GOD'S LAMP

Y ou are Light, and the Giver of light," Simeon uttered as he lifted the trimmer to cut the wick on the center lamp.[1] His hands were steady, like those of a skilled surgeon. The instant the blade touched the wick, a surge of spiritual power jolted through his body. He jerked like a man who had just cut into a live electrical wire. His stomach muscles involuntarily contracted, sucking in his midsection. From his gut, radiating out to his extremities, his body convulsed like someone with a severe case of hiccups. His head thrust forward toward the light. The discharge seemed to emanate from within his spirit instead of the lamp.

He had anticipated the sudden impartation, for he had experienced it before. Yet, no matter how diligently he tried to prepare himself, it always came as a surprise. He knew that all of the other six lamps drew their energy and identity from this central source of power.

The Spirit of the Lord

"The Spirit of the Lord!" he cried like a drowning man, desperately gulping fresh air deep into his lungs. "There's something about this center lamp that has to do with breathing," Simeon realized. "It is Spirit and life! It is the *nephesh*—the *ruach* of God, the breath of the Almighty." (See Genesis 1:2; 2:7[2]; Isaiah 40:13; 48:6; 1 Corinthians 2:16.)

The tended flame burst forth into a bright blaze. The very essence of the Holy Spirit, it danced above the other lamps in constant motion, like the air itself. Simeon could not discern from whence this awesome presence came or where it was headed, only that God had manifested Himself powerfully in this center lamp as it was being trimmed. (See John 3:8.) Although this central flame comforted Simeon, imparting a restful peace, it disguised a storm-like ability. Resident within it was a latent, explosive energy that could part the ocean, split the earth, and move mountains.

Simeon measured the oil in the center cup. Ascertaining that no more would be needed that night, he proceeded cautiously, knowing that his actions and response could inadvertently extinguish the sensitive flames.

The Lamp of Wisdom

Stepping a few paces to the side, Simeon positioned himself in front of the lamp on his far left. He always tended the remaining six lights in a specific order, working from the outside toward the center in an alternating fashion. He lifted the flask and slowly poured a small, steady stream of fresh olive oil into the gold cup of the lamp until it was full. His hands were steady again, calmed by a power from beyond the sacred space. An uncommon skill guided his actions and thoughts. He poured the oil with prudence, as one who was experienced in the ways of the Lord.

"God, You are the Source of all wisdom," Simeon said with genuine humility. (See Job 11:6–9; 12:13; Proverbs 2:6.) The moment he spoke, a drop of oil fell from the lamp into the cupped palm of his left hand, which he had positioned beneath the lamp as a precaution. The glistening oil spread over his skin. Something supernatural was transpiring. His words were inspired by the Holy Spirit. "Your wisdom, Lord, brings success, even prosperity."

Simeon stared for a long time at the droplet of oil, watching it slowly penetrate his flesh. He thought about how his father used to rub oil into the hardened leather of aging wineskins in order to soften them. He wondered if God was not softening his heart, making his spirit teachable. He knew from his priestly training that God expected those who served Him to exhibit His character in the practical affairs of life.

"Please reveal Your wisdom to me, Lord. Enable me to live my daily life according to Your principles of right and wrong." As a deliberate, tangible act of faith, Simeon withdrew his hand from under the lamp with his palm up, intentionally maintaining a receptive posture to obtain a greater measure of the wisdom of God.

The Lamp of the Fear of the Lord

Simeon hurriedly moved to the opposite side of the lampstand. This single flame was a constant reminder to him, and to all of Israel, that God was to be feared. The wick smoked and sputtered in the lamp, emitting a black funnel of soot into the sacred chamber. "It's almost spent," he said with an experienced, skillful tone. He selected a new wick from his pocket and placed it gently into the oil. The pure white color of the braided wick turned beige as the fibers absorbed the oil. He watched vigilantly and wondered whose garments the wick had been fashioned from, recalling that the wicks were made from the discarded sacred robes worn by the priests. "Who should not fear You, O Lord?" he said. "All flesh is as grass before You." (See Isaiah 40:6–7; 1 Peter 1:24–25.)

Only when he was sure it would burn did Simeon transfer the flame to the new wick. He removed the spent, charred one with his tongs and quenched its final, sputtering flame between his fingers. Blowing the smoky soot away from the lampstand, he placed the spent wick into the snuff dish.

A burning sensation seized him before the smell of seared flesh reached his nostrils. He shook his hand violently to cool the skin, rapidly raising his fingers to blow across them. "A small reminder that You are to be feared, Lord," he said, wincing.

The outer, semicircular branch of the almond tree directly connected the lamp he had previously tended on the far left of the lampstand to this lamp on the far right. The design was intentional. As he connected the two lamps, Simeon stated, "*The fear of the LORD is the beginning of wisdom*" (Psalm 111:10).

"I worship You!" he declared, and then he began to chant a song of respect to the Almighty. His Hebrew refrain of worship filled the enclosure. No one else heard; everyone was asleep. But God listened as Simeon's rich baritone voice ascended to the throne room.

You alone are awesome, Yahweh.
You reign over all things.

You enlighten us with wisdom.
You reign over all flesh.
Power and knowledge come from Your presence.
You alone deserve our worship.
I praise You, Yahweh.
You alone are awesome, Yahweh.

With a final glance at the brightly burning flame, Simeon affirmed, "You are a consuming, unquenchable fire, greatly to be feared and worshipped."

The Lamp of Knowledge

Moving to his left, Simeon adjusted the wick in the next lamp with his tongs so that its light was fully directed toward the front of the lampstand. He whispered his thoughts aloud: "Each lamp must shine forward, to illuminate the front of the lampstand and provide light for the priests to perform their duties." (See Exodus 25:37.)

He added a small amount of oil to the cup. "Lord, this is Your supernatural lamp of knowledge. If I were permitted to have a favorite lamp, this would be it. I could never obtain the information that is available here from human intelligence or mental capacity. This kind of knowledge is attained only by those who are intimate with You, like close friends sharing a precious secret."

Simeon's consuming desire for intimacy with God coursed white-hot with passion like the blood pounding through his veins. "My longing for Your presence surpasses the love of a man for his wife," he said, placing his right hand over the center of his chest.

Simeon stared at the shimmering flame, studying its every move. He was not mesmerized into some hypnotic state. Rather, every faculty of his mind was focused. He was fully awake, totally engaged, but his perception went beyond the visible flame before him. He was seeing into the God-dimension. Simeon began to download information from God. He was receiving Holy Spirit-inspired vision and knowledge.

When he finally turned away from the light, *he* was glowing. "There is a knowledge that can be obtained only in the intimate, secret place where God's presence abides," he sighed with soul satisfaction.

The Lamp of Understanding

"'*The* L*ord* *gives wisdom; from His mouth come knowledge and understanding*'!" (Proverbs 2:6) Simeon declared, as he followed the pathway along the second golden branch from the lamp of knowledge to the lamp of understanding, on the opposite side of the lampstand.

"It is possible to hear and see without perceiving. Knowledge is not enough; I need understanding," he petitioned as he stepped up to the flame. He cupped his left hand around it to capture every bit of light, directing it onto his already glowing face.

This lamp possessed a supernatural quality that produced perspicuity and decisiveness. The ability to discern and think clearly seemed to radiate from its brilliance. Scattered thoughts and bits of knowledge, like the pieces of a puzzle, suddenly became sorted and positioned in a logical sequence, as if an unseen hand were arranging them into an understandable form in Simeon's mind. Things that had been confusing to him instantly became lucid and simple. "Aha! Now I understand," he uttered in response to the effortless solution to a problem he had been struggling with for weeks. God had just turned the light on.

Simeon lifted the cruse of oil and poured a generous amount into the gold cup. The fresh supply of oil did not increase the lamp's intensity, but it ensured its continuous brilliance. "It will burn without wavering through the rest of the night," Simeon asserted. Then, without delay, he moved to the adjacent lamp.

The Lamp of Counsel

"'*The* L*ord* *brings the counsel of the nations to nothing; He makes the plans of the peoples of no effect. The counsel of the* L*ord* *stands forever*'" (Psalm 33:10–11). Simeon repeated this passage, as he did every night upon approaching this particular lamp. "The plans of His heart are eternal. They extend to every generation. '*Blessed is the nation whose God is the* L*ord*, *the people He has chosen as His own inheritance*' (Psalm 33:12).

"You are God, and there is no other. There is none like You, Yahweh," Simeon prayed. "You declare the end from the beginning. From ancient times, You have established the things that are not yet done. Your counsel shall stand. You have spoken it; You will bring it to pass. You have purposed it; You will do it!" (See Isaiah 46:9–11.)

Simeon tended the lamp, filling the cup with oil and adjusting the wick to further release the intensity of the flame. All the while, he contemplated the counsel of the Almighty: the lampstand, the secret place, the tabernacle itself, his own life, and the lives of all within the camp. His thoughts expanded to the nations of the earth. "It is all designed with the Creator's perfect wisdom," he reasoned. "It is God who guarantees His work and the fulfillment of His eternal decrees."

The Holy Spirit engulfed Simeon in the light of the burning wick. In this fleeting moment of time, God decided to show Simeon what He would declare to every succeeding generation: the immutability of His counsel. (See Hebrews 6:17.) Shadowy perceptions of prophetic revelation played across the screen of Simeon's mind. He kept repeating the words "Wonderful Counselor" over and over, louder and louder, until it seemed like he would explode if he did not express it. As he shouted into the room, his breath caused the flaming lamp before him to brighten in the stream of air. "Wonderful Counselor!" he declared, gazing in astonishment at the brilliant flame. He felt like one of the trumpet players in the camp, blasting a note loud enough to inform the entire nation.

"Blessed is the man who walks in Your counsel," Simeon affirmed. A renewed hunger for God's Word rose up within him. "Your words delight my soul, Lord. Your counsel is sweet, like honey." (See Psalm 19:9–10; 119:103.)

The Lamp of Power

Peaceful resolution settled over Simeon's spirit. Like a tree planted by a river of living water, Simeon felt nourished, prosperous, and fruitful. He turned to the seventh and final lamp with an undeniable sense that whatever he did would prosper. (See Psalm 1; 119.)

Simeon spoke to the flame as though he were petitioning the Almighty Himself: "*Cause Your face to shine, and we shall be saved!*" (Psalm 80:3). The flame sprang to life, like a warring soldier preparing to engage the enemy.

"Strength and might belong to You, Yahweh," he continued. "*Some trust in chariots, and some in horses; but we will remember the name of the Lord our God*" (Psalm 20:7).

Simeon's muscles flexed. His thighs became rigid; his arms trembled with harnessed energy. "I feel like I could run through a troop and leap over a wall," he said. (See 2 Samuel 22:30 KJV; Psalm 18:29 KJV.) The energetic flame imparted a strength and power like none on earth. Mighty acts of valor and bravery seemed entirely within his ability.

Even though each of the lamps upon the lampstand had a sufficient brilliance, this single flame possessed an authority to light the entire room all by itself. This seventh lamp revealed the power of God's might. To Simeon, it was the assurance that God would give the nation success in warfare. "God is a warrior!" he declared as he poured the last of the oil into the cup.

Millennia later, God's power would rock the planet, send the Son of God to earth, raise the dead, heal the sick, and open the tomb. It would endow a people who did not yet exist with a supernatural ability that would change history and the world forever. But, in this moment, Simeon understood only that with God, nothing is impossible. (See Matthew 19:26; Mark 10:27.) No weapon formed against him could prosper (see Isaiah 54:17), and the flame before him was God's assurance that it was so.

Fulfilled

Simeon spent the remainder of the night at the altar of incense. When the first hint of morning framed the perimeter of the curtained entrance into the Holy Place with a luminescent silver border, he moved quickly back to the lampstand for a final check. He had done his job well in the early night hours. The lamps still burned brightly, each one emitting a pure, steady flame. The wicks had all been trimmed perfectly. Each cup still held an adequate supply of oil.

He stepped to the center of the room for one last look at the portable, inanimate object. It was the center of his world. His life's assignment was to care for this lamp. To most of the camp, it was just a lampstand, albeit a holy one. Although it was the most beautiful, the most skillful, and the most ornamental of all the pieces of furniture in the tabernacle, beaten from a solid block of gold and hammered with artistic skill into its exquisite form, it was still just a lamp with a utilitarian purpose.

"It's the fire that makes the difference," Simeon acknowledged. "The lamp would be mere ornamentation without it. Beauty must be linked with usefulness."

The seven lamps shimmered and danced before him, alive with the presence of the Holy Spirit. "Of all the priestly duties, I am blessed with my assignment," he said with heartfelt sincerity. "Here, in the secret place, I have the privilege of tending to the lamp of God. Supernatural wisdom, the fear of the Lord, knowledge and understanding, counsel and might—they are all available to me in this supernatural light. I am a transformed man. The Spirit of God illuminates my life. In the light of God's lamp, I see what cannot be seen with common human eyesight."

Future Light Keepers

He stayed as long as he dared, and then, reluctantly, he turned to leave. The light from the lamps followed him toward the exit like the eyes of God. When he opened the curtain, the morning breeze blew through the doorway, stimulating the atmosphere of the sacred space. It blew across the lampstand, enticing each flame to life. Simeon watched as the flickering lamps broadcast their message throughout the shadowy interior. Their powerful brilliance illuminated the tabernacle walls with animated splashes of prophetic revelation. The scene was emblazoned upon his mind, and it quickened his spirit.

In an instant, the heavens opened over him. He had tapped into a window of prophetic revelation. The seal on the prophetic scroll was broken, and a voice penetrated the silence of Simeon's spirit like the peal of a trumpet. A preview of things to come engaged his imagination.

There shall come forth a Rod from the stem of Jesse, and a branch shall grow out of his roots. The Spirit of the LORD shall rest upon Him, the Spirit of wisdom and understanding, the Spirit of counsel and might, the Spirit of knowledge and of the fear of the LORD. (Isaiah 11:1–2)

"My God, the lampstand, and the light of Your Spirit," Simeon cried as the vision continued.

Grace to you and peace from Him who is and who was and who is to come, and from the seven Spirits who are before His throne....And from the throne proceeded lightnings, thunderings, and voices. Seven lamps of fire were burning before the throne, which are the seven Spirits of God....And behold, in the midst of the throne and of the four living creatures, and in the midst of the elders, stood a lamb as though it had been slain, having seven horns and seven eyes, which are the seven Spirits of God sent out into all the earth. (Revelation 1:4; 4:5; 5:6)

The revelation of future events, generations removed from this moment, exploded within Simeon. The voices of future light keepers sounded in his ears. He did not fully understand; he could not know it completely right now, in this instant—but, centuries later, far down the hallway of history, his very own offspring, his namesake, would complete his own priestly duties in Herod's temple in Jerusalem. His successor would be the one to unveil the living lampstand.

And thus, it is written,

> *And behold, there was a man in Jerusalem whose name was Simeon, and this man was just and devout, waiting for the Consolation of Israel, and the Holy Spirit was upon him. And it had been revealed to him by the Holy Spirit that he would not see death before he had seen the Lord's Christ. So he came by the Spirit into the temple. And when the parents brought in the Child Jesus, to do for Him according to the custom of the law, he took Him up in his arms and blessed God and said: "Lord, now You are letting Your servant depart in peace, according to Your word; for my eyes have seen Your salvation which you have prepared before the face of all Your peoples,* **a light to bring revelation** *to the Gentiles, and the glory of Your people Israel." And Joseph and His mother marveled at those things which were spoken of Him.*
>
> (Luke 2:25–33, emphasis added)

Simeon struggled to grasp the implication of this prophetic truth. *Could the lampstand be a person?* he wondered. *How would this come to pass?*

His thoughts raced back to John's comment just before the start of his shift: *"Perhaps God will lead us into the Land of Promise soon."* Simeon knew now that there was more at stake than real estate. The implications were far greater than for Israel alone; God's intentions involved the Gentiles, as well. Somehow, a slain lamb with seven horns and seven eyes would reign over all creation. This lampstand would live and walk the earth, to give sight to the spiritually blind of every tribe and tongue.

The God of Surprises

Simeon, still dazed by the significance of the prophetic vision, passed through the gate and stepped out of the tabernacle, back into the camp of Israel. "I forgot the empty oil flask," he said, with worry in his voice. "John will be upset, and I will need more fresh oil again tonight to tend the lamp of God." He looked with uncommon wisdom at his oily palm. "God will provide!" he confessed in faith.

The welcome warmth of the morning sun engulfed the camp, dissipating the cold desert air. Simeon's duties were finished. In a matter of minutes, his colleague on the day shift would extinguish the seven lamps, which would remain that way until Simeon returned again at nightfall to light them once more.

He walked calmly back toward his tent with a deep sense of fulfillment and inner peace. He moved through the morning bustle and business of the awakening encampment with the confidence of one enlightened by the Almighty.

The implications of his experience in God's presence dominated his thoughts. "Things really are not what they seem to be in God's kingdom," Simeon conceded. "It's not just a lampstand; it's the awakening tree. And the seven lamps—they're not simply to light the holy place; the Holy Spirit *speaks* through each of the flaming *eyes* of God."

The tabernacle gate disappeared from view behind a row of tents. Even though his shift was over, the presence and anointing of the Holy Spirit remained upon him. There was a sense of knowing about Simeon. He was the light keeper.

A New Assignment

The vision ended as abruptly as it had begun, but its message penetrated my spirit, just like the holy oil saturated the strands and fibers of the priestly wicks of the lampstand. Simeon's words ignited my passion and captured my curiosity. "It's not just a lampstand," he'd said; "it's the awakening tree."

"All of these years, I've been like the rest of the camp," I confessed, "sound asleep, ignorant, and neglectful of the Light that informs, illumines, and empowers far beyond human capabilities.

"Please, Lord," I prayed, "teach me about this Holy Light. Reveal Yourself in all of Your splendor and radiance. Show me how to tend the lampstand in this present age. Awaken my generation, Lord. Ignite us with the golden fire of the lampstand. It's Your fire that makes the difference."

4

THE LIGHT GIVER

The vision of Simeon and the lampstand consumed my thoughts and raised questions that demanded answers. Why had God brought this vision? What was He attempting to communicate to me? What did the golden fire upon the lampstand, and the power of its lamps to enlighten Simeon, have to do with this present age and with me?

Within a few days, I sensed that the Holy Spirit had intended the vision to be a catalyst. Like all visions and dreams, it required interpretation. The Lord wanted to launch me on an expedition in search of truth. Paul's words of advice to his spiritual son Timothy became my modus operandi: *"Study to show thyself approved unto God, a workman that needeth not to be ashamed, rightly dividing the word of truth"* (2 Timothy 2:15 KJV).

I set about immediately to investigate the Scriptures and every other resource I could access. *I must learn everything I can about light*, I determined with the resolution of Sherlock Holmes, not wanting to miss the smallest detail of information. What I discovered is astounding, and the revelation that came as I sought further instruction from the Holy Spirit was life changing.

At First Light

The origin and essence of light are cloaked in mystery. From the oldest book in the Bible, we hear a Voice out of the whirlwind questioning Job. *"Where is the way to the dwelling of light…? What is the way to the place where the light is distributed…?"* (Job 38:19, 24 RSV).

Before light was, in the beginning, darkness ruled the desolate void called earth with smothering hopelessness. Into this barren womb of unfathomable, terrifying nothingness, the seed of God's creative word penetrated with life-producing brilliance. *"God said, 'Let there be light'; and there was light"* (Genesis 1:3). The stifling blackness on the face of the deep yielded to the unrestrained power of the Spirit of God. What God called "light" came into being. *"And God saw the light, that it was good"* (Genesis 1:4).

"Here is the wonder of existence springing from nonexistence, breathtaking in its suddenness and illuminating power."[1] God is the Creator and the Source of *light!* He is the *Light Giver.* The first thing God did after making the heavens and the earth was to release light.

"God is light and in Him is no darkness at all" (1 John 1:5). The psalmist wrote that God covers Himself *"with light as with a garment"* (Psalm 104:2). And Paul explained that *"He…is the blessed and only Potentate, the King of kings and Lord of lords, who alone has immortality, dwelling in unapproachable light, whom no man has seen or can see…"* (1 Timothy 6:15–16).

In its final chapters, the Bible declares that the glory of God illuminates the heavenly city (see Revelation 21:23), and *"the Lamb is its light.…There shall be no night there: They need no lamp nor light of the sun, for the Lord God gives them light"* (Revelation 21:23; 22:5). From Genesis to Revelation, the Bible abounds with hundreds of references relating to the actual presence and symbolic significance of light.

The Quest

From the earliest times, man has sought to understand light and to unlock its mysteries. "Primitive thinking begins by dividing reality into a dichotomy between light and darkness, viewed as combatants in a perpetual battle for dominance."[2] To the Hebrew mind, light represented the opposite of darkness and was often translated as "daylight." Light ruled over the darkness and was a symbol of

God's goodness and blessing. Israel associated light with truth and understanding, darkness with error and ignorance. "*The unfolding of thy words gives light; it imparts understanding to the simple*" (Psalm 119:130 RSV).

In New Testament times, the Greeks identified light by using the word *phos.* Our word *phosphorous* ("light bearing") derives from this root. The word used for the verb *light* was *photizo*, meaning "shine," "enlighten," or "illuminate." They realized in their era that, primarily, "light is a luminous emanation, probably of force, from certain bodies, which enables the eye to discern form and color."[3] The eye is specifically designed and adapted to receive and interpret light signals. The human eye is the magnificent handiwork of God. It is a specialized, light-sensitive, sensory organ directly connected to the brain by the optic nerves. "Where the eye is absent, or where it has become impaired from any cause, light is useless."[4]

Jesus applied this concept when He explained the following:

> *The lamp of the body is the eye. If therefore your eye is good, your whole body will be full of light. But if your eye is bad, your whole body will be full of darkness. If therefore the light that is in you is darkness, how great is that darkness!* (Matthew 6:22–23)

We have learned a great deal about light since the time of Greco-Roman civilization. We now know that light has no volume. It cannot be reduced, but it can be separated and fragmented into laser-like rays with the capacity to perform precision surgery or burn through the hardest metal surface. We have discovered that light is a wave of neutral particles called photons that travel at 186,282 miles per second. Einstein theorized that in the overall scheme of the cosmos, time is relative to light. At the speed of light, *time actually stops.*

Merriam-Webster's 11th Collegiate Dictionary defines *light* as "something that makes vision possible." We don't see light—we see *with* light! It triggers our brains to register different colors. In fact, the human eye can discern as many as ten million distinct shades of color.

We know the life-giving quality of light—it feeds us by supplying energy for plants to grow, through photosynthesis. Life cannot exist without light! We also are able to harness the power of light through photovoltaic cells and use this energy to electrify and power our world. We can even travel over land and sea, and power our satellites and space stations, using the energy of light.

Light Speaks

One of the most astounding qualities of light is that it can be used to communicate; it can convey messages. Through the use of light, we can talk with each other. Our voices are transmitted on light beams. The use of fiber optics as a means of communication has transformed our world. Words and information are broadcast around the globe by tiny light impulses on thin strands of glass and plastic. Lucent technology is developing so rapidly that the amount of information you can put on a fiber-optic strand doubles every year. In theory, at some point in the future, every phone call in the world could be transmitted simultaneously across one cable. Imagine—the voices of millions of people transmitted over a single light beam at the same time! We actually *hear* through the same medium that enables us to *see*.

Scientists use the electromagnetic spectrum to describe this symbiotic relationship between sound and light. Massless particles, called photons, flow together in a stream moving at the speed of light. They oscillate in a wavelike pattern. The amount of energy they carry determines the length of the wave. Different wavelengths produce different results.

The lowest energy wave is the radio wave. That's right—the photons carry sound! Radio waves are even emitted from stars. The heavens really do sing together. Radio and television use this technology; thus, we hear and see through the spectrum of energy.

That is just the beginning. Microwaves are next, and we have the ability to use this frequency to cook our meals. Infrared light follows—the waves that enable us to perceive heat through night-vision goggles. This is because our skin emits infrared light. We really do glow in the dark!

Next is the frequency of visible light: red (with the longest wavelength), orange, yellow, green, blue, and violet (with the shortest wavelength) comprise the visible spectrum of light. This is the part of the electromagnetic spectrum we can actually see with our eyes. Visible radiation is emitted by everything from fireflies to lightbulbs and stars. If you see it, it is because God designed your eyes to perceive this frequency.

As the electromagnetic wave shortens, we arrive at ultraviolet light. The sun emits UV rays, which are undetectable by human eyesight but can do a lot of damage to our skin. Even shorter, more compact, waves on the spectrum are X-rays, used most commonly in the medical and security professions. Finally, at the very end of the spectrum, high-frequency, high-energy gamma rays are produced by radioactive substances. The power of these rays can be harnessed to make atomic weapons, to provide vehicles with nuclear power, and to produce energy.

Hearing the Light Giver

In the words of political theorist and technological guru George Gilder, "I believe that light was made by God for communication."[5] Simeon the priest did not have to be told this—he knew it from experience! He was the light keeper. Millennia ago, as he stood before the light of the lampstand in the middle of the night, deep within the tabernacle—the abode of the Almighty—Simeon heard the voice of God as he looked into each flaming lamp. All light must have a source of energy, and the Source of the light on the holy lampstand was the omnipotent God! This was far more than an instrument to produce light—it was a place of enlightenment, a transmitter of truth and revelation.

The prophet Samuel had a similar experience as he lay near the lampstand in the tabernacle.

> *Then the boy Samuel ministered to the* LORD *before Eli. And the word of the* LORD *was rare in those days; there was no widespread revelation. And it came to pass at that time, while Eli was lying down in his place, and when his eyes had begun to grow so dim that he could not see, and before the lamp of God went out in the tabernacle of the* LORD *where the ark of God was, and while Samuel was lying down, that the* LORD *called Samuel. And he answered, "Here I am!"* (1 Samuel 3:1–4)

The True Light

Light and the Word existed together at creation.

> *In the beginning was the Word, and the Word was with God, and the Word was God. He was in the beginning with God. All things were made through Him, and without Him nothing was made that was made. In Him was life, and the life was the light of men. And the light shines in the darkness, and the darkness did not comprehend it. There was a man sent from God, whose name was John. This man came for a witness, to bear witness of the Light,*

that all through him might believe. He was not that Light, but was sent to bear witness of that Light. That was the true Light which gives light to every man coming into the world. (John 1:1–9)

The people who sat in darkness have seen a great light, and upon those who sat in the region and shadow of death Light has dawned. (Matthew 4:16)

These Scriptures clearly show that the Word, light, and life are all facets of the same essence—God!

God sent His Son, Jesus—the Living Word—in order to enlighten us. He is the fulfillment of the type and shadow of the lampstand! The same fire of the Holy Spirit that first moved upon the face of the deep to create light, and that flickered in the flames of the ancient lampstand, moved upon Mary so that she conceived God's Son. When Jesus was born, the Word, light, and Life were released upon earth again, this time in the form of the Son of God, the Living Lampstand.

At Jesus' baptism, the Holy Spirit ignited Jesus' life with a sevenfold anointing, depicted by the seven flaming lamps in the tabernacle. Isaiah clearly prophesied this event, saying,

There shall come forth a Rod ["shoot" NIV, NASB, RSV] *from the stem of Jesse, and a Branch shall grow out of his roots. The Spirit of the LORD shall rest upon Him, the Spirit of wisdom and understanding, the Spirit of counsel and might, the Spirit of knowledge and of the fear of the LORD.* (Isaiah 11:1–2)

Jesus made this claim without apology: "*I am the light of the world. He who follows Me shall not walk in darkness, but have the light of life*" (John 8:12). He told His disciples, "*I have come as a light into the world, that whoever believes in Me should not abide in darkness*" (John 12:46). Jesus prepared His disciples for His death and resurrection when He told them, "*A little while longer the light is with you. Walk while you have the light, lest darkness overtake you; he who walks in darkness does not know where he is going. While you have light, believe in the light, that you may become sons of light*" (John 12:35–36).

Before Jesus ascended into heaven, He made this promise:

I will pray the Father, and He will give you another Helper, that He may abide with you forever; the Spirit of truth, whom the world cannot receive, because it neither sees Him or knows Him; but you know Him, for He dwells

with you and will be in you....The Helper, the Holy Spirit, whom the Father will send in My name, He will teach you all things, and bring to your remembrance all things that I said to you.   (John 14:16–17, 26)

The Community of Light

When the day of Pentecost had fully arrived, Jesus kept His promise. The Holy Spirit was brooding over the church, just as He had done on the first day of creation. Suddenly, God gave the signal to create light. The power of the Holy Spirit was unleashed! A sound from heaven filled the room with surging, unrestrained, supernatural power. Like a mighty wind, the Holy Spirit blasted His way past the boundaries of creation and fleshly restraints. The atmosphere crackled with dynamic power. Bodies jerked from the jolting, electrifying presence of God. Tongues of fire from the hand of the Almighty ignited every believer like the lamps on the lampstand. Each person became a living wick, kindled by the fire of God. The oil of the Spirit filled each human vessel to overflowing. Glorious, life-giving light filled the room. God turned the light on in the church!

Immediately, the supernatural light produced communication! The room was filled with words, sentences, and paragraphs of praise. Worship spilled out of the windows and doorways into the streets below. Spirit-filled believers were declaring the wonderful works of God in tongues they had never learned. The Spirit gave them utterance with the languages of foreign nations and peoples. God was releasing His Word to the world through a corporate lampstand made of flesh. Pentecost was all about empowerment and communication. Every disciple was transformed into a *witness*, each one a light. (See Acts 2:1–11.)

The corporate church became a living lampstand—a city set on a hill to give light to the world. Jesus said to His disciples,

*You are the light of the world. A city that is set on a hill cannot be hidden. Nor do they light a lamp and put it under a basket, but on a **lampstand**, and it gives light to all who are in the house. Let your light so shine before men, that they may see your good works and glorify your Father in heaven.*
                              (Matthew 5:14–16, emphasis added)

As Christians, we have been *"called...out of darkness into His marvelous light"* (1 Peter 2:9). We have been *"delivered...from the dominion of darkness and transferred…to the kingdom of his beloved Son*" (Colossians 1:13 RSV). Paul, writing with the understanding of what occurred at Pentecost, clearly established the link between creation and the new creation, between the Old Testament and the New Testament, between the physical reality and the spiritual symbol of light.[6] "*For it is the God who commanded light to shine out of darkness, who has shone in our hearts to give the light of the knowledge of the glory of God in the face of Jesus Christ*" (2 Corinthians 4:6).

I See

It all came together in a flash of inspiration. I connected creation to Pentecost like an electrician completing a circuit. God has always intended to talk with us! But the circuit was disconnected when Adam and Eve sinned. With a few exceptions, from that time, communication between God and His creation was severed—until Pentecost, when, in an instant, God reconnected the circuit. The Light Giver reestablished communion and conversation with His beloved creation!

The importance of the vision of the priest finally became clear. "It makes sense, Lord," I prayed. "No wonder You created light first. Without light, there is no life! Without light, there is no such thing as time! And, most important of all, without light, there is no communication! You created light first because You wanted to talk to us! You reveal Yourself in light.

"Teach me more, Lord," I prayed.

My curiosity was nowhere near satisfied. The intriguing vision of Simeon kept replaying in my spirit, each time more vivid than its first appearance. I was hopelessly consumed with the desire to know more about the Light Giver and the secret of the golden fire on the lampstand.

5

THE MIND OF CHRIST

Only a few days had passed since the vision of Simeon had first appeared. At noon, I hastened upstairs to my secret place. At that time of day, I am usually out and about, taking care of errands and administrative duties, but this day was different. *I'm so eager, Lord, for a deeper understanding regarding Your light*, I prayed silently.

A cool, late-summer breeze gently blew through the window of my secret place. I sat at my computer, my head bowed in prayer, and then I waited in silence for God to speak. The vision of Simeon the priest tending to the lampstand swirled around in my mind like the shadows on the walls of the Holy Place. *The mystery of God's light, the wonder of illumination, the power of His glorious shekinah presence in the tabernacle…it's so overwhelming*, I confessed, struggling to harness my thoughts. *When Your shekinah glory first appeared in its fullness in the tabernacle, even the holy priests could not remain standing in Your awesome presence. Who am I to presume that I can hear Your voice and see Your glory?*

My fingers flew across the keyboard as I attempted to capture the random impressions I received. One common theme ran through all of them: that priests, patriarchs, apostles, believers in Jerusalem on the day of Pentecost, God-chasers, God-pleasers, and even God-persecutors, from creation right up to this very moment, cannot encounter God apart from His marvelous light! The Almighty is the Light Giver, Jesus is the Light Bringer, and the Holy Spirit is the Illuminator!

Spirit Lamps

Suddenly, the Lord interrupted me. His voice was not audible; His words resonated in my spirit. While God rarely speaks to us in an audible voice, we are privileged to discern His message with spiritual ears. His sheep hear His voice. (See John 10:2–4, 16, 27.) The clicking of the keyboard instantly ceased. My fingers froze, motionless in His presence.

"Dale, who tends My lampstand now?" He asked.

"Why, we do, Lord," I immediately responded. "It's our responsibility as believers."

"You are wrong!" He replied.

Oh no, not again, I thought. *I should know better than to answer out of my intellect! I did the same thing when He asked me a few months ago what the showbread does.*[1] *By now, I should know that things aren't what they first appear to be in God's kingdom. His secrets are always a surprise.*

"Lord," I reneged, "please forgive my presumption. I am so quick to rely upon my own intellect."

"Son," He said with patience, "you don't tend the lamp. You *are* the lamp! My Holy Spirit is the One who tends the Lamp."

The revelation of what He had spoken exploded inside of me. Immediately, Solomon's words scrolled in capital letters like a marquis across my mind: *"The spirit of a man is the lamp of the LORD"* (Proverbs 20:27).

"You are My lampstand!" He continued. "My Holy Spirit is the oil and the flame. You are the container, the vessel. The Holy Spirit is the teacher and revelator. The testimony of the Lord is the spirit of prophecy. (See Revelation 19:10.) I have sent My Spirit to illuminate your life and your understanding. He reveals Me and brings My secrets into the light. You cannot experience My presence or understand My mysteries apart from the illuminating presence of My Holy Spirit." (See Psalm 36:9.)

The Hidden Wisdom of God

The impact of this truth gave me new insight into Paul's words to the Spirit-filled believers in the Corinthian church:

We speak wisdom among those who are mature, yet not the wisdom of this age, nor of the rulers of this age, who are coming to nothing. But we speak the wisdom of God in a mystery, the hidden wisdom which God ordained before the ages for our glory, which none of the rulers of this age knew; for had they known, they would not have crucified the Lord of glory. But as it is written: "Eye has not seen, nor ear heard, nor have entered into the heart of man the things which God has prepared for those who love Him." But God has revealed them to us through His Spirit. For the Spirit searches all things, yes, the deep things of God. For what man knows the things of a man except the spirit of the man which is in him? Even so no one knows the things of God except the Spirit of God. Now we have received, not the spirit of the world, but the Spirit who is from God, that we might know the things that have been freely given to us by God. These things we also speak, not in words which man's wisdom teaches but which the Holy Spirit teaches, comparing spiritual things with spiritual....For "who has known the mind of the LORD that he may instruct Him?" But we have the mind of Christ.

(1 Corinthians 2:6–13, 16)

Ask of Me

Centuries ago, King David expressed his passion for the presence of God:

One thing I have desired of the LORD, that will I seek: That I may dwell in the house of the LORD all the days of my life, to behold the beauty of the LORD, and to inquire in His temple. For in the time of trouble He shall hide me in His pavilion; in the secret place of His tabernacle He shall hide me: He shall set me high upon a rock. (Psalm 27:4–5)

Just like Simeon the priest and countless others who were privileged to approach God, David understood that within the depths of the tabernacle, standing before the lampstand, he could inquire of the Lord. There, in the awesome light of His presence, God revealed Himself and brought to light His mysteries. In the golden light of His countenance, He gave revelation and understanding, even to a king!

David's passion was for God's presence. He knew he could not survive without it. Like David, Paul understood and taught that without God's presence and illumination, we are hopelessly lost in the vain imaginings and pursuits of our carnal desires and deficient human intellect. Without the divine wisdom and revelation of the Holy Spirit, we cannot know Jesus, let alone comprehend the deep things of God that He has concealed in mystery. We need the mind of Christ! We need the light of the lampstand!

Neglecting the Light

Tears of repentance formed in my eyes and fell onto the computer keyboard as the Holy Spirit convicted me of my own spiritual condition. *I am a living lampstand,* I thought, *but the flame of God's presence has grown so dim that my spirit is gasping to stay alive. Because of my neglect, the supply of the holy oil of Your presence in my life is dangerously low. I urgently need to be refilled!*[2] *The wick of my human spirit is blackened and charred with the ash of ministry burnout and worldly cares. It needs to be trimmed and refreshed. I am in desperate need of an audience with You, Jesus. You are my High Priest.* (See Genesis 14:18–20; Hebrews 7:1–28.) *You are the Light Giver. The only One who can fill my emptiness is Your Holy Spirit.*

Overcome with regret and shame, I confessed my disgraceful condition. *It's been months since I have spent quality time with You in the well of Your presence, Lord. I am such a hypocrite; how can I point people to intimacy with You and tell them that You are waiting for them when I am such a poor example myself?*

I struggled to find some comfort and encouragement. *Am I the only one who is so undisciplined? Surely, there are others like me, Christians who know they need intimacy with God but fail to pursue Him diligently. Could this be how David felt?* I wondered. *Is it possible that, despite his passion, he also neglected God's presence?*

I Really Miss You

Instantly, the Holy Spirit responded to my pain. He brought to my remembrance a dream I'd had the preceding evening. The night vision had begun with a vivid scene in a beautiful outdoor garden restaurant. I was sitting at a small, circular, white wrought-iron table directly across from a beloved spiritual daughter. We gazed into each other's eyes. As I studied her, I began to cry. "I really miss you!" I said, overcome with emotion. The words came from deep within my soul.

"I know," she replied. After a long pause, she said, "I miss you, too!"

"I love you," I responded.

She looked deep into my eyes, as though she were reading my soul. "You're different," she said.

She's right, I thought. *Something has changed inside of me. It's a good thing. There is clarity in my spirit. I'm able to look into her eyes without breaking eye contact. I'm not hiding anymore or afraid to be seen. I'm able to gaze into her eyes without fear. There's total transparency between us.*

The next day, as I reflected on the night vision, I was impressed with how deep my emotions and feelings had been—pure, uninhibited, and honest. I had truly loved without fear, and with genuine transparency. I had searched her soul, and she had searched mine.

Suddenly, I realized that the beautiful woman in the dream represented God. The dream had been an expression of the true longing in my heart for Him. From deep within my spirit, I was saying, "I really miss You, Lord! I love You." The deepest part of me was calling out to the depths in Him. But, in reality, the dream had served as a warning. I really wasn't changed inside, and I knew it. I was living in disobedience. I was neglecting my first love.

A Smoking Flax He Will Not Quench[3]

"Lord, I'm afraid that You will no longer speak to me because of my neglect," I confessed. "But I cannot hide it from You. You know my heart better than anyone else. It's You I really miss deep inside! I'm so sorry, Lord!

"I'm heartbroken. Why am I so disobedient? I have neglected Your invitation to intimacy. I desperately need Your help. My lifestyle must change! I know that You're asking for total surrender. I must make the choice: Will I spend the remainder of my life in selfish pursuits, or will I be sold out to You? Will my focus be self-preservation or abandonment to Your will for me?

"No more neglect," I vowed. "No more reluctance or halfhearted worship. No more making ministry my priority. My desire, my real longing, is a lifestyle of loving You, Jesus. I want to be recklessly abandoned to You. I want to walk with You like Enoch walked with God. (See Genesis 5:24.) I have come to the end of myself! No more hiding or faking it. I cannot go on without intimacy with You."

Living Lampstands

His response was instantaneous. "My son, I know your heart. If you will serve Me unreservedly, the revelation of My secrets will broaden and deepen in the well of My presence. You know the path into My presence. It is still open. I am waiting for you. Would you turn your sons away? Neither will I turn My own sons and daughters away from My presence. Because of your neglect and lack of discipline, others have drawn up the vessels of revelation which I had assigned and intended for you; but do not be afraid. I knew that this would happen. I trust that you have learned this lesson well.

"I am calling you to come before Me and minister to Me. Wait before Me in the secret place. I want you to become like the lampstand, filled and saturated with the oil of My Holy Spirit. Let My light shine upon you. Inquire of Me. In My light, you will see light. My Spirit will enlighten and ignite you with the sevenfold light of revelation.

"I am summoning My sons and daughters into My presence. I am going to give My church prophetic insight and strategy. The Holy Spirit is preparing My end-time laborers for the last and greatest harvest of souls. He will bring the needed illumination. Get ready! My Spirit is about to move in fresh, new bursts of power. I will release the mighty wind of My Spirit upon the earth. Entire nations will be impacted by prophetic truth."

God's Invitation to You

Do you hear the invitation of the Holy Spirit? He is summoning *you* into God's presence! He wants to reveal His thoughts and ways to you. "*For 'who has known the mind of the LORD that he may instruct Him?' But we have the mind of Christ*" (1 Corinthians 2:16).

Don't delay. The Lord is waiting to reveal to you the deep things in His heart. Seek His face! Invite the Holy Spirit to anoint you, enlighten you, and reveal God's strategies to you. He will open your spiritual eyes. He is the Light Giver. He wants you to become a seer!

PART TWO

THE SEERS

*"I will stand my watch and set myself on the rampart,
and watch to **see** what He will **say** to me."*
—Habakkuk 2:1, emphasis added

6

A TALE OF TWO MEN

We don't see light; we see with it! But seeing can be deceptive. Our vision can be impaired or unreliable. What we think we see may be an illusion. Both the eyes and the mind can play tricks on us. What the physical eyes discern may be far from the truth because the brain must filter every perception—and, in the process, thoughts and feelings come into play. Opinions and convictions often distort reality. If seeing is believing, then why are there so many skeptics and unbelievers? A deciding factor is what kind of light you are using. If your mind and spirit are darkened, no amount of external light can adequately illumine a subject for you to form an accurate perception.

The Bible provides some instructive examples of blurred perception. Observe and consider as we compare two men, both of them unique and coming from very different backgrounds. One man perfectly illustrates the distress of blindness, while the other illustrates the danger of seeing but not perceiving. The first man is anonymous—a face in the crowd who, because of the persistence of his daring friends, was suddenly thrust upon the stage of history. The second man became world famous, but, to his eternal embarrassment, his actions as a young man once earned him a reputation as a murderer. His arrogant convictions had blinded him.

The scenes are set in our imagination. In the first scene, life seems common and uneventful, as it often does. But that is about to change. A blind man is about to see.

Scene One: Opening Blind Eyes

The eastern sunlight filtered through the blanket of mist above the sea and cast morning shadows on the waking town. Day dawned in the city of Bethsaida, just like the countless sunrises that had preceded it. What had for years been a small village on the shores of the Sea of Galilee was now a bustling city, enlarged and beautified by Philip the Tetrarch in honor of Julia, daughter of the Roman emperor Augustus. But the accomplishments of political power and wealth would pale in the light of the event that was about to occur in this city. From this day forward, Bethsaida would forever be known for a different reason.

The inconspicuous fishing boat landed on the northern shore of the Sea of Galilee. Its occupants stepped from the small craft into the gentle surf, stretching away the stiffness of the night crossing from Dalmanutha on the distant, western coast. They breathed deep of the fresh morning air, then made their way into the town. It wasn't long before they were recognized. Their previous visit had left a lasting impression. Word spread rapidly through the city. A crowd quickly gathered.

Excitement exploded as many vividly recalled how, just a few months prior, a multitude had followed Jesus and His disciples to a deserted place outside of town. They had sat for hours in the hot sun as He taught them about the kingdom of God. Many had been healed that day as He prayed and touched them. Who could ever forget the moment when, looking up to heaven, He had prayed a simple prayer of blessing upon the five loaves and two fish, and gone on to feed five thousand men, not to mention all of the women and children who were there, as well? (See 14:1421.) It was a miracle! And now, the Miracle Worker had come back.

A commotion erupted at the periphery of the crowd as several men pushed their way abruptly through the throngs of people. "Make way!" they shouted, their voices determined and urgent. They jostled and shoved their way toward Jesus. For years, they had led their blind friend around. They had served their brother as best they could, guiding him through the simple duties of life as they cared for his needs. Yet, despite their attempts to comfort and encourage him, their own hearts ached continually to see him in such a helpless state.

Hope pulsed through their veins as they rehearsed in their minds the testimonies of many who had been healed by Jesus' touch. *If only we could bring him to the Healer* had been their perpetual desire. Now, nothing would stop them from bringing their friend to Him. They would not be denied. They fell at Jesus' feet and, with heartrending cries of desperation, begged Him to heal their friend. "Please, Master," they cried, "please, touch him! Have mercy upon him, Lord." The crowd stood in a hush. Every eye was fixed on the Master. The blind man stood in silent helplessness before Jesus.

The Trees Are Walking

Jesus reached forward with a slight smile on His face. His eyes sparkled like a fountain, pouring forth liquid love that washed over everyone. He tenderly grasped the hand that had known only the touch of his beloved friends but now felt the warmth and pulse of the Son of God. The crowd watched in awe. The atmosphere was electric; those standing close by gasped to catch their breath. Jesus spoke softly, and then, turning, He led the blind man by the hand through the crowd and headed for the outskirts of town.

The blind man followed his new guide, stumbling now and then on the stone-covered roadway. An unearthly peace descended upon him. His countenance was radiant. Heat emanated from his face. He felt like he was on fire. He followed unhesitatingly.

The Master led His blind companion away from the seaside town, until the rooftops were barely visible in the distance. Finally, they stopped by the side of the road. Only a few had followed them. The crowd back in the city had somehow sensed that this was for the invited only, even though the Master had not said so.

The blind man waited expectantly. His useless eyes were closed, but he discerned the time of day from the heat of the late-morning sun. Without warning, moistness covered his eyelids, and he felt a puff of breath upon his face. He flinched backward, as though hit by a thousand volts of electricity. Stunned, he reeled from the impact and almost fell, but he was steadied by two hands that grasped his head and gently stroked his eyes. Slowly his eyelids opened. It was like waking from a long sleep. Light penetrated the darkness as he squinted with discomfort.

"Wait—what is that?" He paused. "Shapes moving in the distance."

"Do you see anything?" Jesus queried.

"Yes! Oh, yes!" he cried. "I see men walking! They look like trees."

Jesus reached down once more and touched his eyes a second time. "Look again!" the Master commanded.

"I can see clearly now!" he shouted with unashamed exuberance. "I see everything clearly!"

They sat together talking for a long time. Jesus spoke of the future, the kingdom of God, and the love of the Father. They laughed together and, at times, cried. Tears of joy fell from the healed man's eyes and dampened the dry ground. *My life is restored*, he thought. *What should I do now?* He wanted to run, shout, and proclaim to the entire city what the Master had done for him.

Before he could ask the Master, Jesus was already walking back toward the city. He glanced back over His shoulder and spoke His last words to him: "Don't go back to town! Don't tell anyone in the city what happened to you. Go home!"

As he *watched* Jesus casually walk away, he knew he would never be the same again. Every waking moment of every day would be a miracle to him. He could see! But why had the Master forbidden him to return to town? Was it to prevent him from going back to his old ways and habits? Was it to avoid the chance of a large crowd gathering and overwhelming Jesus or preventing Him from fulfilling His mission?

How can I possibly keep quiet and not tell the entire city? he wondered. He was filled with so much zeal. Everything within him wanted to shout aloud and declare what Jesus had done. *How can someone who was blind but now sees not declare the revelation of who Jesus is? Perhaps those who might hear it are not ready to receive it yet.*

That night, around the family table, he retold for the third time the events of the day. His wife, with tears of joy streaming down her face, continually spoke the praises of God. As he held his daughter tightly and gazed into her beautiful face for the very first time, he said, "I love you." Later that night, he drifted off to sleep, knowing that the answer to a long-hidden mystery was forever settled in his heart. It was a seed, a microcosm of the coming revelation. "I met the King," he whispered, "and soon the world will know of His presence, even if I can't tell them myself." (See Mark 8:13–26.)

Jesus continued His journey. From time to time, His thoughts traveled back to that moment outside of Bethsaida when He spoke to the man who was blind and restored his vision. Jesus knew that He had accomplished more than just a physical miracle that day. He had opened the man's spiritual eyes and revealed His lordship. But the city was not ready for this revolutionary truth yet. Jesus wasn't interested in creating excitement and encouraging false expectations of approaching political deliverance. He was on a mission that would transform all mankind forever. Many things had yet to be accomplished before the full manifestation of who He was would be declared.

The curtain closes on scene one. A blind man can see because of Jesus.

The stage is rearranged for the next scene, a completely different scenario: A man and his companions race toward a distant city on horseback. The thundering hooves betray their deliberate, ominous intentions. Their hearts are consumed with murderous thoughts.

Scene Two: Blinding Light

I must protect the true faith of my fathers, Saul thought, as his horse sped down the road to Damascus. He was a man possessed. Perspiration dotted his forehead, making small, brown streaks in the dust that had settled on his face. Even though he was small in stature, his attire revealed his religious status. He carried no weapons; instead, he was armed with papers granting him authority from the high priest to capture and put in chains those who polluted the synagogues and claimed to be people of "the Way." He did not speak to his companions, but they knew his intentions well. Murder was in his heart. He was eager to cover the 150 miles between Jerusalem and his destination in as little time as possible.

Saul's thoughts came in rapid succession: *All my years of training and education at Gamaliel's school…how could anyone believe this heretical nonsense? Our fathers made known the only true way to God.*

There was a smug satisfaction as he recalled the moments of victory recently won. The blasphemous words of a zealot called Stephen echoed in his mind. "The audacity of that heretic, to even think that he could interpret God's plan for Israel," he grumbled in disdain.

Saul grimaced at the thought of such blasphemy. He could still feel Stephen's warm garments being placed in his arms and hear the bone-crushing thud of the lethal stones thrown by the crowd of religious zealots as they smashed into Stephen's head and torso. He watched the heretic's blood puddle on the ground under his broken body. The crowd screamed with righteous indignation and then fell silent when they were finished. The smell of death lingered in his nostrils. It was then that he realized that the campaign in Jerusalem would not be enough. He was eager to do more. (See Acts 6:8–7:60.)

Yet, deep inside, beneath Saul's reasoning and logic, there was an uneasy gnawing. He could neither explain it nor identify its source, but he knew something was wrong. A surging, unstoppable tide of emotion inside him pressed against his rib cage and steadily, unrelentingly, sucked the life from him. No matter how hard he tried, he couldn't assuage its persistent onslaught. His thoughts were battered by this barrage of emotion like an unsecured tent door flapping in a strong wind, demanding attention before it tore completely off. No matter how hard he tried to reason, he just couldn't explain it away.

Saul also struggled to understand what could drive a young man to willingly give his life for such a cause. What could evoke such loyalty and devotion? He could not erase that final moment from his memory. He could still see the glance from Stephen. Their eyes had met for only a moment, but what compassion and mercy had emanated from this man in his moment of death!

The sight was indelible. Stephen had spoken his last words in excruciating pain as blood trickled from his broken and battered jaw. He had barely whispered his final request, but Saul had heard it. Those words kept repeating like blaring trumpets in his head: "Lord, don't charge them with this sin. Lord Jesus, receive my spirit."

The man didn't die, he mused. *It's as if he fell into a peaceful eternal sleep.* The thing that troubled Saul the most were Stephen's haunting words: "Lord, don't charge them with this sin."

Spiritual Roadblock

Suddenly, Saul was encompassed in pure brilliance. The shaft of magnified light completely surrounded him. His horse, stunned by the unexpected brightness, lurched sideways and stumbled in the road. Saul was thrown to the ground. His eyelids instinctively closed tight. Time froze. He lifted his face toward the light, and then he heard someone call his name. "Saul! Saul! Why are you persecuting Me?"

That undefined gnawing deep in his gut exploded into his consciousness. He struggled to speak. Finally, hesitatingly, he stuttered, "Who are You, Lord?" His entire body trembled in fear.

"I am Jesus," came the response. "I'm the One you persecute. It has been painful for you to disregard your conscience, Saul. You have been fighting against Me."

A different kind of light flashed into Saul's spirit. The enigma of the last few months dissolved into revelation. A peace settled into him like the calm that follows the fierce storms that often assault the Sea of Galilee. Immediately, with an inner clarity he had never experienced before, he understood Stephen's peaceful departure. Now he realized how Stephen had been able to forgive the worst of offenses.

Saul saw the terrible ugliness of his sin. He surrendered. The inner war was over! Taken captive by the Master, he could never go back. Like a man whose death sentence had been commuted, he breathed deeply and then spoke, with a transformed heart, "What do You want me to do, Lord? I am Yours to command."

"Get up, Saul. Go into Damascus. You will be told there what you must do."

He felt the hands of his companions on his shoulders. They did not speak as he stood to his feet. He forced his eyes open but saw only deep darkness. *He was blind!*

Waiting to See

His companions led him into Damascus and found lodging for him at the home of a man called Judas, and then they departed. For three days, Saul waited in the house of a man he did not know, isolated by his blindness, waiting for a word from God. He ate nothing. He spent all his time alone in his room, praying. In the silence of his prayers, God spoke to Saul. In a vision, he saw a man coming into the house to lay his hands on him. He was told his name: Ananias. This was all he had to cling to. And so he waited.

Saul heard the footsteps outside his door. His hearing was extra keen now. He heard the sound of a strange voice, a man talking to Judas just outside his room. The door swung open, and someone approached him.

"Saul, I am Ananias."

"Thank God you have come," Saul replied. "I have been waiting."

"The Lord, who appeared to you on the road, has sent me to deliver a message to you, Saul. He wants you to know that you are His chosen vessel. You are to bear witness to His name before Gentiles, kings, and the children of Israel. In the days to come, He will show you the things you must suffer for His name."

Saul buckled at the impact of Ananias' words. "Me, a chosen vessel?" he asked. "I am the least of all. How could He choose me for such an honor, after all I have done?" An overwhelming compassion rose in his heart for his race. *My people*, he thought. *God save my people. But how, Lord? They will never listen to me, a traitor.* Instantly, he thought of his Roman citizenship. A sudden, inexplicable urge to travel came upon him. He felt a burning sensation as his feet were anointed with fire. *I have to go! I must go!* he thought. *The world must be told about Jesus. But how can I go? I cannot see!*

Ananias reached forth his hands and laid them upon Saul's head. He spoke with distinct authority. Saul knew that he spoke on God's behalf. "Brother Saul, in the name of Jesus of Nazareth, receive your sight and be filled with the Holy Spirit!"

Saul was overcome by the presence of the Holy Spirit. He thought for a moment that Ananias had poured hot oil all over him. His skin tingled with supernatural anointing. His limbs trembled with electricity. His face felt flushed. The power of God surged through him, quickening his whole being. "I am totally alive!" he shouted.

After days of not being able to see, Saul felt the crusty scales that had formed over his eyes fall to the floor. He opened them wide, indulging in the restored joy of viewing his surroundings. There was a strangely familiar glow in the room. It reminded him of the light that had initially blinded him on the road into town. It was emanating from Ananias' face.

This is a new beginning, he realized. An unquenchable urge came over him. No, it was more than that—it was an unction, a special grace, a divine mandate, an inescapable destiny. *I must tell the world. I must proclaim the truth. Jesus is alive!*

Saul had begun his journey to Damascus as someone who thought he knew his assignment. He hadn't realized that he had been consumed by a purpose that was destroying him. He thought back to that critical, world-changing moment on the road, and then, with stunned realization, he spoke. "I was so wrong, God. You had to blind me so I could see."

"I must finish my assignment," Ananias said. "Follow me, Saul." They stood in the shallow pool of water, and Ananias braced Saul's back as he lowered him into the water. "I baptize you, Saul, in the name of the Lord Jesus Christ!" Ananias declared. The cool water testified to Saul's spiritual death and resurrection as Ananias lifted him from beneath the surface of the pool. Saul was a new man. His real journey was about to begin. (See Acts 8:1–3; 9:1–22.)

The curtain closes on scene two. The play is ended.

⌒

These characters are real. These events are recorded history. We have imagined what these two men experienced. Their raw emotions and vivid thoughts are almost palpable, and it's reasonable to assume they are accurate. But, looking beyond the theatrical license, we need to extract the central message. What can we deduce from these two strikingly different scenes? What vital lesson does God want to communicate? Let's dig deeper.

7

CLEAR VISION

Our comparison in the previous chapter of the two blind men and their respective handicaps clearly demonstrates the danger of flawed vision. Jesus' response to their blindness is a warning for all of us to heed. It is a lesson in what it takes to acquire clear vision.

The first man, whose name we do not know, was blind physically. He was totally dependent on others to guide him through life. Even though his human helpers had the best of intentions, they were unable to restore his vision. The best they could do was to make his life as comfortable as possible. But providence smiled upon them. There was a glimmer of hope when they heard about a Man called Jesus who possessed the power to heal. They even spoke with various townspeople who testified how He had healed them personally and performed many miracles. When the opportunity came, they seized it. Oh, what delight filled their souls when Jesus healed their friend! But what an unusual procedure He performed. Breaking all codes of etiquette, He actually spit into the blind eyes. He massaged His saliva into the eyelids, and the breath of His mouth brought vision. What is even more amazing is that it took a *second touch*. Why?

Could it be that the Master was imparting more than just the physical ability to see? Was it necessary for the blind man to be touched twice to have really clear vision? Surely, the Son of God could have healed him with the first burst of breath from His mouth. There has to be a deeper meaning here! What is God trying to communicate? Beyond the wonder of this marvelous miracle lies a foundational truth to life that helps us to make sense of our purpose and existence. It has to do with the way we *see* things.

Some of us are blind to our world and cannot discern the times in which we live. We may even go through our entire life never realizing that God can enable us to see clearly. It is His heart's desire for us to be oriented to our world from His perspective, to understand the times in which we live, and to know what to do with our lives. Yet, instead of seeking Him for understanding, we rely on human guides who lead us here and there. However good their intentions, we are no better off. Philosophies come and go, championed by great thinkers. Political theories and economic cycles ebb and flow like tidal pools set in the ocean of history, and still we struggle to make sense of it all. The experts have not helped us, and Satan seeks to keep us in the darkness.

There are some people among us who have a limited dimension of understanding. They are not blind. They see men "as trees walking." Their perspective is fuzzy, at best. Yes, it is better than blindness, but they are still left with an imperfect picture. They are the ones whose eyes have been touched the first time, but their vision has not been completely restored. It is better to see men as trees walking than to see nothing at all, but Jesus was not satisfied with that, and neither should we be. It takes a second touch to see clearly. It requires a full impartation of the Holy Spirit to have an accurate understanding of our world and God's purpose for us in it.

Jesus breathed upon the apostles in the upper room and said, "*Receive the Holy Spirit*" (John 20:22). Many of us have been touched in a similar way. This is our first encounter—the new birth that opens our spiritual eyes. At that moment, we think we have it all. Eventually, we discover that we see men as trees walking.

It should not surprise us that Jesus requires us to receive a second touch. The disciples waited for fifty days until the Holy Spirit came *a second time* and opened their eyes clearly to see their world, to understand the times in which they lived, and to interpret their destiny and purpose in the context of eternity. In an instant, everything came into focus.

The World in Focus

Jesus often used His actions to teach an important prophetic truth. His three-day "delay" in raising Lazarus from the dead was intended to be a shadow and a type of His own coming death and resurrection. When He was criticized for waiting too long, He responded, *"Lazarus is dead. And I am glad for your sakes that I was not there, that you may believe"* (John 11:14–15). Those who followed Him did not understand the spiritual significance of His delay until His death, burial, and resurrection.

I am convinced that, in a similar fashion, Jesus was communicating to us by His actions when He healed the blind man in Bethsaida that, in order to see clearly, we need more than a single touch from God. We need more than the eyes of a newborn spiritual baby struggling to find focus and make meaning of the world. We need the all-empowering, eye-opening fullness of the Holy Spirit—a Pentecostal revelation that brings our world into focus from an eternal perspective. I am not referring to a denomination or an emotional experience. I am speaking of that awesome moment when the Master comes and touches our eyes and we no longer see men as trees walking. We truly see clearly, and life comes into focus. Only the fullness of Holy Spirit can bring this kind of vision!

Blindness of the Soul

But what of Saul, the man possessed with a search-and-destroy mission that he hoped would ultimately lead to the death and destruction of this new cult, "the Way," which threatened his beloved Judaism? How does he factor into this spiritual equation? Saul's problem was the simple fact that he was wrong! He had a blindness that far exceeded that which crippled his physical abilities. His was a blindness of the soul. He was blinded by his own opinion.

Nothing is as insidious as deception! It is a subtle evil whereby the one deceived has no idea that he is blind. Deception is believing a lie and crusading for its global acceptance as if it were absolute truth. It is dogmatic and often abusively pharisaical. Jesus addressed this crusading blindness when He said to the scribes and Pharisees, *"You are mistaken* [literally, "deceived"], *not knowing the Scriptures nor the power of God"* (Matthew 22:29).

How tragic to live an entire lifetime accepting as truth what is really false. To be cheated in the fullest sense of depravity because you bought into a lie and didn't know it—this is the ultimate waste. It is the tragedy of a life lived in darkness, only to be ended by a sudden burst of reality when it is too late. It is the ultimate life crisis. Truth makes all the difference.

This was Saul's world. He was a man driven to defend the truth, as he understood it. He didn't know he was blind. What would it take to open his eyes? What could stop his rapid rush to destruction? What could harness this powerful drive and turn it in the right direction? The solution was blindness! He needed to be disconnected from the external, superficial environment. He had to be stopped in his tracks. And so, God broke into Saul's world. With all the force of eternity, He interrupted Saul's life and altered his worldview. In a moment, on a dusty road leading Saul to further hopelessness, God stepped in and blocked his path. Life, as Saul had known it, was over. The true Light had arrived. In his physically blinded condition, he saw reality and encountered the Way, the Truth, and the Life for the first time.

This experience was more than just being thrown from a horse. Saul was being launched into a dimension he didn't even know existed. It was the discovery of ultimate truth that finally opened his spiritual eyes. His deception was exposed in the light of revelation. He would no longer be cheated by the lie.

God Wants Us to See

What does it take for God to open our eyes? For some, it is the violating of cultural norms and the sudden impact of "spit" on our eyes and the "breath" of God in our face. God comes and is even willing to touch us a second time so that we might see clearly because He knows that having a distorted view of our world is partial vision.

To see men as trees walking and have no hope of any clearer view is to live in a world of half-truths with no final resolution or clarity. It is life out of focus, where we wander, condemned to an eclectic confusion of ideas without any absolutes. It is a dim existence spent groping for resolution and constantly seeking to look through different sets of glasses, hoping to find the right frame of reference that will finally help us make sense of our world. In His mercy, God refuses to leave us with partial vision. He sends His Holy Spirit to fully open our eyes.

For others, it may require a cataclysmic encounter. Life may have to come to a halting, grinding stop. We may have to be stripped of our self-assuredness and blinded to our own biases so that the real truth can shine forth. We may need to be knocked from our "horse" and thrown to the ground of reality. God has a way of humbling us by reminding us of our humanness. In that posture, we finally cry, "Lord," like Saul did, and He can open our spiritual eyes at last.

One thing is certain. God wants us to see! He wants us to see not only with our physical eyes but also with the eyes of our spirit, so that we may live circumspectly with the kind of "knowing" that characterized Simeon the priest. In the light of His revealed wisdom and knowledge, we not only discover our true purpose in the scheme of things; we also live with supernatural determination and intention.

Spiritual Vision

The light of prophetic revelation is a gift from God that suddenly breaks through into our existence. He initiates it! He lifts the curtain and offers us a glimpse of His ultimate purpose and divine nature, and, suddenly, all of life comes into focus. Our world begins to make sense because we *see from His perspective*. This is called "spiritual vision." It is the ability to see with the eyes of the spirit.

Within the biblical volume of wisdom called Proverbs is an invaluable passage. Amidst the abundant precious gems of truth effortlessly mined from this literary landscape, it is the "mother lode"—a vein of ore that provides unfathomable riches. It speaks of an ability to *see* that comes from beyond the human frame of reference. It is an ancient key to unlock reality and purpose. It aptly describes the insatiable longing of the one who penned it, King Solomon.

This ancient king hungered for a discernment that superseded his peers' and that would enable him to judge, lead, and govern a nation with justice and integrity. To Solomon, this knowledge was the pure ore of *revelation*. Nothing—not riches, fame, or success—could compare with possessing this, the greatest of all treasures. He knew that without the ability to discern, he would be a personal and public failure. His life would be wasted on the trivial, and he would go to his grave a frustrated man. When God granted him one request as the newly installed king of Israel, there was no hesitation; he spoke from his heart and asked for wisdom. God, the Source of wisdom, was so pleased with his request that He granted him riches, wealth, and honor, as well.

No doubt his father, David, had described to Solomon the previous ages when men and nations had dwelled in darkness, lacking an understanding of their times and void of any true sense of God's purpose or direction. Israel's own history spoke of a time when judges ruled the people. *"In those days there was no king in Israel; everyone did what was right in his own eyes"* (Judges 21:25). Solomon heard the story of Samuel, who, as a boy, ministered to the Lord before Eli. "*The word of the* Lord *was rare in those days; there was no widespread revelation*" (1 Samuel 3:1). King David even expressed his own frustrations as he recited the contemplation of Asaph with his little son Solomon on his knee: "*We do not see our signs; there is no longer any prophet; nor is there any among us who knows how long*" (Psalm 74:9).

When Solomon was about to take the throne, he was faced with his own inability and weakness. How could he presume to govern so great a people? The only way it would be possible was with a higher knowledge and insight than man could attain on his own. He knew that "*where there is no vision, the people perish*" (Proverbs 29:18 kjv). He needed to see from God's perspective, and only God could grant that insight. Solomon realized that he didn't need a good idea or some all-consuming passion or project to occupy his life. What he needed was a revelation of God's will and eternal purpose that would give meaning and make sense out of his life and frame his kingship in the context of a bigger picture. This would enable him to lead the people in disciplined lives of productivity.

It was this kind of vision, this ability to see, this wisdom that transcends the learning of man, which became for Solomon the pure gold of life. God granted it to him. Solomon placed it in the soil of Proverbs near the end of the book. He wrote, "Without revelation we perish." A more complete translation of this text reads, "Without a prophetic vision the people dwell carelessly."

Solomon's words imply that unless we have supernatural revelation, we will live in a world limited by our own definitions and mental landscapes. We will struggle to maintain any kind of purposeful existence. We will eventually succumb to our human weaknesses and yield to our fleshly appetites. We will become a lawless race, lacking our bearings, just drifting on the sea of time and eternity without a compass.

A Famine of *Vision*

The prophet Amos gave a clear warning:

"*Behold, the days are coming,*" *says the Lord* God, "*that I will send a famine on the land, not a famine of bread, nor a thirst for water, but of hearing the words of the* Lord. *They shall wander from sea to sea, and from north to east; they shall run to and fro, seeking the word of the* Lord, *but shall not find it.*"

(Amos 8:11–12)

Amos was not speaking of the absence of Scripture or someone to teach from the Torah. He was speaking of a *closed heaven* and a *silent God* who refused to speak into man's predicament and bring divine direction.

History can be chronicled not only by the actions of men and nations, of armies and epochs, or discoveries and inventions, but also by the absence of revelation or by those divine, time-altering moments when God breaks through the curtain of darkness to speak to us. It is this God-initiated revelation that restores sight to the blind and delivers us from a world out of focus. When it comes, God's prophetic vision instantly obscures all other vistas. Like Saul, we are locked in with ultimate reality. We cannot escape reality, nor do we wish to. We now discern it with the eyes of our spirit.

The Cry of My Heart

What God enables us to see makes all the difference. Without vision, we will waste our lives and our generational purpose on paltry pursuits that are self-serving and, at best, make a temporary improvement in the condition of mankind. The cry of my heart is that God will enlighten us with His revelation. We desperately need our spiritual eyes to be opened by a secret-place encounter with the living God.

My hope is that not only will you perceive your need of prophetic revelation but also that the Holy Spirit will immerse you in His supernatural light so you may see the kingdom purposes and perspective of almighty God for our times. Only that vision can blind us to lesser goals.

People with this type of vision not only understand the events of their times and interpret them from God's point of view; God uses them to affect history. There was such a group of people centuries ago who had this kind of influence. We can learn much from their example. They are the sons and daughters of Issachar. They possessed such a high degree of spiritual insight and wisdom that they were sought out and consulted by kings and commoners alike. They were seers. They exemplified the ability to see with spiritual eyes. We need to understand this ability and seek the same grace and anointing that God imparted to Issachar.

8

ISSACHAR AND SONS

Allow me to introduce you to the tribe of Issachar. The members of this tribe are history influencers that exemplify vision in action. Uniquely identified by their exceptional ability to see and discern, Issachar's progeny knew how to access the Light Giver and consequently lived life with their spiritual eyes wide open. Their understanding exceeded the unenlightened perceptions of their times.

Is it possible to possess this ability in our generation? Dare we conclude that God wants us to be like them? Let's find out. The life and history of Issachar and his progeny will help us to understand what it means to be a seer. To fully comprehend the significance of the anointing upon Issachar, we must search the history of Israel. The story begins with his father, Jacob.

Patriarch Jacob

Young, virile, handsome Jacob, the future patriarch and father of Israel, was on a mission. He was in search of a wife. He journeyed eastward and came to a desert oasis. There, by an ancient well in the land of the east, he was smitten by the beautiful Rachel. It was love at first sight! Casting protocol and social correctness to the desert winds, he enfolded her tightly in his arms, not caring that the other shepherds could see, and kissed her passionately. Lifting his eyes to God, he wept with joy and gave thanks to the Almighty for leading him to this beautiful treasure.

Jacob was delighted to discover that Rachel was the daughter of Laban, brother of his mother, Rebecca. Jacob stayed in Haran, in his uncle's house, laboring for seven years as a shepherd in order to obtain the hand of Rachel in marriage. But when the time was fulfilled, Laban tricked Jacob. He insisted that if Jacob wanted Rachel, he would have to marry Leah also and agree to work for another seven years. Jacob agreed to the offer and married both Rachel and Leah. Jacob got the desire of his heart. He loved Rachel deeply. During the seven years that Jacob served his deceitful uncle, God blessed him with great prosperity. (See Genesis 29.)

The Problem with Two Wives

Bitter resentment arose between Rachel and Leah. Jacob loved and favored Rachel, but she was barren. When the Lord saw that Leah was unloved, He opened her womb. She bore Jacob four sons: Reuben ("behold a son"), Simeon ("God hears"), Levi ("attached"), and Judah ("praise"). In ancient days, personal names were given with a clear intent, and they revealed the purpose and character of the one so named. The names of Leah's sons chronicle her emotions: "Behold, Jacob, God has given us a son; now you will love me. God has heard and answered my prayer. Surely, you and I will be attached to each other. Now I can praise the Lord!" Then Leah stopped bearing children.

Rachel was wild with envy. She sent her maid Bilhah to Jacob in her stead, so that she might have children on her behalf. Dan ("judgment") and Naphtali ("my wrestling") were born as a result. Rachel expressed her feelings by their names: *"God has judged my case; and He has also heard my voice and given me a son.…With great wrestlings I have wrestled with my sister, and indeed I have prevailed"* (Genesis 30:6, 8).

Leah had no recourse but to send her maid, Zilpah, to Jacob, as well. Another two sons were delivered: Gad ("a troop comes") and Asher ("happy"). "I have given Jacob a troop of sons, and now I am happy. The daughters will call me blessed," she asserted.

By now, you would think that a truce between Rachel and Leah would be declared. And what about Jacob? His emotions and divided loyalties must have been painful, as well. But it was not to be. Jacob still favored Rachel.

Who can quench the zeal of a woman scorned? One day, Leah's son Reuben was gathering the wheat harvest. He spotted the purple and whitish flowers of the mandrake growing among the wheat. He knew the potent ability of this valued herb of the nightshade family. It was a powerful stimulant to promote conception. Its root also produced a powerful narcotic that was used as an ancient tranquilizer. He carefully picked the flowers and carried them home to his mother.

When Rachel found out, she was incensed and demanded some of the mandrakes. Leah pleaded with her, "You have taken away my husband; will you take away my son's mandrakes, too?"

Rachel made her a deal: "I will let you lie with Jacob tonight if you will give me some of the mandrakes."

Leah gladly accepted the offer. She met Jacob that night as he came from the fields. His masculine appearance awakened her desires. The odor of ripening wheat clung to his clothes, and there was a musky earthiness that permeated him.

She was dressed in finely woven silk. The light purple fabric draped her shoulders and wrapped around her supple body in an alluring way. Before their eyes met, Jacob could smell her perfume drifting on the evening breeze. He was aroused, not so much by her beauty as by her simple faithfulness. She was there to meet him.

She did not wait for him to make the first move. Her eyes spoke her undying devotion. With tenderness she reached to touch his callused hand, toughened by the hard labor of the harvest. "Come home, Jacob," she said seductively. "You must come home with me."

His eyes met hers, and together they walked toward the house, arm in arm. He lay with her that night. (See Genesis 30:14–16.)

It's a Boy!

Nine months later, Jacob awoke to the cries of a baby boy. "His name shall be Issachar," Leah said, "for God has given me my wages and fully repaid me for giving my handmaid to my husband."

Issachar arrived in this world as a gift from God to a woman with a pure heart whose only motive was to please her husband, Jacob. All she longed for was the love and acceptance of her husband. Issachar—the just reward, the full payment—was God's response to a broken heart; the ninth son of Jacob, his fifth by Leah. She held little Issachar in her arms and smiled as only a mother can. Jacob watched and grinned with satisfaction.

Leah went on to have a sixth son, Zebulun ("abode"). He was to her like insurance, securing her place with Jacob beyond measure. Finally, she bore a daughter, Dinah ("judgment"). But God had not forgotten Rachel. He took away her reproach and opened her womb. She gave birth to Joseph ("God will add"), and Jacob formed a special bond with the little boy immediately. (See Genesis 30:17–24.)

Twelve sons grew up in Jacob's house, each with a prophetic name and a unique personality. While Joseph was Jacob's obvious favorite, his older brother Issachar was still loved and nurtured at the side of his wise and anointed father. He had been born with destiny in his veins. He carried himself differently than the others. One day, he and his own sons would produce an entire tribe in Israel. They would stand in their own right among the tribal leaders of the nation.

Fathers Speak to Our Destiny

Very little is recorded concerning Issachar's personal history following his birth. No doubt he joined in the conspiracy with his brothers to sell Joseph into slavery in Egypt. When famine struck the land, he and his four sons, Tola, Puvah (also called Puah), Job (also called Jashub), and Shimron, along with their families, joined Jacob's caravan and took refuge in Pharaoh's house. (See Genesis 46:13.) With Joseph's blessing and Pharaoh's permission, they settled in the land of Goshen with their flocks and herds. It was there that Jacob became ill and prepared to die. He called his sons to him, that he might bless them, saying, "*Gather together, that I may tell you what shall befall you in the last days: gather together and hear, you sons of Jacob, and listen to Israel your father*" (Genesis 49:1–2).

One by one, each of the twelve men stood before the weakened patriarch as he prophesied to them. First Reuben, then Simeon and Judah, listened carefully. Zebulon came next, and then it was Issachar's turn. The old man stretched forth his hand. He spoke with a wisdom and discernment that penetrated Issachar's soul. "*Issachar is a strong donkey, lying down between two burdens; he saw that rest was good, and that the land was pleasant; he bowed his shoulder to bear a burden, and became a band of slaves*" (Genesis 49:14–15).

Issachar trembled with a sense of new awareness. His destiny was settled. He was filled with prophetic revelation and purpose. Jacob had deposited in his son's spiritual genetic code a promise with divine potential. The Light Giver had spoken through a spiritual father. Time and providence would confirm its accuracy. Issachar's prophecy would come to pass, but Jacob would not live to see it. He died in peace, and his twelve sons buried him in Canaan.

Issachar himself was finally laid to rest alongside his brothers in Goshen, but the prophecy didn't die with him. No doubt, just like his own father, Issachar stretched forth his hand and blessed his own children, imparting to them the spiritual inheritance he had first received from Jacob. The prophecy would be fulfilled through his offspring generations from this moment. Fathers speak to our destiny!

Part of the Crowd

It wasn't long before Issachar's tribe, as well as those of his brothers, experienced the hardships of slavery and bondage in Egypt. But they were chosen people with a divine destiny. God saw their horrible estate and answered their desperate pleas for help. He sent a deliverer, Moses.

The enslaved brick makers were free at last! They wasted no time getting out of Goshen. They dug up Joseph's bones, put them on a cart, and headed for the wilderness. Moses had no compass or map, but his rod and his ability to hear God's voice were more than enough. They crossed the Red Sea, leaving the pursuing armies of Egypt to drown in their footsteps.

Moses immediately set their course toward the mountain of God. His goal was to return as quickly as possible to the place where God had first spoken to him. He realized the importance of leading God's people to Mount Sinai, the place of enlightenment. Once there, they would receive further direction from God, the Light Giver. (See Exodus 1–15.)

If God can cause a bush to burn and not be consumed, surely He can light our pathway through this desert wilderness, Moses must have thought. *Only in God's presence will our destiny be fully revealed. We need God's direction,* he surely acknowledged with absolute conviction, and kept prodding the caravan deeper into the wilderness, in total dependence upon Jehovah.

The ragtag column stretched across the desert sand as far as the eye could see. The descendants of Issachar were somewhere among this eccentric throng of displaced humanity, livestock, and wagons overloaded with the spoils from the wealth of Egypt. One thing was certain: the sons of Issachar would never forget this miraculous journey.

9

DESIGNER CLOTHES

The Israelites finally arrived at the foot of Mount Sinai. They pitched their tents on the desert floor beneath the flaming mountain of God. Issachar's sons dug deep into the sand and set a single post in place. They proudly raised the banner bearing the standard of their father, Issachar, on the tall flagpole for all the camp to see. They were a courageous, sometimes stubborn, lot, with a fierce loyalty to their leaders and an unusual clarity about them. Their tribal commander, Nethanel, the son of Zuar, had his hands full overseeing 54,400 soldiers, all descendants of Issachar.

At first, the nation waited in fear and trembling at the base of the mountain as Moses ascended into the fiery presence of God to seek His counsel. But Moses' lengthy absence caused the people to grow impatient. Aaron condescended to their idolatrous behavior, and, with his instructions, they forged a golden calf and began to worship it. While Moses stood in God's presence on behalf of Israel, they were reveling in a sexual orgy of satanic proportions, totally oblivious to the severity of God's judgment that would soon come upon them.

Divine Designs

For forty days and nights, Moses stood in the presence of the Light Giver, receiving massive revelation and specific strategy and direction for Israel's culture and future. God gave Moses ten laws—commandments that would govern the Israelites' relationship with God and with one another. He revealed to Moses the blueprints for a place of worship. It was to be a mobile tent, readily adaptable to the people's nomadic lifestyle. Israel was to build this sanctuary where God would "tabernacle" (dwell) in their midst. Precise plans were given detailing this holy place of worship, along with its furniture and accoutrements.

In addition, God chose Aaron and Levi and their sons to serve Him as priests. He told Moses how to design their priestly garments and make the habiliments that they would need to fulfill their duties in His presence. God gave minutely detailed instructions regarding how the priests were to serve Him, along with the appropriate sacrifices and offerings that He required from His people.

When the time came for Moses to return to camp, God dispatched him from His presence with a singular command: "Do all of this exactly as I have instructed. Don't change or alter a single thing!" His face glowing with the light of God's presence, Moses stumbled toward the camp, gripping the words of the Light Giver tightly to his chest. He was God's courier, the bearer of the revelation of God's plans and strategy, and he was on a holy mission!

He could hear the sound of pagan worship and drunken revelry long before he could see the camp. Moses' anger raged against the sons of Jacob. That day, three thousand men were executed by the sword. Then God sent a plague upon the encampment. It had taken only a few days to deliver them from Egypt, but it would take a generation to get Egypt out of the sons of Jacob. Despite this setback, God continued to guide and speak to these stubborn and rebellious nomads. He chose them over all of the nations of the earth for a special purpose. They were to be the bearers of the Light for all of mankind. God would forge a holy nation in the heat of the desert. (See Exodus 19–34.)

Supernatural Garments

According to the instructions God gave to Moses on Mount Sinai, the names of all of the sons of Jacob were to be represented before Him in the tabernacle in two distinct ways. First, their names and symbols had to appear in two locations on the garments of the high priest. Issachar was recognized, along with his brothers, as a tribal leader.

The priesthood, with its robes and rituals, was not a religious invention of the people; it was God's requirement. It provided the only means whereby God allowed Israel to access His presence. The whole purpose of the priests' existence was to perform their duties—to establish and maintain an atmosphere pleasing to God and to minister to God in that atmosphere on behalf of the people. This demanded a life-or-death awareness of the holiness of God and the strict observance of His requirements.

The clothing of the high priest was designed to represent three things: the nature and character of God, the nation of Israel, and a symbolic and prophetic type of Jesus Christ our Great High Priest.

> The quality of the whole of these vestments, whether it was of texture or material or workmanship, was the very best of its kind—fine linen, pure gold, precious stones, costly ointment, made with cunning workmanship all used by wise hearts. This was because it was all a type of Christ's character, and nothing but the very highest quality would do to portray Him.[1]

Issachar's Birth Certificate

The high priest's vestments included a coat, with its sash; a robe; an ephod; an intricately woven belt; the breastplate that carried the Urim and the Thummim (used to discern God's will and worn over the heart of the priest); the mitre; and the holy crown. (See Leviticus 8:7–9.)

The ephod was an opulent, intricately bejeweled, dazzling vest. It was far more than a customized piece of ornamentation. Stunning in its brilliance and representational significance, it was a showcase of God's intentions toward Israel. It consisted of four pieces attached by a golden chain into one unit: the ephod, girdle, shoulder stones, and breastplate. It was placed over the shoulders of the high priest and attached at the waist by a masterfully crafted belt. It was highly visible and prophetically symbolic.

Consider the shoulder stones, which God instructed Moses to have engraved.

> *Then you shall take two onyx stones and engrave on them the names of the sons of Israel: six of their names on one stone, and six names on the other stone, in order of their birth. With the work of an engraver in stone, like the*

engravings of a signet, you shall engrave the two stones with the names of the sons of Israel. You shall set them in settings of gold. And you shall put the two stones on the shoulders of the ephod as memorial stones for the sons of Israel. So Aaron shall bear their names before the LORD on his two shoulders as a memorial.   (Exodus 28:9–12)

Engraved into solid black onyx, framed by pure gold, the names of Israel's twelve sons appeared in chronological order. On one shoulder were Reuben, Simeon, Levi, Judah, Dan, and Naphtali. On the other shoulder were Gad, Asher, *Issachar*, Zebulun, Joseph, and Benjamin. These memorial stones were worn like epaulets on a uniform. When the high priest entered into the holy presence of God in worship and intercession, the shoulder stones served as a reminder to God of each of Jacob's sons and his tribal offspring. It was a symbolic prayer inscribed on the priests' shoulders that said, "Lord God Almighty, remember the sons of Jacob and the tribes of Israel. Have mercy on them and bless them. Do not forget Your promises and the covenant You made with Abraham, Isaac, and Jacob."

Closer examination of the design of the two shoulder stones reveals a significant truth. All of the names were engraved on the *same* type of stone in the *same* handwriting. All of Israel's sons were framed in gold. No son or tribe was exalted above another. They were all precious to God, and there were no favorites in His sight. In the order of their birth, God chose to remember them as His beloved, and each one was valued equally.

Every time the high priest entered the Holy of Holies, Issachar's name appeared before God, along with the names of all of his brothers. When God saw this onyx "memo pad" and took notice, every single son of Jacob was thought of. Not one was overlooked! I wonder what His thoughts were toward Issachar.

Supernatural Birthstones

The breastplate was the centerpiece of the ephod. Moses crafted it exactly as God instructed.

You shall make the breastplate of judgment. Artistically woven according to the workmanship of the ephod you shall make it: of gold, blue, purple, and scarlet thread, and fine woven linen, you shall make it. It shall be doubled into a square: a span shall be its length, and a span shall be its width. And you shall put settings of stones in it, four rows of stones: The first row shall be *a sardius, a topaz, and an emerald; this shall be the first row; the second row shall be a turquoise, a sapphire, and a diamond; the third row, a jacinth, an agate, and an amethyst; and the fourth row, a beryl, an onyx, and a jasper. They shall be set in gold settings. And the stones shall have the names of the sons of Israel, twelve according to their names, like the engravings of a signet, each one with its own name; they shall be according to the twelve tribes....So Aaron shall bear the names of the sons of Israel on the breastplate of judgment over his heart, when he goes into the holy place, as a memorial before the LORD continually. And you shall put in the breastplate of judgment the Urim and the Thummim, and they shall be over Aaron's heart when he goes in before the LORD. So Aaron shall bear the judgment of the children of Israel over his heart before the LORD continually.*   (Exodus 28:15–21, 29–30)*

God's personal selection and placement of the twelve gemstones in the breastplate served an entirely different purpose from that of the two engraved onyx shoulder stones. Both settings contained all of the names of the tribal founders, but that was their only similarity. While the two shoulder stones represented Israel's sons equally and by chronological order of birth, in contrast, the gems on the breastplate typified each man's uniqueness and function in God's *prophetic* purpose. On the ephod, the order of their names was not based upon birth rank. Instead, each tribe was represented as having unique abilities, and each was assigned a divinely chosen place according to God's design and plan. The stones on the breastplate symbolically expressed the prophetic words of their patriarchal father, Jacob.

Like a modern army with different branches of military expertise, Israel's sons carried uniquely specific anointings to accomplish needed services in God's campaign. The sovereign placement of each tribal leader upon the breastplate actually determined the order in which Israel's column would be formed when they were marching though the wilderness and eventually into Canaan. (See Numbers 10:14–28.) The twelve tribes quickly realized and acknowledged that their order and rank were not based upon their seniority but upon God's sovereign choice and placement.

A Topaz for Issachar

Each one of Jacob's offspring was represented by a unique, precious stone with his name inscribed upon it. There is a definite connection between the character of that individual and the nature and characteristics of the stone God specifically chose to represent him. Like a signet ring, each stone served as an indicator or *sign* of the identity, quality of character, authority, and function of its possessor.

Issachar was characterized by a topaz. This particular stone was found in Ethiopia and varied in shade from transparent yellow to brownish yellow. The very meaning of the word *topaz* is quite revealing. It comes from a Greek word meaning "to seek." Legend records that the stone was discovered on an island located in the Red Sea that was often hidden by fog. Sailors who had difficulty finding the obscured island named the gem they found there "topaz" to symbolize their reward for diligent pursuit. It is easy to draw the conclusion that Issachar, whose name meant "reward" and whose stone symbolized "to seek," was identified by God's choice of a birthstone as "the one rewarded for diligently seeking."

A Hidden Message

The Bible is a supernatural book inspired by the Holy Spirit. There are hidden meanings and secrets encoded within its text that escape the detection of the casual reader. The apostle Paul spoke about a hidden wisdom not of this world:

> For the Spirit searches all things, yes, the deep things of God. For what man knows the things of a man except the spirit of the man which is in him? Even so no one knows the things of God except the Spirit of God. Now we have received, not the spirit of the world, but the Spirit who is from God, that we might know the things that have been freely given to us by God....But the natural man does not receive the things of the Spirit of God, for they are foolishness to him; nor can he know them, because they are spiritually discerned.
> (1 Corinthians 2:10–12, 14)

It is possible to have eyes and yet not see. This is exactly how Jesus described the religious people of His day.

> And the disciples came and said to Him, "Why do You speak to them in parables?" He answered and said to them, "Because it has been given to you to know the mysteries of the kingdom of heaven, but to them it has not been given. For whoever has, to him more will be given, and he will have abundance; but whoever does not have, even what he has will be taken away from

him. Therefore I speak to them in parables, because seeing they do not see, and hearing they do not hear, nor do they understand.…But blessed are your eyes for they see, and your ears for they hear."   (Matthew 13:10–13, 16)

In recent years, the book *The Bible Code* has stimulated great interest in the possibility of hidden messages existing in the pages of the sacred Scriptures. The author claims that only in recent history have we obtained the appropriate skills and necessary computer technology to unlock and interpret these secrets. From a humanistic, scientific point of view, this may be true, but from a spiritual perspective, God's secrets have always been revealed to His prophets. Amos wrote, *"Surely the Lord GOD does nothing, unless He reveals His secret to His servants the prophets"* (Amos 3:7).

Cracking the Breastplate Code

The God-inspired and designed breastplate is far more than a piece of priestly clothing. I believe that it contains an encoded message from God! In order to decipher the message, we must look past its surface symbolism to discern its prophetic content. God has often used symbols to communicate truth. If we look closely, we can discern that the nature and destiny of each of the twelve sons of Jacob is symbolically revealed by the order and nature of each stone. Remember, the gemstones are not randomly placed but are divinely ordered.

The encrypted message must be decoded from right to left and from top to bottom, in the same way that the ancient Hebrew language is read. First, we must read across the top row, where Issachar's stone holds the middle position. Adjacent to Issachar on the right is Judah. Judah means "the praise of Jehovah," and he is characterized by a sardius (colored red, typifying blood). On the left is Zebulun, or "dwelling," typified by a carbuncle (symbolizing glittering, lightning, or flashing).

Next, we must read from Issachar's position downward through the stones that are set beneath him. We find Simeon directly beneath Issachar. His name means "hearing," and he is represented by a sapphire (to cut or divide). In the center of the third row is Manasseh. His name means "forgetting my suffering," and he is characterized by an agate (a stone harder than steel that is rough and unattractive when first found but, when split and polished, is a source of delight). The entire column of four stones, with Issachar at the top, rests upon Asher at the bottom. Asher means "happy" or "blessed." He is represented by an onyx (to shine with the luster of fire or a flashing forth of splendor).

We can now decipher the encoded message of the breastplate by taking the meaning of each person's name and combining it with the unique characteristic of his assigned gemstone. When every name and symbol is translated into the words that describe it in the exact sequence they appear, the words can be used to form sentences. The resulting information regarding Issachar reads as follows:

> (From right to left): To the praise of Jehovah, the one who covers our sins with blood, Issachar the diligent seeker shall be rewarded by dwelling in the place of great insight and revelation and be for his brothers as one who understands his world and acts wisely.

> (From top to bottom): Issachar's wisdom will be based upon his ability to hear the voice of God and rightly divide and interpret His words. Although he will get knowledge and understanding at great cost, the price will seem insignificant in light of the great revelation that will burst forth from him and bring blessing to the nation.

It is strikingly clear that when God designed the breastplate, He was intending to reveal much more than His skill at designing clothing! The breastplate contains a hidden prophecy for every one of the twelve sons of Jacob. Each message can be deciphered using the same formula: read from right to left and from top to bottom, using the symbolic meaning and characteristic of each stone.

One must wonder what other secrets and mysteries may be locked in the encryptions of the breastplate. Could there be strategies and revelations regarding God's plans and purposes for our own generation and even the end times? The light keepers of today must seek the Light Giver to unlock the code. These secrets can be discerned only through the enlightenment of the Scriptures and the Holy Spirit.

Issachar, the Enlightened

From the encoded message on the breastplate, it is clear that Issachar's unique place among the tribes of Israel was one of great insight and understanding. Their father, Jacob, was the first to acknowledge it, and God confirmed it through the breastplate. He granted to Issachar and his descendants one of the highest honors—that of wisdom and revelation. The sons of Issachar would be known as light keepers—seers with spiritual eyes to discern what God was saying. In the future, their advice and counsel would impact the history of Israel.

Moses carried out God's instructions with perfection. Issachar's name and symbol were expertly crafted and positioned on the garments of the high priest. Issachar's sons were portrayed as enlightened ones who could advise Israel regarding what they should do and how they should live in times of war or peace. They possessed a prophetic ability to see and understand the times and could give knowledgeable, wise counsel to God's people. As the nation began to discover its new identity in the wilderness, the other eleven tribes began to recognize Issachar's family for their supernatural ability to provide counsel and understanding.

10

A RESERVED SEAT
AT GOD'S TABLE

According to the instructions God gave to Moses on Mount Sinai, the names of all of the sons of Jacob were to be represented before Him in the tabernacle in two distinct ways. We have just examined the first method: their names and symbols were expertly crafted in two locations on the garments of the high priest. But God insisted on a very special second means of representation for the sons of Jacob. In addition to the design of the priestly garments, each tribe, including that of Issachar, was assigned a seat at God's family table. God designed a special piece of furniture called the table of showbread, and He told Moses to set this table inside the Holy Place. This table was *reserved* for all twelve of Israel's sons and their offspring.

The Holy Place was a sacred space surrounded by opaque walls and covered with a multilayered roof. It served as an anteroom or vestibule. It was a place of transition—a time tunnel, of sorts—where the priests ministered before God. It provided the only means of access into the Holy of Holies, where the ark of the covenant rested and where God was enthroned upon the mercy seat.

The only sources of light in this totally dark, secret strategy room were the veiled entrance opening to the east and the golden lampstand. The atmosphere inside this Holy Place was continually perfumed and permeated by sweet incense burning on an altar at the back of the chamber. A table covered with gold stood along the north wall opposite the lampstand. (See Exodus 25:23–30.) This was the table of showbread.

Many of the utensils needed to minister in this priestly enclosure were positioned on or near this table. There were two gold dishes, used to carry the twelve loaves of showbread. Adjacent to the gold trays were gold flagons shaped like cups. These were used to hold wine for the drink offering. Golden bowls with spouts that held the oil used to fuel the lampstand, as well as wick trimmers and snuffers, were also placed in readiness there. Finally, there were golden spoons, each one holding about a handful of incense, which were to be used at the altar of incense for special offerings. Incense was also sprinkled upon the loaves of showbread.

God's Bakery

The showbread itself was composed of oil mixed with fine wheat flour. (See Leviticus 24:5–9.) All of the twelve loaves were the same weight and size. The bread was baked every Friday evening and placed upon the table early on the morning of the Sabbath. Four priests arranged the loaves in two rows of six. Two priests placed the new loaves on the table and sprinkled frankincense on them, while the other two simultaneously removed the old loaves and placed them on the gold carrying trays.

After the loaves had rested in God's presence for seven days, they were no longer considered showbread. They were then transformed into the "*bread of the Presence*" (Exodus 25:30 NIV, NASB, TLB, RSV), or the "bread of faces."[1] The priests were commanded to eat a portion of the transubstantiated bread they had just removed from the table in His presence inside of the Holy Place. The remaining pieces of each loaf were then taken outside and distributed among the priests.[2]

The priests cherished this sacred event each week. It was a Sabbath dinner with Jehovah. In this manner, God renewed His fellowship with the Israelites. He became, in a symbolic way, a part of them. Just as we value those special times when we take our own assigned seat at the family table and fellowship with our earthly father, the sons of Israel looked forward to this appointed time in God's presence. Because they were in attendance at Jehovah's table, they carried His presence with them through the rest of the week, until the next time they gathered for dinner with God.

A Loaf of My Own Bread

Everything about the tabernacle—its atmosphere, furniture, and functioning priests—is filled with prophetic revelation and spiritual insight. It was a place of supernatural power and impartation. Each piece of furniture identified a unique type and station of ministry. God's supernatural power worked through each one. Ministry at the table of showbread was more than a religious ritual or a merely symbolic act, as some might suppose. It was a place of intimacy with God and of transformation as the priests acted as surrogates for the nation.

Issachar was represented by his very own loaf of showbread on this supernatural table of God's presence. He rested alongside the other eleven brothers before God twenty-four hours a day for seven days. His tribe was secure in the knowledge that their placement at God's table was specified and reserved and would remain constant and unchanging.

God maintained a face-to-face relationship with Issachar, and just as the priests feasted on the bread of God's presence representatively, Issachar fed upon God's presence in reality. As incense was sprinkled upon the bread, so the sweet fragrance of God was imparted to Issachar and his descendants. While the priests were nourished and strengthened by the loaves, Issachar and the other sons of Jacob were also nourished and fed by God. The showbread served as a constant reminder of God's covenant-keeping faithfulness and as an affirmation that the tribe of Issachar and all of the sons of Israel could trust God to meet their physical and spiritual needs.

Of greatest significance is the fact that the showbread clearly indicates the divine fellowship between God and His people. While pagan gods could not speak or talk, the true God of heaven was and is a living God who communicates with His people and dwells among them. The Canaanite gods of wood and stone kept silent, despite their devotees' anguished pleas. But Yahweh heard and answered prayer. His wisdom, counsel, and intervention in the affairs of Israel were evident. Issachar worshipped a God who speaks to His children, a God who does not withhold knowledge.

It was from Jehovah that the sons of Issachar sought and gained uncommon understanding and insight for living. God was their source of wisdom, and He remains the only source of true wisdom to every succeeding generation. God is the Light Giver for all who will seek Him in the secret place and choose to rest in His presence continually, like the bread of faces.

God Moves In

When all the preparations for the tabernacle and the priesthood had been completed, Moses called for the tribes to bring an offering for its dedication.

On the second day Nethanel the son of Zuar, leader of Issachar, presented an offering. For his offering he offered one silver platter, the weight of which was one hundred and thirty shekels, and one silver bowl of seventy shekels, according to the shekel of the sanctuary, both of them full of fine flour mixed with oil as a grain offering; one gold pan of ten shekels, full of incense; one young bull, one ram, and one male lamb in its first year, as a burnt offering; one kid of the goats as a sin offering; and as the sacrifice of peace offerings: two oxen, five rams, five male goats, and five male lambs in their first year.

(Numbers 7:18–23)

"And it came to pass in the first month of the second year, on the first day of the month, that the tabernacle was raised up" (Exodus 40:17). The priests were cleansed, clothed, consecrated, and commissioned for their service before God in the Tent of Meeting. All the furniture and holy utensils were positioned in readiness in their assigned places. So it was that Moses finished the work.

Then the cloud covered the tabernacle of meeting, and the glory of the LORD filled the tabernacle. And Moses was not able to enter the tabernacle of meeting, because the cloud rested above it, and the glory of the LORD filled the tabernacle. Whenever the cloud was taken up from above the tabernacle, the children of Israel would go onward in all their journeys. But if the cloud was not taken up, then they did not journey till the day that it was taken up. For the cloud of the LORD was above the tabernacle by day, and fire was over it by night, in the sight of all the house of Israel, throughout all their journeys.

(Exodus 40:34–38)

No One Is Perfect

When the nation was at rest on their journey through the wilderness, Issachar's assigned place of encampment was east of the tabernacle, alongside of Judah and Zebulun. From this vantage point near the entrance to the tabernacle, they could observe the daily functions of the priests on the people's behalf. The pillar of fire lit their campsite and warmed them at night. They remained covered by the holy cloud throughout the hot desert days. When the nation moved to follow God's direction, these three tribes broke camp first. Issachar was just behind Judah in the procession. The tribe kept rank and followed their commanders at God's bidding. Israel's combined army numbered 186,000.

When Israel finally arrived at the Jordan River, Moses chose a leader from each of the tribes to go and spy out the land of Canaan. From Issachar, he chose Igal, the son of Joseph. To the ultimate regret of the entire clan, Igal was among the majority of the twelve spies who came back fearful. Only Joshua and Caleb gave a positive vote.

The consequence of the ten skeptics' advice was devastating to the nation. Because of their rebellion against God, Israel turned back into the wilderness, condemned to wander through the barren desert for forty years. Igal, the cowardly spy, along with his family and an entire generation of Issachar's descendants, were sentenced to death. One of Issachar's great-grandsons signed their death sentence. No one is perfect, not even among the enlightened sons of Issachar. They would all perish in the shifting desert wastelands before another opportunity would be given to the next generation of Issachar's offspring to possess the family inheritance in Canaan. (See Numbers 13:1–36.)

This is a solemn warning for those of us who are called to be light keepers in our generation. Unless we stay close to the Light Giver and refuse to rely on our own human perceptions and reason, we, too—like Igal of Issachar—may be guilty of providing deadly counsel. How easy it is to follow the crowd and succumb to peer pressure, especially in a religious context.

11

ISSACHAR'S HOMELAND

Forty years of wandering in circles left a tragic, mournful path of graves strewn across the desert. It was the trail of Israel's tears, a stark testimony of their failure to obey God. Even Joseph's calcified bones cried out from his battered sarcophagus, demanding their final resting place. Despite all of the death and decay, the distinct sounds of the struggle for life burst through the door flaps of countless tents of nomads. With every newborn baby's cry, Israel drew that much closer to a second chance to possess their inheritance. At last, with the memory of their parents' deaths still fresh in their minds, a whole new generation of Israelites stood on the mountain across from Canaan staring down toward the fertile ribbon of land that was the Jordan River Valley. They were a determined army now. This time they would obey God. They had learned their lesson the hard way.

Israel encamped across from Jericho, on the plains of Moab by the Jordan. God commanded Moses and Eleazer, the son of Aaron the priest, to take a second census according to tribal lineage to determine the size of their army.

The sons of Issachar according to their families were: of Tola, the family of the Tolaites; of Puah, the family of the Punites; of Jashub, the family of the Jashubites; of Shimron, the family of the Shimronites. These are the families of Issachar according to those who were numbered of them: sixty-four thousand three hundred. (Numbers 26:23–25).

Altogether, there were 64,300 men in Issachar's tribe twenty years old and above who were capable of engaging in warfare. This new generation of Issachar's offspring were about to make a miraculous crossing over the Jordan River to mount an assault on Canaan.

A Prophetic Word from the Leader

Moses prepared to die on Mount Nebo with the Promised Land in sight. His final act was to prophesy to and bless each of the tribes before his death. He spoke the word of the Lord to Issachar:

> *Rejoice, Zebulun, in your going out, and Issachar in your tents! They shall call the peoples to the mountain; there they shall offer sacrifices of righteousness; for they shall partake of the abundance of the seas and of treasures hidden in the sand.* (Deuteronomy 33:18–19)

With this encouraging promise resounding in their hearts and minds, the sons of Issachar prepared, along with the rest of Israel's army, to subdue the inhabitants of a land that flowed with milk and honey.

The Assault Begins

With God's blessing, General Joshua launched the assault. After a miraculous crossing at the Jordan River, the army of Israel took the fortified city of Jericho without losing a single soldier. It was the equivalent of D-day with no casualties. Once Jericho, which guarded the entrance to Canaan, miraculously fell before God's army, Joshua quickly moved inland to capture Ai and Bethel. It wasn't long before the enemy confederacy of Amorite kingdoms succumbed to Joshua's forces. Ensuing battles occurred at Makkedah, Libnah, Lachish, Eglon, Hebron, and Debir.

The army fought its way northward, eventually arriving at the waters of Merom to face the northern confederation of kingdoms. Like its southern counterpart, Hazor and the other northern cities succumbed to Israel's young and rising power among the nations.

Among the valiant warriors of Joshua's army, the sons of Issachar fought courageously and won for themselves and their tribe the right to possess their allotted parcel of land within Canaan. They would soon be home.

Home at Last

The whole congregation of Israel assembled at Shiloh and set up the tabernacle of meeting. Joshua commanded Judah to remain in the territory to the south; the house of Joseph was to remain to the north. A survey team consisting of three men from each tribe was sent to walk through the land and divide it into seven parts to accommodate the seven tribes that had not yet received their inheritance. The survey team recorded their work *"in a book in seven parts by cities; and they came to Joshua at the camp in Shiloh"* (Joshua 18:9). Joshua cast lots for them before the Lord. He divided the land of Israel according to their tribal divisions. (See Joshua 18:8–10.)

The fourth lot came to Issachar. (See Joshua 19:17.) The land apportioned to Issachar lay south of Zebulon and Naphtali, and north of Manasseh. Its eastern border was the Jordan River. It included a large part of the extremely fertile Plain of Esdraelon, which still remained mostly held by the Canaanites. Along the southern edge of the Esdraelon plain there were fortresses occupied by part of the tribe of Manasseh.[1] There were sixteen cities with their villages located within the boundaries of Issachar's inheritance. Mount Tabor, in the north, served as a point of convergence and a common boundary for Zebulun, Naphtali, and Issachar.

Looking from the highest point of the Tabor Mountains in Nazareth, the sons of Issachar surveyed their land. They were blessed indeed, for it contained two fertile valleys: the Valley of Jezreel, to the south, and Chesulloth, to the north. The topography was partly flat and partly hilly as the land stretched southeast of lower Galilee. The life-giving Jordan River ran along the eastern border and watered the landscape, painting it with verdant foliage and producing luscious fruit. The center of the Jezreel Valley was the source of the River Kishon. This was their expansive inheritance. This was what they had fought and died for. This was home!

They settled into their land, dispersing throughout the cities and towns, and life became predictable again. From time to time, Manasseh, in the south, kept pushing its borders into their territory, and there were still Canaanites dwelling in the land who kept growing in numbers and infecting the tribe's single-hearted devotion to God. Issachar could not succeed in driving them out, despite their attempts. This insidious infestation of Canaanites would soon become powerful enough to demand tribute from them. But the future appeared even more ominous due to the tenuous bond between themselves and the other tribes of Israel. The sons of Jacob couldn't get along with each other.

Deborah's War

Following the death of Joshua and the elders who had served under his command, the confederacy began to weaken. Judges—individuals with military skill and godly anointing—rose up to lead the nation. One of the shining lights of that troubled period was the prophetess Deborah, a *"mother in Israel"* (Judges 5:7). She was the fourth and greatest of the judges, serving as the divinely appointed deliverer and executive leader of Israel. Her name means "honeybee," and her influence and authority were used by God to "sting" Israel's enemies. Deborah stands out as the God-inspired fighter for her country's freedom and her people's survival. The veritable prototype of Joan of Arc, she could easily be called the first woman military commander and the first woman Supreme Court justice.[2]

Deborah was a deeply spiritual woman who had an intimate walk with God. She held court under a palm tree named after her between Ramah and Bethel in the mountains of Ephraim. The children of Israel would come there to seek her wisdom and judgment. God endued her with uncommon insight and wisdom. Her decisions were based on justice, righteousness, truth, fairness, and equity. Deborah had supernatural discernment. Not only was she a judge; she was a prophetess and a songwriter, as well. She was a seer who could hear God's voice, discern His will, and give wise counsel to individuals and the entire nation. She influenced and shaped her times. *She was a light keeper from the tribe of Issachar.*[3]

Supernatural Military Strategy

At this time, King Jabin of Hazor was oppressing Israel's northern tribes. Summoning Barak of Naphtali, Deborah prophesied that an offensive from Mount Tabor at the northeastern limit of Esdraelon would lure Sisera's and Jabin's army to annihilation on the plains below (the land belonging to Issachar). Barak agreed to her battle plan with the stipulation that Deborah accompany the troops into combat. She reluctantly agreed, warning Barak that his demand meant that the honor for victory would be given to a woman. (See Judges 4:9.)

Barak mustered an army of ten thousand men from the northern tribes and, at Deborah's direction, strategically positioned them on the fortress hill of Mount Tabor, only ten miles from the source of the Kishon River. Deborah knew that this was an easily defensible position against which the superior forces of the enemy and their chariots had no chance of success. From here, they would have a flanking position against hostile movement along the Jezreel Valley and excellent visibility in all directions. This would be a perfect position to stage an attack on an enemy encamped at the foot of Mount Tabor.

Deborah also knew that sudden rainfall could quickly fill the dry riverbed of the Kishon River in the valley. It was the rainy season. She waited in preparation for the approaching Canaanite coalition and prayed for God's intervention.

There were two separate divisions of the Canaanite army. Those under Sisera's command advanced southward along the shore of the Sea of Galilee. The allied northern kings approached from the west, advancing along the coast of the Mediterranean Sea. The two enemy forces joined between Megiddo and Jezreel, just south of Israel's position. Deborah and a small detachment of troops lured Sisera's army into the valley of Jezreel. *"And the princes of Issachar were with Deborah"* (Judges 5:15). The stage was set. The trap was about to be sprung.

The Sound of Battle

On the plain beside Mount Tabor, the sound of battle rose up from the land. At a prearranged signal from Deborah, Barak's army charged down the mountain to engage the enemy. Sisera's troops were forced to retreat to the edge of the Kishon River. Suddenly, another sound exploded from the mountains and echoed through the valley. Thunder and lightning filled the skies overhead. As the armies engaged each other, a heavy rain began to fall upon the battlefield. That day, God warred on behalf of His people.

The deluge of water cascaded down the slopes as far away as Mount Carmel, joining with the runoff from Mount Ephraim and Lower Galilee. Filling the dry riverbed, it quickly became a raging torrent. The turbulent current rushed along with the deadly force of a flash flood, sweeping away everything in its path. The Kishon became a wall of water as it rushed through the valley of Jezreel. The flood took Sisera by surprise. His horses and nine hundred chariots of iron, already hampered by the swampy soil near the river, were swept away. His archers vanished in the deluge. The heavily armed infantry was immobilized in the quagmire. The soldiers' iron spears and shields, along with their helmets and coats of mail, sealed their death sentence. They were no match for the armor-less Israelites, who fought on foot with bronze and copper daggers, swords, and slings. They were cut down as they tried to flee; not a soldier was left.

Sisera, the only one to escape, foolishly abandoned his own chariot and fled on foot. Lured into Jael's tent, presuming to have found a safe refuge, he died a shameful death at her hands. She covered him with a blanket and gave him some milk to quench his thirst. Pretending to stand guard at the tent door, she took a tent peg and a hammer and stealthily crept up on the sleeping Sisera. Jael drove the tent peg right through his temple and into the ground. With one swift blow, his head split open like a coconut. Deborah's prophecy was fulfilled, for the Lord had delivered Sisera into the hands of a woman. (See Judges 4:17–22.)

Israel was victorious! They had seen the hand of God. Deborah knew that this was more than just a quirk of nature. It was a miracle! She composed a song to commemorate their success. It was a tribute to God. Deborah and Barak sang the song of victory that day as the soldiers rejoiced in the great defeat of Sisera's army:

> *They fought from the heavens; the stars from their courses fought against Sisera....Thus let all Your enemies perish, O LORD! But let those who love Him be like the sun when it comes out in full strength.*   (Judges 5:20, 31)

On the muddy, bloodstained battlefield of victory, among the reveling troops, the sons of Issachar joined in the chorus.

Another Judge from Issachar's Tribe

Issachar's soldiers returned to their homes and enjoyed a forty-year respite from war. Leaders came and went in the time of the judges. Following Deborah's legacy, another offspring of Issachar's assumed leadership in the struggling nation. Tola, the son of Puah, the son of Dodo, rose up to save Israel. He led the nation for twenty-three years.

Tola was not a military leader. Instead, he was full of wisdom and a true peacekeeper. He maintained and administered the law, performing judicial duties in Israel. His acts of deliverance were confined to resolving internal strife and idolatrous conditions in the fledgling nation. He called Israel back to its heritage in God. When he died, he was buried in Shamir, located in the hill country of Ephraim.

The children of Israel continued to dwell in the land, each tribe in its own allotted homestead. Around the tables of Issachar's sons, the story was told of the great victory in the valley—how God had raised up Deborah and Barak and the miracle of how He had come to their defense through the rain and the flood. Tola was lauded for his wisdom and leadership abilities as the children listened intently and cherished their proud inheritance. But the days grew more and more troubled as Jacob's sons struggled in their separated condition. Despite the intermittent leadership of a few of Issachar's sons and daughters, the confederacy lacked unity. *"There was no king in Israel; everyone did what was right in his own eyes"* (Judges 21:25).

12

DISTINGUISHED SERVICE

Times were turbulent in Israel in the days of the judges. Unrest pervaded the landscape, and the fledgling nation, cloaked in a darkening cloud of evil, teetered on the brink of chaos. The people lived in great confusion and fear. Then, Israel made a fatal mistake. Constantly comparing themselves with the pagan nations around them, they demanded, "Why can't we have a king of our own, just like the other nations?" God heard the contentious complaints of His people and, despite His jealousy for their total devotion, granted their request. But along with it He issued a warning. They would pay a high price for their demand.

The Age of the Kings

God gave them Saul to be the first king of Israel. It had been a long time since they had followed Joshua. Now, at last, Israel was united once more under a single leader. Things seemed to go well at first, but that didn't last long. Within the first two years of his reign, Saul disobeyed God. Instead of waiting for the prophet Samuel's arrival, after seven days Saul built a fire and offered a burnt offering. His cunning attempt to maintain the devotion of the people angered God.

Samuel's fiery words of judgment rang in Saul's ears:

You have done foolishly. You have not kept the commandment of the LORD your God, which He commanded you. For now the LORD would have established your kingdom over Israel forever. But now your kingdom shall not continue. The LORD has sought for Himself a man after His own heart, and the LORD has commanded him to be commander over His people, because you have not kept what the LORD commanded you. (1 Samuel 13:13–14)

Saul's anointing to be king was withdrawn.

God commissioned Samuel to anoint a new king. Making his way to the small village of Bethlehem, he selected from the sons of Jesse the most unlikely candidate. The youngest of eight sons, David was the one chosen. God determined the qualifying criterion. The Lord said to Samuel, *"Do not look at his appearance or at the height of his stature....For the Lord does not see as man sees; for man looks at the outward appearance, but the LORD looks at the heart"* (1 Samuel 16:7).

David's brothers watched in disbelief as Samuel took the horn of oil and poured it upon the ruddy, bright-eyed shepherd boy kneeling before him. As the fragrance of the holy oil filled the rural house with the scent of God, the Spirit of the Lord came upon David. For the rest of his life, he would carry the memory of that moment in his heart.

David's Rise to Power

Things developed quickly after that eventful day in Bethlehem. David went on to serve as Saul's armor bearer. After he killed Goliath, he married King Saul's daughter, Michal. David soon became Saul's greatest general and the closest friend of Saul's son, Jonathan. The cheering praises of the crowd reverberated in the streets and in his mind: *"Saul has slain his thousands, and David his ten thousands"* (1 Samuel 18:7). His successful military leadership and popularity among the people provoked deep resentment and jealousy in Saul, who began to fear David. The contention that arose between the house of Saul and David deeply divided the kingdom.

When Saul realized that the people were scattered from him, he devoted his remaining energy to the quest to eliminate his rival, David. He was possessed by a jealousy that drove him mad. His envy of David consumed his every thought.

A Band of Brothers

Despite Saul's attempts to kill David, the young man refused to retaliate. He fled and took refuge in Gath, feigning madness. From there he took up hiding in the cave of Adullam. In the isolation of this remote cave, a band of brothers gathered around his leadership. It was a ragtag group at first, about four hundred men in all. Those in distress and debt, and everyone who was discontented, pledged allegiance to David. From that time on, David's army continued to increase.

When Samuel the prophet died and was buried at his home in Ramah, the nation grieved. The news deeply saddened David. He sought comfort in the wilderness of Paran and pondered the unforgettable moment when Samuel had anointed him to be king. Then Saul and his son Jonathan were tragically killed on the field of battle against the Philistines. David mourned their deaths with anguished cries: *"How the mighty have fallen, and the weapons of war perished!"* (2 Samuel 1:27). Only a man with a pure heart could have done so. It was obvious that God had made a wise choice in David.

Judah, the southern half of the nation, rose to the occasion. Coming to Hebron, they declared David to be their sovereign leader. He was thirty years old when they anointed him king of Judah. A bloody civil dispute ensued between Israel and Judah. *"There was a long war between the house of Saul and the house of David. But David grew stronger and stronger, and the house of Saul grew weaker and weaker"* (2 Samuel 3:1). For seven years and six months, David led half of the divided nation.

Time to Take Sides

The continuing conflict between the house of Saul and the house of David drove a bitter wedge between the tribes. The kingdom was deeply divided between north and south. This set the stage for the sons of Issachar to distinguish themselves among the tribes of Israel. This was the high hour of their appointed destiny, and they did not fail to rise to the occasion. They were anointed and generationally prepared for such a time as this.

God had bestowed great favor and blessing upon the descendants of Issachar. His four sons, Tola, Puvah (Puah), Job (Jashub), and Shimron, each fathered a sizable clan within the tribe. By David's time, Tola's offspring alone numbered *"thirty-six thousand troops ready for war; for they had many wives and sons. Now their brethren among all the families of Issachar were mighty men of valor, listed by their genealogies, eighty-seven thousand in all"* (1 Chronicles 7:4–5).

Issachar's courage and strength alone may have been enough to distinguish them among their fellow Israelites, but another characteristic caused them to stand out from among the other tribes. This one quality made them invaluable and indispensable. The sons of Issachar had a unique ability to understand the times. Not only did they understand their world and the momentous age they were living in; they knew what Israel needed to do to succeed! They were men with the distinct ability to *see* and *discern*. They were enlightened by God's insights and guidance. Even though they were smaller in number compared to the other tribes, their influence, wisdom, and circumspection distinguished them. They were seers. Just like Simeon the light keeper, they possessed an uncommon wisdom. They sprang into action.

The Cry for Unity

The voices of the sons of Issachar resounded throughout the land. Leaving their tents, these men called the people to the mountains and challenged them to act righteously. They pleaded with the northern tribes to acknowledge David as God's appointed king. The unique gift that had sprung from their father and persevered through their predecessors who wandered the desert and settled their homeland fully manifested itself. The prophetic purpose revealed by the blessing and prophecy of Jacob played a major part in changing the tide of prejudice, envy, and separatism in their nation.

Jacob's Prophecy Fulfilled

The ancient prophecy came to pass. Issachar's inheritance in the land of Canaan had fallen to them in a strategic geographical position. Right in the center of the nation, between the northern and southern tribes, they were crouched down like a strong donkey between two burdens.

It should be pointed out that the animal referred to as a donkey in the Bible is considerably different from the familiar donkey of the Western world. Our donkeys are normally smaller and are known for their stubborn meanness. They are accused of being stupid for good reason. In the Eastern world, however, these animals developed into stately creatures. It is no accident that the Bible never refers to the stubbornness, meanness, or laziness that we today associate with the word "ass." These are characteristics that the Eastern world never observed in this animal.[1]

Issachar was a strong ass with a noble name and a distinguished past. A beast of considerable value and unquestionable character, the sons of Issachar were about to bow their shoulder to bear a prophetic burden. Their appeal to Israel succeeded.

Peace at Last

The army of the sons of Issachar marched to Hebron along with the other northern tribes to turn over the kingdom of Saul to David, according to the word of the Lord. Choosing to become subservient to David, they brought rest to the land that was so pleasant to them. They became slaves of a new king, but, more than that, they helped to crown the one from upon whose throne the King of Kings would reign. (See 1 Chronicles 11:1–9.)

How incredible that Issachar, the symbolic "donkey," helped to make David king. Centuries later, Jesus, who sat upon David's throne, would also arrive in Jerusalem riding on a donkey.

The sons of Issachar, crouching between two burdens (Judah and Israel), submitted to God's choice and called the nation to acknowledge a new king and establish a united kingdom. The prophecy of Jacob was fulfilled!

Finally, the civil war ended, as the northern tribes of Israel accepted David as their king. He immediately chose Jerusalem as the capital city of the restored nation. At last, peace began to settle upon God's beleaguered people as Judah and Israel were united under one sovereign. The evil cloud began to lift.

The Historical Records

The book of Chronicles records David's praise to God for the victory over his enemies and for the restoration of the nation. He rejoiced that the ark of the covenant had been restored to its rightful place in the City of David. Even the disgraceful acts of his predecessor, Saul, were recorded. David's honorable actions to honor Saul's position as king despite his hatred of David are clearly described. His ruthless honesty about his own humanness and failings as a man is a testimony of his passion for God's presence. David openly admitted to his lustful behavior toward Bathsheba and his murderous actions toward her husband. His prayer is scribed, "*Create in me a clean heart, O God, and renew a steadfast spirit within me. Do not cast me away from Your presence, and do not take Your Holy Spirit from me*" (Psalm 51:10–11).

Kudos to the Team

King David, now the commander in chief, turned his attention to those who had served him in battle faithfully and with distinction. It was time to show honor where honor was due. He acknowledged those who served under his command. He cited them for meritorious service in a time of national crisis. He recalled the heads of the mighty men by name—men like Jashobeam, the son of a Hachmonite, who killed three hundred at one time with a single spear. Eleazer and his men, who took up a position in a barley field and defeated an entire Philistine army. David spoke of the three mighty men who risked their lives to bring him a drink of cool water from the well in Bethlehem, in the heart of the enemy's camp. And who could forget Benaiah, who had climbed into a pit in the midst of a snowstorm and killed a lion with his bare hands?

As he applauded the military heroes and valiant warriors, David also numbered the divisions that were equipped for war. (See 1 Chronicles 11:10–12.) These chapters read like a military history replete with names and details of battles and acts of great courage. David made special mention of the unique contributions that each division had contributed to his campaign. Among the honored individuals receiving medals that day was a group of men who had highly distinguished themselves. David recognized this group as one of his most valuable resources. These men were the sons of Issachar.

There were only two hundred chiefs who led this division of the army, but every one of their brethren was distinguished by his respect for military protocol. All of them knew how to keep rank and obey their commanders. But there was something more than their regard for rank, their serial number, and their obedience that made these men different from the other divisions in David's army. They stood out among their peers. David valued their contribution so highly that their place and function were highlighted for future generations to see and remember.

David's tribute to Issachar and his descendants is well deserved. He referred to them as *"the sons of Issachar who had understanding of the times, to know what Israel ought to do...and all their brethren were at their command"* (1 Chronicles 12:32).

The sons of Issachar were brave soldiers. They grasped the importance of military protocol. But they carried themselves with a circumspection that went beyond military procedures. David described this quality as *"understanding."* He relied upon Issachar's unusual wariness.

Insight from God

The Hebrew meaning of the word *understand* is "to separate, to distinguish, and hence to discern."[2] It describes an ability to perceive based upon insight. Understanding is more than mental discernment in the Hebrew culture. It is the capacity to "hear" with the heart, not just with the head; to perceive with spiritual eyes and not mere human reason. The person who truly understands would act prudently and circumspectly. He would "mark" time with foresight. Life would be lived in the context of a larger framework. It follows logically that a person who has genuine understanding would be successful.

How blessed David was to have such a group of advisers like Issachar's sons who could counsel him on what the nation should do. "It seems reasonable to infer that their job was to perceive trends, discuss major issues, evaluate information, and consider strategy."[3]

Issachar's acumen was more than an acquired knowledge. It was a grace imparted by God Himself. Not only did they understand the sacred teachings and scrolls, but they also understood the world in which those teachings needed to be applied. Thus, they were able to frame the events of their day in the context of God's greater will and purpose for mankind. Issachar's sons were light seekers, and God enlightened them with revelation and understanding. They perceived an eternal kingdom and an approaching King.

The Anointing Remains

The sons of Issachar appear again in the days of King Hezekiah's reign. The first thing Hezekiah did as king of Judah, after the dreadful reign of his predecessor, Ahaz, was to restore and cleanse the temple and reinstate worship. Although they belonged to the northern kingdom, many from the tribe of Issachar attended Hezekiah's Passover. (See 2 Chronicles 30:18–20.)

Later, Ezekiel prophesied regarding the restoration of the land to captive Israel. Issachar was allotted one section in the restored city, and a gate in the city wall was assigned to the tribe. (See Ezekiel 48:25, 33.) The honor of sitting in the gates was considered a privilege reserved for the wise and discerning. The elders who were appointed to do so were responsible to protect the city.

Tradition holds that in Jesus' day, representatives from Issachar were the wisest members of Israel's highest ruling body, the Sanhedrin. What a legacy! The anointing and insight of Issachar's sons survived sibling rivalry, slavery, invasion, civil war, and captivity. Surely, God's gifts and callings are irrevocable. (See Romans 11:29.)

The closing reference to Issachar's descendants is in the book of Revelation:

After these things I saw four angels standing at the four corners of the earth, holding the four winds of the earth, that the wind should not blow on the earth, on the sea, or on any tree. Then I saw another angel ascending from the east, having the seal of the living God. And he cried with a loud voice to the four angels to whom it was granted to harm the earth and the sea, saying, "Do not harm the earth, the sea, or the trees till we have sealed the servants of our God on their foreheads." And I heard the number of those who were sealed. One hundred and forty-four thousand of all the tribes of the children of Israel were sealed:…of the tribe of Issachar twelve thousand were sealed.

(Revelation 7:1–4, 7)

The Lost Generation

Issachar and his descendants serve as a prophetic example and a challenge to us. Loved equally among all of God's children, they were treasured by God as a topaz. As diligent seekers of wisdom, they sought the heart of God, and He gave them understanding beyond that of their peers. Their God-given insight enabled them to walk circumspectly and provide counsel and direction for the entire nation. They understood the times and knew what to do. They were seers illuminated by the Light Giver.

Today, in a world filled with confusion and darkness, we desperately need the sons of Issachar to come forth. We face challenges and changes in this century of such magnitude that the situation is chaotic and desperate. The moral and spiritual anchors that have stabilized our world are being hoisted in the name of relativism and eclecticism. We are set adrift on the sea of history with no attachment to past or future. Lacking the ability to "mark" time, we have turned to occult sources and humanistic philosophies to obtain wisdom and guidance. We are a generation lost in a wilderness of moral decline without a compass. We have abandoned our leaders. Our ranks are in disarray.

We need more than just a self-serving, individualistic idea of what God wants "me" to do. We need to get beyond a narcissistic spirituality that promotes stardom and superheroes of faith. We need a Damascus Road encounter that forever launches us into the purpose of God and calls us to a selfless surrender to His lordship. We need our vision restored!

Calling a New Generation of Seers

There is good news. A new generation of Issachar's sons is being raised up in the earth. But they are not those who by birth are of the lineage of Issachar. Instead, a host of men, women, and children from every tribe and tongue, whose eyes have been opened by the revelation of God's ultimate purpose, are coming forth to speak into the confusion of our age.

These individuals are anointed with discernment like Issachar of old. They are not flaky, emotional people who are solely subjective and ethereal. Instead, they are individuals whose critical faculties and spiritual intuition are acute. They have studied the Scriptures and know them well. But, beyond that, they have attuned their ears to the heart of God. They are not blown about by every wind of doctrine and the cunning craftiness of man's ideas and motives. (See Ephesians 4:14.) Like the blind whose eyes have been opened by the Light Giver, they see clearly, and in their seeing, call us to walk circumspectly, redeeming the time, for the days are evil. (See Ephesians 5:14–16.)

God has not changed. The Issachar anointing is available to you. You can be anointed with revelation, just like the sons of Issachar! You can hear with the heart and not just the head. If you have lost your way in life, God will restore your spiritual compass and establish your bearings on the map of His eternal purpose.

It is time to return to the secret place and to seek the Light Giver. The lampstand is lit. You are God's priest. Rise to your calling. This generation needs you!

⌣

On the very first page of his novel *The Time Machine*, published in 1895, H. G. Wells wrote, "There are three planes of Space, and a fourth, Time." The sons of Issachar understood this fourth dimension of time. Among the many talents and gifts that this distinguished tribe of Israel possessed, there is one that stands out above the rest. They were much more than astute historians who interpreted the times, seasons, and ages through a particular worldview. They had the weighty responsibility of being the spiritual "timekeepers" for Israel.

According to the Targum, the sons of Issachar were biblical astronomers. They kept track of the times and the seasons:

> ...the sons of Issachar, who had understanding to know the times, were skilled in fixing the beginnings of years, the commencement of months, and the intercalation of months and years; skillful in the changes of the moon, and in fixing the lunar solemnities to their proper times; skillful also in the doctrine of the solar periods;...that they might show Israel what to do.[4]

Why was this so vitally important in the life of the nation?

The answer has to do with God's commands. God required Israel to observe certain feasts throughout the year. Because Israel observed a lunar calendar, the dates of the nation's feasts changed annually. Issachar's skill and understanding of the heavens qualified them to be *keepers of the calendar*. They were the ones who made known the appointed times and seasons when Israel should observe the feasts of the Lord.

The feasts, which are described in Leviticus 23, are observances that have great significance. These holy days are full of revelation. Each of these special times has historical and prophetic implications. Historically, they were a continual reminder to Israel of God's intervention and miraculous provision for them, His chosen people. Prophetically, they are a clear indication of the coming of the Messiah.

As the keeper of this sacred calendar, Issachar was entrusted with the task of keeping the nation on track. The sons of Issachar were the stewards of the nation's memory and memorials. They made sure that the nation was tied to its *spiritual and historical roots*. In doing so, Issachar had the distinct responsibility of maintaining Israel's relationship with and dependence upon the God of Abraham, Isaac, and Jacob. By keeping the feasts, they assured that Israel would remain rooted in God and His sovereign guidance and miraculous power.

Since the Lord's feasts reveal God's plan of redemption, the sons of Issachar had an anointing that gave them a unique insight into God's timing of events past, present, and future. Their knowledge of God's Word caused them to become the primary cultivators of Israel's spiritual treasures, and their counsel and interpretations of Scripture were received as authoritative.

If we are to follow Issachar's example in our contemporary world, we need to realize our responsibility to hold our nation accountable and to call our world to dependence upon God. It is of the utmost importance that we recognize the nature and significance of the "times" and "seasons" and that we hold the appropriate worldview—one that will enable us to correctly interpret the signs of our times. Our discernment is the critical issue. The intention of the Light Giver is to impart understanding so that we may discern and interpret the times in which we live—from His perspective. Where are we in terms of God's calendar? The spiritual sons and daughters of Issachar should know! But how can that happen?

What is time? How is it related to light and, more important, to the Light Giver? How is time kept and chronicled? Is there a "right" way to interpret history? Why are our philosophical and spiritual worldviews so important? Let's find the answer to these questions. It's *time* for us to explore this fourth dimension. I want you to meet the timekeepers.

PART THREE

THE TIMEKEEPERS

"When it is evening you say, 'It will be fair weather, for the sky is red'; and in the morning, 'It will be foul weather today, for the sky is red and threatening.' Hypocrites! You know how to discern the face of the sky, but you cannot discern the signs of the times."
—Jesus of Nazareth (Matthew 16:2–3)

13

REDEEMING TIME

When we awaken from a long night's sleep to the light of a new day, the first thing most of us do is to check the clock and then the calendar. We want to know what time it is and what day it is. In a similar sense, when our spiritual vision is restored, it's like opening our eyes to a new world. Time becomes extremely important. When the Light Giver opens our spiritual eyes, enabling us to understand the age we are living in and granting us the ability to correlate contemporary events with His ultimate plan, it's like an alarm clock going off inside of us. It is a commission to rise and face the task that awaits us, His servants. I often say out loud at the beginning of a new day, "Thank You, Lord, for giving me life and the desire to serve You. Let's go see what damage we can do to the devil's kingdom." God gives us vision for a reason. He wants us to understand the time in which we live and to know how to redeem it.

What is time? How did it come into existence? Why should we, as God's servants, view time any differently than the rest of mankind? Is it even possible to view and interpret the ages correctly? Perhaps a good place to begin to search for the answers to these questions is to go back in history to a period when time was considered sacred. Let's take a journey back to the Dark Ages for a quick glimpse into daily life at a monastery.

The Setting

The fortresslike structure is built of hand-hewn stone quarried from a nearby mountain and carried by wagon to the site. The gray walls are fifteen feet high, and the only entrance is a large oak door left standing open during the daytime. In the center of the compound is a church, its tall steeple dominating the skyline.

The monastery sits on a hill overlooking the rural valley. It's early spring, and a light fog blankets the cultivated fields, made bare with the scars of fresh plowing and seeding. In the far distance, a river winds lazily through the town. It's nighttime. Every now and then, a dog barks, but that's the only sound rising from the sleeping village.

Welcome to the Monastery

The vigilant monk clasped his woolen blanket—the earthly possession he cherished the most—and pulled it tightly around his neck to ward off the cold, damp night air. He rolled over and cast a quick glance at the awakening clock (*horologia excitatoria*) near his cot. Fastened by a crude chain to the clock above it, the heavy weight that powered the mechanism moved slightly in the sudden gust of air that intruded under the door of his cell from the drafty hallway outside. *The abbot chose me to be the guardian of the sacred clock (*custos horologii*)*, Brother Stephen affirmed. *My duty is to keep time in the monastery.*[1]

Night passed slowly for the monks in the darkened monastery, but, for the timekeeper, vigilance was an absolute necessity. Enveloped in the predawn darkness of *Matins* (the night watch hour), all of the usual details of life were hidden, and he immersed himself in the mystery of the Almighty. *I must learn to listen with my heart,* Stephen thought, embracing the darkness as a friend who had come to sequester him in quiet meditation. But his welcome womb of silence was abruptly invaded by the alarming sound of the awakening clock, alerting him to perform his duties. "Time is the now of eternity," he muttered, casting aside his blanket and slipping his feet into the sandals he had positioned by his bedside only a few hours before.

"I must summon the others to prayer and worship," he whispered as he made his way through the doorway of his cubicle. He headed quickly down the gray stone passageway and turned left through the archway into the corridor leading toward the bell tower. He moved with the stealth of a shadow past the doorways along the hallway, not wanting to awaken the brothers prematurely. He stepped into the circular chamber beneath the great bell and stared upward into the darkness that desperately fought to cling to the night, with no hope of victory. He thought once more of the verse from the Holy Scriptures that he held in reverence as part of his calling: *"The Light shines on in the darkness, for the darkness has never overpowered it"* (John 1:5 AMP).

A Monk's Life

At the first tinge of sunrise, just as the light was barely visible through the arched windows at the top of the belfry, when each opening was outlined with a halo of luminescence gloriously announcing the dawn, his hands grasped the rope. Clutching the hemp, now worn smooth from years of service by generations of timekeepers, Stephen pulled with a determination that required all of his weight. His feet lifted from the stone floor for a moment, and then the full force of his lunging effort moved the bell on its axis. The heavy clapper struck a sledgehammer blow. A booming resonation, loud enough to wake the dead, let alone the sleeping, reverberated through the monastery and far beyond it, across the freshly plowed fields and to the farmhouses, beyond the humble dwellings of peasants and the palatial abodes of royalty alike, finally cascading into the streets and houses of the townsfolk in the distant village. The night vigil was finished.

It was sunrise—the dawn of a new day, a gift from God. It was *Lauds*, the coming of the light, and life within the monastery and beyond began once more to measure and mark its time by the bell in the monastery. Stephen pulled the massive rope again and again with steady rhythm until, filled with certainty that no one was still asleep, he loosened his grip, letting the bell fall silent for now.

The sacred meaning of the passing hours was heralded by the timekeeper throughout the day. Brother Stephen would make his way to the bell tower six more times. Shortly after a meager breakfast, Stephen would ring the bell to call the brothers to assemble at *Prime* in the Chapter Room. This marked the transition when work duties were assigned to the monks. The bell signaled a deliberate beginning to their work.

Then, at precisely the third hour, the bell would sound again to announce *Terce*. Like students at the end of a class period, the monks dropped everything to prove to themselves that they were not slaves to the law of work. They were free to let go. Work did not master them; they mastered it. As deliberately as they had begun, they ceased their labors, now free to focus their prayers on the Holy Spirit. *Terce* reminded the entire monastery of Pentecost, when the disciples were accused of being drunk—which was impossible, since it was only the third hour of the day.

Stephen, his stomach growling from the morning's work and prayer, hastened to the bell tower once more. The cold night chill had long since fled, and the cool refectory would be a welcome refuge from the blazing sun directly above the stone walls and black-gray slate roof of the monastery, which Stephen had called home since he'd first passed through the huge oak entrance doors fifteen years ago.

Sext came at noon, in the middle of the day. *This is the hour of fellowship,* Stephen thought with joyful anticipation. *I will be glad to see Brother Jonas again. I must remember to ask him about his journey to our sister monastery in the distant mountains.*

The refectory was buzzing with chatter as the monks exchanged greetings and gathered bits and pieces of information and news from one another. "I wonder what's for dinner," Stephen announced more than asked, beating a quick path to his assigned place at the table near the far window. *Even though I am really hungry, this is far more than just an occasion to grab something to eat,* he thought. *It's more like a celebration than a main meal. It's a time to serve one another.*

Gathered around the tables in the refectory, the monks took turns waiting on each other, sharing their common faith. The room turned suddenly silent as one of the older brothers, his balding head and crown of remaining hair lending a dignified air to his actions, opened the leather-bound text before him and began to read, picking up at the place where he had left off the day before. The remainder of the meal was eaten in silence as Brother Bartholomew read from the worthy Book. Stephen pondered the words of the divine reading and wrestled with his own inadequacies, hoping to become a better servant of God as he listened. When Bartholomew finished, the monks stood for prayer and petitioned the Almighty for peace.

Some free time, Stephen thought as he left the dining hall. *I think I will spend it in the garden again. I love the wonderful smell of the roses, and I can check on how the herbs are coming along. They may need watering.* He lingered in the garden, sitting on a stone wall to listen to the mockingbird in the nearby monastery orchard, until the last minute, then hastened to the bell tower again. It was mid-afternoon, and the bell would announce *None*.

The lengthening afternoon shadows marked the occasion for reflection, and Stephen, along with the brothers whose cubicles were along his passageway, exchanged a few quick comments before they closed their doors and retreated into the solitude of their private cells. Each man faced his own shortcomings and weaknesses. The cell provided a place apart; not an escape from reality, but a place where reality could be faced, a sanctuary where the love and mercy of God were rediscovered and forgiveness abounded.

Indeed, the afternoons of our lives are often a place where forgiveness is essential. It is a time of personal introspection, Stephen thought. Then he prayed, "Search me, O God. Try my heart, and see if there be any wicked way in me, and lead me in the paths of righteousness, for Your name's sake. Only then will I teach transgressors Your ways." (See Psalm 139:23–24; 51:13.)

It was just before sunset when Stephen heard the small bell on the awakening clock beside the bed, where he had been kneeling for several hours, deep in prayer and immersed in the presence of God in his secret place. *The lamps must be lit in the monastery,* he noted, hurrying to the bell tower to perform his duty once again. "My brothers," he called out. His voice echoed around the walls of the bell tower and was suddenly drowned out by the power of the clanging bell far above him. "It is the hour of *Vespers,* a time of peace of heart and serenity." The bell proclaimed the message for all to hear.

The monastery chapel would soon be filled with the wonderful sound of singing. "Blessed be the Lord, for He has visited His people; He has come to their rescue," Stephen chanted as he walked along the corridor leading to the chapel and Vespers.

"The day's assignment will soon be complete," Stephen said with gratitude as he shuffled once more toward the bell tower. "I must see if Brother Michael can fix this strap on my sandal tomorrow before I end up tripping some morning and waking the brothers prematurely." (Stephen always sought to put others before himself. The abbot had noticed and had even commented that he was pleased with his spiritual growth.)

Life is good, Stephen thought, *so ordered and peaceful, so fulfilling and meaningful. Each day is like an entire season, ordered and offered to God, who gave it to us.*

Why should I worry when I can pray? he reasoned. *My life is simple, but so full of joy and happiness. Why, even work has become an offering to the Savior.*

The final peal of the bell came at *Compline*, or completion. It marked nightfall. Stephen made his way back toward his cell. Before retiring for the night, in the privacy of his cell, each monk examined his own conscience under the shelter of God's protection. Stephen closed the door gently. The monastery was quiet now. Checking the awakening clock to be sure it was functioning, he pulled the chain and reset the weight to its highest position. "I am safe, and I am loved," he said, affirming Father God's goodness and mercy. The "night question" now answered, he tugged the woolen blanket up around his shoulders and fell fast asleep. The full circle of the day was complete.

Ordering Life in the Midst of Chaos

Somehow, in the midst of the ungodly, superstitious culture of the Dark Ages, a group of faithful followers of Christ established a rhythm for each day. Within the boundaries of their ordered life, they managed to redeem the time, for the days were evil. (See Ephesians 5:16.) Within this microcosm of experience, time was lived as a sacred succession of days, each day viewed as a gift from God, the Giver of light and Redeemer of life.

In the monastery, time was sacred![2]

14

THE TIME MACHINE

"Time is the greatest innovator," wrote Francis Bacon in his treatise "*Of Innovations*" in 1625.

> The first grand discovery was time, the landscape of experience. Only by marking months, weeks, and years, days and hours, minutes and seconds, would man be liberated from the cyclical monotony of nature. The flow of shadows, sand, and water, and time itself, translated into the clock's staccato, became a useful measure of man's movements across the planet. The discoveries of time and of space would become one continuous dimension. Communities of time would bring the first communities of knowledge, ways to share discovery, a common frontier on the unknown.[1]

Boorstin's analogy of time as the "landscape of experience" is a perfect description of life within the walls of the monastery. In his opinion, time is the scenery on the stage of life, the panorama of understanding. In essence, he declared that "time" changes everything. It is the great innovator. But what is time, and where did time come from? How did mankind discover time and learn to measure it? In order to answer these questions, we must start at the very beginning, with the "time machine" itself.

The Origin of Time

Time began! We measure time; we divide it into segments and chronicle our life and history by it. But who created time and started the clock? Paul answered the question for us.

God...has saved us and called us with a holy calling, not according to our works, but according to His own purpose and grace which was given to us in Christ Jesus before time began. (2 Timothy 1:8–9)

He wrote to Titus,

Paul, a bondservant of God and an apostle of Jesus Christ, according to the faith of God's elect and the acknowledgment of the truth which accords with godliness, in hope of eternal life which God, who cannot lie, promised before time began. (Titus 1:1–2)

Time is a created dimension! God made it. The Alpha and Omega, who exists outside of the time-space continuum, is not limited by time's constraints. He can compress and expand time and intersect it, entering and leaving it at His discretion. He is the only One who governs and controls the cosmic clock. Our only option is to keep the appointments that God has scheduled for us. King Solomon summarized this principle for us when he wrote, *"To everything there is a season, a time for every purpose under heaven: a time to be born and a time to die..."* (Ecclesiastes 3:1–2; see also Hebrews 9:27).

It appears that the monks got it right. They honored the One in whom time originated and saw it as a sacred gift to be spent within the framework of a single day. They gave careful attention to its Inventor and honored Him with each passing hour.

The Cosmic Clock

What is the relationship between time and the Light Giver—and, for that matter, with light itself? The answer can be summed up in a simple statement: Without light, there is no time! The very first act of creation occurred as an *enlightening* moment! God, who is Light, said, *"Let there be light"* (Genesis 1:3). Time, space, matter, and energy all came into existence at once. The event that scientists have named the "Big Bang" was, in essence, God starting the cosmic clock. The cosmos came into being at the speed of light—186,282.4 miles per second. According to Einstein's theory of relativity, light is the ultimate speed limit of the universe, and no particle or piece of information can go any faster.[2]

Time and light were inextricably bound together at creation. Time would not exist apart from light. H. G. Wells was right when he wrote, "There are three planes of Space, and a fourth, Time." Time became the fourth dimension.

The planets, stars, comets, and galaxies, bathed in light and contrasted upon a canvas of black space, are the mechanisms of the Master's timepiece. Their movements chronicle the passing of time on a grand scale. Like the miniature gears and springs of a watch, they keep *universal* time, and every other timepiece that exists is set to their precise movements. In this divinely ordered system, there are no random events within the timepiece, only occurrences that we have not yet come to understand. These so-called anomalies appear and disappear as part and parcel of the Grand Designer's architectural plans for all of existence.

Using our giant telescopes, we attempt to trace the first light beams that emanated from the quantum beginning of zero time. At the instant of creation, the first lasers shot across the expanding universe, speeding toward the limits of the cosmos and their final consummation in eternity. Only God knows when that will happen. Could it be possible that, when it does, time will be captured by eternity once more, and the clock will stop at light speed, just as it began? When the light stops, light-years no longer exist. They become irrelevant. Could this be the end of time as we know it?

John described this event in the last chapter of Revelation, with alpha light returning to its Creator-source and dissolving into the Omega of eternity.

> *They shall see His face, and His name shall be on their foreheads. There shall be no night there: They need no lamp nor light of the sun, for the Lord God gives them light. And they shall reign forever and ever....I am the Alpha and the Omega, the Beginning and the End, the First and the Last.*
> (Revelation 22:4–5, 13)

Measuring Time

God never said, "Now I am going to create time." He created light, and man discovered time. Things change and events occur as they respond to light in a sequential manner. All living organisms sense time by recognizing and responding to this phenomenon. This order of events in our environment can be measured by using light as the standard. We call this observable occurrence "time." Time is a way of identifying and measuring the duration between the events and motion happening all around us. We do not measure some absolute phenomenon called "time"; what we measure is the rate of some physical change in the universe as it is observed and related to light.

We've Got Rhythm

It is accurate to say that we are designed with an internal clock. The rhythms and cycles continuously occurring inside our bodies give us an awareness of constantly changing conditions and a sense of the passing of time between these occurrences. More than one hundred functions are known to oscillate within our bodies every day. Brain waves, heartbeat, breathing, sleep stages, and the twenty-eight-day reproductive cycle are just a few of the biorhythms of life. This endogenous, internal timer is our first awareness of something passing, something moving back and forth and coming and going within us, that gives us a sense of timing.

Another basic cadence within us is the human response to day and night. *Circadian* rhythm, from the Latin words *circa*, meaning "about," and *dies*, meaning "day," describes the innate response of plants, animals, and humans to the cycle of a single day. Some plants automatically raise and lower their leaves on a day-and-night schedule. The sunflower bows at night and then raises its head to follow the sun through the heavens until darkness returns. Just try going three days without sleep, and you will quickly discover that you require rest within every twenty-four-hour cycle.

The Calendar

The heavens declare the glory of God; and the firmament shows His handiwork. Day unto day utters speech, and night unto night reveals knowledge. There is no speech nor language where their voice is not heard. Their line has gone out through all the earth, and their words to the end of the world. In them He has set a tabernacle for the sun, which is like a bridegroom coming out of his chamber, and rejoices like a strong man to run its race. Its rising is from one end of heaven, and its circuit to the other end; and there is nothing hidden from its heat. (Psalm 19:1–6)

Observing the heavens, ancient cosmologists and astronomers from many different cultures quickly discerned the cycles of the cosmic clock that God set in motion. The cycle of a day, delineated by the trajectory of the sun, was immediately obvious. Through careful surveillance, they concluded that a particular planet ruled each day, and they named each day after the planet that ruled its first hour. The sun ruled Sunday, the moon ruled Monday, Mars (Anglo-Saxon *Tiw's* day) ruled Tuesday, Mercury (Woden's day) ruled Wednesday, Jupiter (Thor's day) ruled Thursday, Venus (Frigg's day) ruled Friday, and Saturn (Saturne's day) ruled Saturday.

Eventually, it was discovered that the moon passes through a twenty-eight-day cycle. Fishermen and sailors detected its effect on the tides as it progressed through the heavens. The month was devised to identify the phases and cycles of the moon. Along with the observation of the repeating seasons of winter, spring, summer, and fall, the passing of a full cycle of days, months, and seasons marked a complete year. Man had devised a time-marking device to chronicle these changes in the heavens. The calendar is simply a measuring device, a record of movement in the universe. It is man's attempt to measure time and keep our lives synchronized with nature—and, ultimately, with the Light-powered cosmic clock.

Hours and Minutes

Perhaps somewhere in the ancient past, a nomadic wanderer stuck his staff into the desert sand and sat in the shade of a nearby ledge to rest. After some time passed, he wiped the sweat from his brow and returned to the position of the upright rod. He observed that its shadow had moved since he had first thrust it into the ground. The discovery of a shadow moving in conjunction with the sun was the beginning of our ability to measure smaller increments of time.

The sundial was first used by the Sumerians and Egyptians as a crude instrument to measure the passing hours. Ancient obelisks still stand today in Egypt as a testimony to their function in society as religious symbols and giant sundials. But there were several problems with this method of measuring time. Most notably: no sun, no shadow. Also, the early morning and late afternoon shadows were difficult to detect. In addition, the sun moved so slowly that it was impossible to measure minutes, let alone seconds. Nevertheless, the evolution of the sundial progressed, and by 30 B.C., the historian Vitruvius could describe thirteen different types of sundials in use in Greece, Italy, and Asia Minor.[3]

Mankind needed to find a way to liberate itself from reading shadows and depending on the sunshine for time-telling. It was soon discovered that the passage of time could be measured by the amount of water dripping from a pot, and thus the *water clock* was conceived. Stone vessels with sloping sides were fashioned to allow water to drip at a constant speed from a small hole near the bottom. Markings inscribed upon the inside of the container indicated the passing hours, and it worked at night as well as during the day. Still, there were problems. The water pressure and temperature could vary, affecting the flow of water, and the hole in the instrument could become clogged, restricting the flow entirely.

The search for a more accurate means of timekeeping led to the use of sand instead of water. With the development of glassmaking, it became possible to seal the *hourglass* and prevent moisture from slowing the rate of flow. Sandglasses were not practical for measuring long periods of time, but they served well when used to measure small increments of hours and minutes. Another device also used to measure small increments of time was the *candle clock*, which tracked the rate of burn by markings on the side of the candle.

Seconds Arrive

The invention of the calendar enabled us to track large spans of time in days, months, and years. In the succeeding millennia, we refined our abilities, measuring hours with simple instruments as we slowly progressed to more sophisticated means. With the advent of the water clock and the hourglass, we were finally free from dependence on the sun's trajectory, and we could keep time through the night hours. But the demand for greater precision and smaller and smaller divisions of time led to further ingenuity and invention. The race was on for an even more precise delineation that would divide hours into seconds.

In the fourteenth century, monasteries and religious communities eager to perform their duties to God in a timely fashion demanded a precision timepiece. Thus, the precursor to the modern mechanical clock was invented. Monks like Brother Stephen became timekeepers for the entire society. Keeping vigil with their small, weight-driven alarm clocks, they rang the monastery bell to announce the hour. Time was sounded by a bell rather than indicated by a dial. The word *clock* is actually derived from the Dutch word *clok*, meaning "bell."

The invention of the "escapement," a cogged wheel device that interrupted the force of the weights powering the clock, revolutionized timekeeping. This mechanism allowed the weights to "escape" the force of gravity momentarily. By checking the downward motion for a moment and then releasing it again, a clock could be kept running for hours with just a small descent of the weight. The resulting ticktock—the staccato sound emitting from the escapement—became the voice of the "second." The modern-day clock was born. Soon, large, weight-driven mechanical clocks were constructed in city towers throughout Italy.

Portable Time

In the sixteenth century, the use of different means to power the clock made sweeping changes in the way we tell time. The heavy driving weights were replaced with much smaller coiled springs, which could be wound to restore tension on the mechanism. This made the clock portable.

In the seventeenth century, the first pendulum clock was invented. It had less than a one-minute error each day. Further refinements resulted in a marine chronometer that kept time onboard a moving vessel to within one-fifth of a second per day. Its inventor, George Graham, won the 1714 British Government prize, worth over two million dollars in today's currency. British mariners used the chronometer to determine longitude to within half a degree on a test voyage to the West Indies. Until then, without the availability of a portable clock, ocean navigation was an educated guess. The problem of longitude was finally solved! The chronometer, along with the compass and the cosmic clock (the stars), became the early navigator's Global Positioning System of the seas.

In the 1930s and 1940s, quartz crystals replaced weights, springs, and pendulums as an even more accurate means of timekeeping. When a quartz crystal is subjected to an electrical field, it vibrates, generating a constant frequency signal. This electrical pulse is used to control the clock's display. By the 1950s, wristwatches powered by miniature batteries were introduced. There was no longer a need to rewind Grandfather's pocket watch, which was left in the jewelry box or relegated to a collector's showcase.

With the advent of readily available electricity, modern families plugged their kitchen and bedside clocks into the electrical outlet. The electric clock still created the comforting, womblike ticking sound, but electricity was unreliable. The old grandfather clock in the dining room, dependant on its swinging pendulum, and the cuckoo clock in the living room, which required one to reset the metal pinecone-shaped weights dangling from the chain, were a sure backup system.

Time was always available to a modern society in which precision and promptness were demanded. This was both a blessing and a curse. We could no longer escape time's constant imposition and demand upon our lives.

Atomic Time

Hidden within the invisible particles of the universe, a pendulum of sorts, invisible to the naked eye, began oscillating when the Creator started the cosmic clock.[4] Every chemical element and compound is designed to absorb and emit electromagnetic radiation at a unique frequency. This internal atomic and molecular process is highly stable and unaffected by normal external conditions. The oscillations of a cesium atom today (9,192,631,770 cycles per second) are exactly the same as one from millennia ago or even one that may exist in an unknown galaxy. The intrinsic nature of the smallest particle in the universe enables it to keep time.

Based upon this knowledge, in 1949, the first atomic clock was built using the ammonia molecule. In 1957, after a decade of research and development, the cesium atom clock was perfected and became the laboratory standard. It is so accurate that it loses only one second in thousands or even millions of years.

Time, Light, and the Cosmos

Centuries ago, courageous explorers set sail upon a vast ocean believing that the earth was flat. They dared to press the limits. To their great astonishment, they did not fall off the end of the earth. Instead, they discovered new islands and continents rich with diverse cultures and resources. Their understanding of the world instantly changed. Their knowledge of time and their ability to measure it made exploration more of an adventure than a dangerous, life-threatening risk.

In our fledgling attempts to explore outer space, a similar question demands an answer: What exists beyond the cosmos? Is it possible for us to "fall off the edge" of the universe or be sucked into a black hole and be catapulted into nothingness? How does our understanding of time apply to this great adventure?

According to Newtonian physics, the universe is static. It is everything there is. Time is an absolute constant within it. For centuries, we believed his theory. Like our adventuresome predecessors who thought that the earth was flat and that if you went too far, you would fall off, we believed that you could fall off the end of the universe. But our misconception was about to be shattered.

One of the greatest discoveries of the twentieth century was observed through the powerful lenses of the Hubble telescope as it peered into the distant reaches of space. What did Hubble measure? It tracked the light traveling through space and affirmed that it was moving away from us. This conclusion revolutionized science and physics. The universe is not static; it is expanding! This concept really plays havoc with the traditional understanding of time. But Einstein had already solved this problem.

The Hubble discovery that the universe is not static proved what Einstein's theories of specific and general relativity suggested regarding time. Einstein directly associated time, including its starting and stopping, with the idea that the contents of the cosmos are in motion. He believed that *space-time*, as he called it, is determined by the relativity between energy and matter moving throughout the universe. The only way an observer can measure space-time is to factor in the speed of light. Einstein's equation, $E=mc^2$ (energy equals mass times the square of the speed of light), confirmed the inseparable relationship between the three basic elements of creation: energy, matter (or mass), and light.

Einstein's theory of relativity adequately explained the large-scale dynamics of the universe. In so doing, he concluded that "there is no such thing as absolute time. Instead, all moving reference frames have their own relative time."[5] He further proposed that at the speed of light, time stands still, thereby affirming that light and time are inextricably bound together. Time cannot exist without light!

In a moment of introspection, Einstein, reflecting on the amazing insight of his relativity principle, said, "The thought is amusing and seductive; but for all I know, the good Lord might be laughing at the whole matter and might have been leading me up the garden path."[6]

The God Particle

Einstein's theory of relativity concentrates on the big picture. Quantum physics, in contrast, deals with the smallest particles in the universe. It is based on the subdivision of matter into radiant energy on an atomic or molecular level. It measures the transfer and transformation of energy from these finite quanta. Massive particle accelerators smash atomic particles together at speeds approaching the speed of light. Scientists have recently claimed that they have discovered the "God particle," believed to be the beginning of matter itself. Their goal is to arrive at a "theory of everything."

In quantum theory, the nature of time is a mystery. Stephen Hawking, one of the world's most brilliant physicists, has proposed that our ordinary concept of time is transcended in a quantum-cosmological setting.[7] It becomes just another dimension of space. In essence, time is space. If we could return to the beginning, time would be indistinguishable from space. In other words, time did not exist—only space existed! *Quantum theory permits us to describe a universe that has been created from nothing!*

Einstein came to a revealing conclusion as a result of his research: he claimed that he had discovered God! He had spent his last years trying to prove that God didn't exist. In like manner, quantum theorists cannot explain the origin of the universe except to say that it happened. Nothing became something. We have come full circle!

Time and History

Man has discovered time and learned to keep track of it by observing the cosmic clock. The concept of time, and the mechanisms that have been invented to measure it, are the framework and instrumentation that we use to chronicle the events of life and the activities of mankind. We call this *history*—"His story."

But again, we encounter a major difficulty. Can there actually be a factual, unbiased, objective, impartial record of what happens in the passing of time? Or are we doomed to view the events occurring in the chronicles of life through jaundiced eyes? If time is the landscape of experience—the scenery on the stage of life, as Bacon suggests—then history is the record of the action occurring on the stage. How the action is viewed and interpreted all depends upon which seat you occupy in the theater.

Power-hungry potentates, as well as various politicians, educators, and religious leaders who are motivated by political correctness, prejudice, and religious convictions, manipulate society by bending and shaping history to further their diabolical intentions. Historians, victims of their educational viewpoints, as well as their cultures and their racial, political, philosophical, and religious persuasions, record history in terms of belief rather than fact. In this malaise of opinion, is it possible to arrive at a correct understanding of man's behavior within the inexorable framework of the time machine? Even more important, is there a way to discern the times that will enable us to spend our days and years wisely and successfully, like Issachar's offspring?

The answer is simple. *It depends on your viewpoint!*

15

THE WAR OF
THE WORLDVIEWS

All of us sail on an ocean of time upon which we make our voyage through life. We are affected by tides and currents over which we have little control, if any. We all aspire to reach our chosen destination successfully. We hope that the sails we unfurl and the course we steer will be a positive influence and that we will be history makers, not mere observers. Our ultimate goal is to advance the kingdom of God and achieve eternal fulfillment. Understanding history and exercising good timing are critically important on this lifetime expedition. How can we understand the times we are traveling through accurately? And, as Francis Schaeffer asked, "How should we then live?"

Ticket to Ride

An imaginary ride in *The Time Machine* is the place to begin. Let's take a trip back in time to explore some of the *philosophical viewpoints* traditionally used to interpret history from the past right up to the present: secular humanism, socialism, communism, modernism, and postmodernism. We will then compare these humanistic viewpoints to the Christian perspective.

Considering the scope of this book, our intention is to provide a brief summary of each viewpoint. There are many other sources available if you wish to do an in-depth study of each philosophy. My goal is limited to introducing you to these views and exposing their fraud. If we are unaware of the deceptions they impose upon us, we will be doomed to repeat the mistakes of former generations and will buy into their erroneous philosophies. The result will be a distorted worldview that will cause us to misinterpret the present. We will be like the blind leading the blind.

Be forewarned—the shifting tides and currents of philosophical interpretation are perilous and can be very enticing and misleading. The traditional methods of perceiving history provide us with a partial, distorted view. Our ultimate destination, though, is to navigate through the smokescreen of man's interpretation of history to the core of reality—to the Light Giver and the Timekeeper Himself. Only in His presence, seeing from His perspective, will we finally and accurately come to discern what history, our times, and time itself are all about, just like Issachar and the prophets of Israel were able to do.

The Ship's Log

Are you ready for your journey in the time machine? Then let me welcome you aboard our particular ship, called "Earth." Please take note of the stacks of books on the shelves in the library of our vessel. These are the chronicles of the human adventure, a travelogue of time. The ship's log contains the journals of the history of civilization; it records every experience on Earth.[1] Each entry chronicles an event or change that has occurred on mankind's journey through the ages. The log helps us to remember. It is the map we use to travel back into the past.

Reading a history book is like opening a time capsule intentionally left behind by a former generation. It is like a time machine, transporting us all the way back as far as the beginning of a written record. We could say that the information recorded in Earth's log is accurate and speaks for itself, but that would be a lie. "The facts never come to us pure. They are always refracted through the mind of the recorder."[2] The element of interpretation enters into every facet of history. You may read these books at any time you wish during your journey, but remember, you are subject to the same tendency as those who wrote them.

The Way You See It

I want to call your attention to something you may not have been aware of. All of you who have boarded the time machine for our journey into the past are wearing glasses. They aren't actual glasses, of course, but imaginary ones. Nonetheless, though unseen, they are very real. Be aware that, just like those who kept the ship's log, you wear a pair of lenses—your personal point of view—through which you will observe and interpret everything you see on your journey. Let me remind you that the key to rightly interpreting history and, ultimately, the times we are living in is to establish the correct viewpoint!

Throughout the ages, a battle for the hearts and minds of mankind has raged with fury. There are worldviews in conflict, and you are a soldier in this fight. The philosophical glasses you are wearing determine your chosen point of view and shape your opinions according to your personal preference or belief. Because of this, your conclusions about history and time itself are automatically predisposed.

Let's identify the different types of philosophical lenses so that, when you read Earth's logbook, you will be aware of your own viewpoint and be able to detect the bias of the one who wrote the entry.

Secular Humanism

The first lens is *secular humanism*, which is the dominant view of most schools, colleges, and universities. This viewpoint denies the existence of God and focuses on man. It claims Darwin's theory of evolution as the only reasonable explanation for the existence of mankind. Self-actualization is the method of achieving personal fulfillment and happiness. This view claims that there are no moral absolutes and that social ethics are relative. Socialism, globalism, and world government are the ultimate utopia.

History, according to secular humanism, is interpreted from a strictly naturalistic viewpoint. God does not exist; only matter exists. Evolutionary process and spontaneous generation is the source of life. Because there is no purpose or design, mankind's only hope of survival is to evolve into the place of superiority over nature and create a future paradise through science.[3]

Socialism and Communism

The second viewpoint was designed by two lens crafters, Karl Marx and V. I. Lenin. Their viewpoint, like secular humanism, subscribes to atheism and biological evolution, but their main emphasis is class warfare. The struggle of social classes between the proletariat (non-owners) and the bourgeoisie (owners) will be brought to an end through socialism and communism. Private property will be eliminated and, with it, crime and the need for law. Home, church, and state will be abolished. A new world order will destroy national barriers and transform capitalism into socialism.

Marx and Lenin viewed history as an outworking of dialectical materialism. This attempt to explain all of reality proposes that the material universe is infinite and matter is eternal and indestructible. Based upon Darwin's evolutionary theory, dialectical materialism is the struggle to evolve. Through the recurring process of thesis, antithesis, and synthesis, the great force of dialectical materialism, along with some help from social engineering and eugenics, will propel matter and man toward a communist paradise. This is historical determinism; neither God nor man has any influence in determining nature or history.

Modernism

The lens of modernism existed in the nineteenth century and was intimated by Marx, Darwin, and others, but the emerging philosophical viewpoint really found a fertile breeding ground in the early twentieth century as a consequence of the atrocities and social upheaval of World War I. In some measure, it was a reaction to the use of technology in the war and the growing discontent with the prevailing worldview. Then, Einstein's theory of relativity changed everything. Society was instantly cut loose from the three-centuries-old moorings of Isaac Newton's mechanical, unchanging universe. *Relativity* became the buzzword for every aspect of society. Nothing was certain anymore except progress.

Modernism rejected the certainty of the Enlightenment and revolted against the conservative values and traditions of the Victorian Era. The existing Victorian culture emphasized nationalism and cultural absolutism. Everything could be defined in clear-cut dichotomies: right and wrong, good and bad, civilized and savage. Modernist views stood in stark contrast to these values, endorsing the idea that the old ways of thinking were to blame for slavery, racism, imperialism, and the war itself.

Rejecting "misguided" Enlightenment thinking, modernists encouraged the reexamination of every aspect of existence, including the arts, architecture, science, philosophy, commerce, literature, and religion. Traditional social structures and daily life were considered outdated in the new economic, social, and political conditions of an emerging, fully industrialized world. Anything that was regarded as holding back progress had to be removed. Modernism challenged the basic foundations of society.

The belief that man possessed the power to improve his environment through knowledge and experimentation gripped the hearts and minds of a world set free from its classical moorings. Self-awareness became a hallmark for modernist thinkers, leading to experiments with form and production that drew attention to the processes and materials used in creating and designing everything from furniture to buildings. Progressive thinkers and artists like Einstein, Picasso, Matisse, Stravinsky, Schoenberg, Joyce, Eliot, Proust, Freud, and Wittgenstein led the way.

Modernism totally rejected the existence of a Supreme Being. In the view of modernists, God does not play an active role in the world. In fact, there is no meaning or reason behind history. No one is born for a specific purpose. Everyone must define his or her own meaning in a world of cultural relativism. Religious ideas are made to bow to modern culture and adapt to modern ways of thinking.

The belief that the world had drastically changed since the time Christianity ruled the culture led to the questioning of the authority of the Scriptures and the creeds. The Bible is portrayed as the work of writers who were limited by their times. It is considered neither a supernatural nor an infallible record of divine revelation. It does not possess absolute authority. Reason and experience must rule, not religious authority. All beliefs must pass the tests of reason and experience and are subject to newfound facts and truth, regardless of where these may originate.

Modernism also engendered theological liberalism. The authority of the Scriptures, creeds, and the church were diluted into the "essence" of Christianity. This resolved the contradiction between faith and natural law, revelation and science, sacred and secular, and religion and culture. God is portrayed as present and dwelling within the world, not apart from or elevated above the world as a transcendent Being. He is its soul and life, as well as the Creator. God is found in the whole of life, not just in the Bible or a few revelatory events. Because God is present in all that happens, there is no distinction between the natural and the supernatural. He reveals Himself in rational truth, artistic beauty, and moral goodness.

Modernism succeeded in the destruction of the idea of the immanence of God, characterizing Him as an indifferent, anemic deity who exists in nature. It made religious authority a slave of relativism. While some modernists held steadfast to the core of Christian doctrine, the ultimate outcome of progressive theological liberalism was pantheism.

Postmodernism

The lens of postmodernism is very hazy. Trying to define it is like trying to catch a greased pig. Every time you think you've got a hold of it, it slips away. By its very nature, postmodernism resists definition because the very act of defining involves restricting or limiting a word, object, or idea to a specific meaning. Postmodernists consider limitations or restrictions as anathema. This insidious worldview has gone viral in our society.

Let me simply explain that postmodernism is the progeny of two distinct historical periods—first, the premodern era, which began with the collapse of Rome in the fourth century. Because of Emperor Constantine, the dominant worldview at that time was Christian. But as the church grew and developed an ecclesiastical hierarchy, the Catholic Church began to exert control and dominance over Christianity. The consequence was that society eventually divided into two streams, the Reformation and the Renaissance.

The modern era began in the fourteenth century with the Renaissance. This cultural evolution shifted the focus from a biblical worldview to a progressive, modern one. The importance of God and the Bible diminished, and attention shifted to the value and significance of the individual. René Descartes, a prominent philosopher and mathematician during that time, reduced absolute certainty to a simple equation: *Cogito, ergo sum.* "I think, therefore I am." The only thing he was sure of was that *he existed.* All other knowledge was suspect. Everything had to be questioned. Faith without proof was invalid.

The result of the ensuing societal skepticism was the scientific revolution, secularism, and naturalism (the belief that everything has a natural cause and that man is a product of evolution). By the mid-twentieth century, the belief that mankind was capable of solving every problem and accomplishing every goal was pervasive.

Like so many philosophical viewpoints, postmodernism began in the intellectual Petri dish of academia, but it soon spread to the general population. It quickly infected society like a virus attacking a susceptible host that had no positive antivirus to fight it off. The 1960s appear to have been the tipping point that thrust us into a social revolution. The hippie movement, sexual freedom, mind-altering drugs, political unrest, demonstrations, and protests over the Vietnam War heralded its full arrival. Mass media spread the infection. Scientific skepticism and natural causation were replaced with tolerance and nihilism (the viewpoint that traditional values and beliefs are unfounded and that existence is senseless and useless. Nihilism denies any objective ground of truth, especially moral truth).

The Russian author Alexander Solzhenitsyn described our present condition as "a world split apart." We have become socially schizophrenic, torn in two by drastically opposing worldviews. We are in conflict with our Judeo-Christian roots and biblical faith and the absolute supremacy of the individual, along with a total, eclectic tolerance for anything and everything.

The virus of postmodernism thrives on chaos. It considers the pursuit of truth to be a pointless activity. The only absolute truth is that there are no absolute truths. What we individually perceive *is* reality. Consequently, a correct description of reality is impossible. Opinion supersedes authority. We get to make up our own rules and obey only the ones we like. *Tolerance* is the number one virtue. Whatever you believe is okay, even if it's diametrically opposed to someone else's beliefs. Since what you believe is right, you can do anything to achieve your goals. God is dead. The concept of morality is absurd. Truth, authority, national pride, honesty, and intolerance are outmoded ideas, merely part of our immature past. They have no place going forward.

The problem with postmodernism was summed up well by Lucretius: "If anyone thinks nothing is to be known, he does not even know whether that can be known, as he says he knows nothing." We are left with nothing! There is no possibility of ever determining absolute truths about how we should think and live wisely on earth.

I Am!

There is a saying that without the right questions, the right answers have no place to go. Another is that someone who knows that he "does not know" actually knows more than another who thinks he knows but is wrong.

Jesus asked the right question. It is the most important question you and I will ever answer: *"Who do you say that I am?"* (Matthew 16:15). He affirmed Peter's response, which was, *"You are the Christ, the Son of the living God"* (Matthew 16:16). Jesus personally identified Himself as the way (the means), the truth (absolute reality), and the life (the journey). (See John 14:6.)

Jesus told us to say "Our Father" when we pray. We have a Father-child relationship with the I Am. Truth is a living, dynamic Person, leading us on a never-ending adventure in time and eventually in eternity. Is not our Father's revelation of Himself as "I Am" the *existential place* to be? Is it not absolute truth?

Christianity

The Christian worldview is in stark contrast to secular humanism and its off-spring, communist socialism, with its idealistic founders. It also stands in stark contrast to modernism and postmodernism. For starters, the lens of Christianity is not based on a philosophy concocted by man. It has nothing to do with human ability or the evolutionary process to manipulate society. It does not depend upon the laws of nature to ultimately create some utopian existence where superior beings who have survived evolution's process live in an Elysium paradise of total equality. Nor can a hopeless quagmire of tolerance and nihilism destroy it. Christianity is based upon factual, historical information and documentation. *Christianity does not begin with philosophy; it begins with fact.* It is historically documented, and the events are verified.

The centrality of a single Person, Jesus of Nazareth, is the cornerstone upon which the authenticity of Christianity rests.

But when the fullness of the time had come, God sent forth His Son, born of a woman, born under the law, to redeem those who were under the law, that we might receive the adoption as sons. And because you are sons, God has sent forth the Spirit of His Son into your hearts, crying out, "Abba, Father!" Therefore you are no longer a slave but a son, and if a son, then an heir of God through Christ. (Galatians 4:4–7)

Jesus was born; He lived; He was crucified and buried, and He rose again! He was seen ascending into heaven. Many eyewitnesses testified to the verity of these historical facts, and millions through the centuries have borne testimony to their truth. No competent scholar would think of denying the historicity of Jesus, and those who have examined the evidence surrounding the resurrection have not been able to disprove it.

Christianity's proof text is the Bible, a literal, inspired account of history that has been proven time and again for its authenticity and accuracy. Modern archeology, geology, astronomy, physics, and biology continually confirm its correctness.

The Christian worldview is clearly defined by Scripture. God created everything. *"By faith we understand that the worlds were framed by the word of God, so that the things which are seen were not made of things which are visible"* (Hebrews 11:3). He created man and woman and every living thing. Marriage and family were God's idea and form the basic unit of society. (See Genesis 1–2; Romans 1:18–27.) Man has sinned and needs a Savior. (See Genesis 3; John 1–3; Ephesians 2:4–10.) There are ethical absolutes. (See Exodus 20.) All authority and government are established by God's design. (See Romans 13:1–7.) The end of time as we know it will culminate in the resurrection and judgment of every individual. (See 1 Corinthians 15:51–52; 2 Corinthians 5:10; Romans 14:10; Hebrews 9:27.) Christians believe that God has always been active in history and that, by His intervention, He is unveiling and fulfilling His will.

> *He has made from one blood every nation of men to dwell on all the face of the earth, and has determined their preappointed times and the boundaries of their dwellings, so that they should seek the Lord, in the hope that they might grope for Him and find Him, though He is not far from each one of us; for in Him we live and move and have our being, as also some of your own poets have said, "For we are also His offspring."*   (Acts 17:26–28)

While secular humanism and communist socialism believe that man can save himself, Christianity believes that this is impossible. God's intervention is necessary, and the redemption of mankind is made possible only because God acted by sending His Son, Jesus Christ.

Postmodernism may deny the existence of God, but despite its attempts to destroy absolute truth, the only correct, proven-to-be-accurate viewpoint is Christianity. This lens enables us to interpret the events on the grand stage of time, where mankind lives in the context of God's creative, amazing, redeeming love, His pure justice, and His kingdom reign.

Choose Designer Glasses

We have compared only a few of the multitude of philosophical viewpoints that have been foisted upon us by godless, atheistic scholars and so-called intellectual experts. Only one proves to be accurate. Not only is the Christian viewpoint historically and factually correct; it is the only way to properly interpret and understand the true meaning of time and its relevance for our predecessors, ourselves, and our progeny.

The words of the apostle Paul, who lived in an age when superstition and Greek philosophy ruled the thoughts and viewpoints of mankind, are more applicable than ever: *"Beware lest anyone cheat you through philosophy and empty deceit, according to the tradition of men, according to the basic principles of the world, and not according to Christ"* (Colossians 2:8).

Choose your glasses carefully! Regardless of which logbook you choose to read and navigate by, or how far back in time you wish to travel, remember, viewpoint is critical. Interpretation is in the eye of the beholder. Enjoy your ride. You can depart whenever you like. Our time machine, Earth, is moving. The chronicles of the human adventure are readily available. Godspeed!

The Picture Frame

History can be likened to an artist's painting of a scene from the past. As we have just discussed, how we interpret that scene, whether it is an event, object, landscape, or person, is significantly determined by our philosophical persuasions. But there is another aspect of historical interpretation we must consider. Every artist's painting is *framed* before it is hung on the wall. There are many different kinds of frames used to enhance and define an artist's conception of what he is portraying. These frames have nothing to do with the portrait's philosophical meaning or content. Instead, they serve as a *frame of reference*—a border, providing a definite boundary for the painting. Everything is viewed and interpreted inside this parameter.

Historians use a similar technique. They use frames of reference to associate and interpret sequences of events that belong together. Not only does this make an individual event more definitive; it also places it in historical context with the multitude of events from the same time period or age.

Let's take a closer look at the frameworks of history.

16

THE FRAMEWORKS
OF HISTORY

The sons of Issachar were astute at deciphering the times and seasons. They were able to detect patterns in the actions occurring around them in Israel and Judah. These anointed servants of God looked beyond isolated events, interpreting them as signs pointing to something much more significant. They understood that these indicators were clues pointing to a greater purpose, as designed and orchestrated by the Light Giver. God was always up to something, and they were always able to discern what it was.

Just as the individual pieces of a puzzle reveal much more than their unique shape and identity when they are all joined together, Issachar's offspring correlated the events occurring in their world and were able to see the definitive "big picture." Once events were viewed in context, a *paradigm*, or pattern, emerged. It was like looking at the completed picture on the puzzle box. It's so much easier to figure out where each individual piece fits when we have a model to follow.

An awareness of this framework provides us with a paradigm or pattern for *discerning and interpreting the times*. Random events make sense when viewed within a theoretical framework. But it's essential to choose the correct frame. Holding the wrong paradigm can be misleading and even disastrous.

Advanced History

My introduction to the concept of various paradigms that frame the events of history happened when I was a senior at the University of Pittsburgh. As a student majoring in history and sociology, I was taught by some of the best and brightest professors, who exposed me to ideas and insights that hadn't occurred to me before. Like the apostle Paul, I sat at the feet of the "experts" to learn the intricacies of the process of interpreting the times.

One particular senior class, Advanced Historical Frameworks, served as a turning point for me. It came at the culmination of five years of studying, reading hundreds of history books, and attending countless lectures. By that time, I was overloaded with information. I needed some way to categorize it all—to put it in a comprehensive mental filing system of sorts. I had to find a frame of reference, a pattern, that would help me make sense of various social theories of human behavior and all of the many periods and areas of history I had studied. I had the pieces of the puzzle; I just needed the puzzle box top. This upper level class provided it.

I invite you to audit Advanced Historical Frameworks. Come with me back to that college classroom. Experience it vicariously through my eyes and ears. You will be introduced to the paradigms this class provided for me, along with my introspective reflections as I pondered each framework. The classroom is located in one of my favorite buildings in the world. Are you ready? Let's go! We don't want to be late for class.

Welcome to Campus

I searched everywhere for a parking space and finally found one, located so far from the Cathedral of Learning that I had to hustle for more than a mile through the frigid, winter air just to get to class on time. The solid, slate-gray sky was an ominous warning of the approaching blizzard sweeping down from the Great Lakes, about to descend upon Western Pennsylvania. I spun through the revolving doors of the Gothic limestone skyscraper, the second-tallest education building in the world, and gratefully welcomed the heat emanating from the roaring fireplace in the magnificent, three-story Commons Room.

I love this building, I thought. *It's more like a castle than a modern classroom. The ambiance is transforming.* Stepping inside this citadel of education was like being transported back in time to an era of lords and ladies, King Arthur and the

Knights of the Round Table, a time of valor and bravery. I quickly forgot that I was in a major cosmopolitan city in the twenty-first century.

Vaulted stone arches were visible in every direction, each one leading to some out-of-the-way corner or dark chamber where a student could seek solitude and peaceful contemplation. Huge chandeliers, their design copied from some medieval castle, hung from husky chains dangling thirty feet above the stone floor. They cast a dim yellow glow that gave barely enough light to navigate, let alone read a book. Many students were sequestered in the shadows of nooks and crannies, poring over textbooks and notes. Others were chatting with friends near the crackling fire. The oak chairs and tables in the center of the huge room seemed centuries old, scarred by generations of neophytes hoping to learn something, and lovers whose names, carved into the surface, were now darkened by decades of use. These furnishings had obviously been designed for longevity rather than comfort.

No time to linger, I reminded myself before scurrying up the stairs to the second floor, where a broad hallway circumnavigated the cavernous space below. My class was in the far corner of the passageway. I arrived with rosy cheeks and a runny nose, still exhaling condensation from my burning lungs. I took a seat in one of the upper rows of the lecture auditorium, so far from the professor that I could barely make out his facial expressions. I struggled out of my heavy coat, then threw it over the back of the empty seat next to me. I retrieved my notebook and pen from my briefcase just as the doors were closed and the class began. "Historical Frameworks," I scribbled with my trusty Bic pen across the subject line on the cover of my spiral-bound notebook. All talking ceased as the professor began his lecture.

"Welcome to advanced history," the professor said with a tone of authority. His light brown corduroy slacks, matching sport coat, and plaid wool sweater seemed appropriate in light of his prominent position as head of the history department. His silver-gray hair was an unruly banner crop, and he kept throwing his head to the right to clear his glasses of this white awning of wool that hung down over them.

"Most of you have spent your early college years in our history department learning about the world and particular events in the past," he continued. "The purpose of this course is different. My job is to teach you how to interpret history! It is far more than knowing dates and occurrences. History begs for understanding and interpretation. It is the chronicle of human behavior, a compendium of decisions and actions fraught with all the emotion and motivation of humankind. It is life in the raw, unmasked, and waiting to be understood. We are *detectives of time*, searching for clues that reveal reason and motive. The life lessons and experiences of former generations wait to be unraveled, decoded, and made relevant to today's world. Voices from past generations have left us a legacy of life lived for us to analyze with the desperate hope that we will not repeat their mistakes.

"Like a foreign language, history must be translated so that we can understand the reasons behind the events, their causes and effects, and what the ultimate consequences are for us. We must learn to read between the lines of cultural context, language barriers, and ancient worldviews. The educated historian seeks to understand *why* things happened the way they did and the lessons these insights may teach us.

"My goal as your professor is to shed some light upon the subject of history itself. I want to provide you with the interpretive tools that professional historians use to understand the big picture of the past. These traditional tools of interpretation help us to make sense of the minutiae of daily life, as well as the cataclysmic events that have transformed our world.

"Historians use a set of models or blueprints to interpret history. Like the Rosetta stone, which is used to decode the mystery of the hieroglyphs, these imposed patterns guide our thoughts as we study the events of past generations. How we decode history is significantly determined by the template we choose to frame it in. We call these frames of reference *historical paradigms*. First, let's examine the most common paradigm."

The Shortest Distance Between Two Points

"The first mathematical law that we learn in geometry class is that the shortest distance between two points is a straight line. This basic principle, when applied to history, simply states that time moves in a straight line from beginning to end. This viewpoint, called the *linear paradigm*, is the most traditional template used to interpret history.

"In this paradigm, time is considered to be chronological: seconds, minutes, hours, days, months, years, decades, centuries, millennia, light-years. Each change or occurrence in real time becomes a continuous evolution of linear events.

History is considered to be the recording and study of these accumulated events and their interactions and influences on each other. Since time began, history has been moving inexorably forward toward a future and, depending on your persuasion, even an apocalyptic culmination.

"In a cosmic setting, astrophysicists call this linear concept the *arrow of time*. Everything in the cosmos is continually moving from low entropy (a high degree of order in a system) to high entropy (a low degree of order). They base this on the second law of thermodynamics, which claims that everything tends to move from order to disorder.

"The entire cosmos is degrading into chaos, disorganization, randomness, and, ultimately, nothingness. Physicists claim that this process is irreversible. Entire solar systems, stars, and planets, including our sun and the earth itself, are very slowly dying. This process will take trillions and trillions of years. Eventually, dark stars and black holes will be all that remain of our cosmos. They, too, will vanish, marking the total disappearance of light, life, energy, and time. This will be the end of the age of starlight. In essence, we are on a straight-line course from beginning to end in which all action occurs between these two goalposts. Everything is dependent on light, and when the light goes out, time will cease. There will be nothing left. There will be no change to measure. History, as we know it, will end."

The *Chronos* Connection

Aha! That reminds me of the Greek word chronos, I thought, comparing what the professor had just said to my knowledge of the Greek language.

The Greek word *chronos* means "chronological." It denotes a space of time, short or long, or a succession of things. It has a sense of quantity or duration of time in which events occur in sequential order—a calendar, if you will. Thus, chronology becomes the skeletal structure upon which we place the body of history. "No second is seen as being worth more than any other. The clock and calendar essentially dictate the rhythm of our lives."[1] Genealogy, ancestral tracking, and the family tree are of paramount consideration within this framework.

Luke, the biblical historian, used this chronological, linear template when he recorded events occurring in the first century A.D. His goal was to set in order—in the proper sequence—the details in the life of Jesus. He wrote,

*Inasmuch as many have taken in hand to set in order a narrative of those things which have been fulfilled among us, just as those who from the beginning were eyewitnesses and ministers of the word delivered them to us, it seemed good to me also, having had perfect understanding of all things **from the very first**, to write you **an orderly account**, most excellent Theophilus, that you may know the certainty of those things in which you were instructed.*

(Luke 1:1–4, emphasis added)

The former account I made, O Theophilus, of all that Jesus began both to do and teach, until the day in which He was taken up, after He through the Holy Spirit had given commandments to the apostles whom He had chosen.

(Acts 1:1–2)

Here We Go Again

The professor continued his lecture. "Let's consider the second framework of interpretation, the *cyclical paradigm*. This perspective views time as a cycle of events that keep occurring over and over, not in exactly the same way but in similar ways. It suggests that we are doomed to repeat the mistakes of the past. What goes around comes around. Sound familiar?

"This paradigm is affirmed by observation. Our lives are encompassed by constantly repeating procedures. The daily twenty-four-hour cycle of the earth, the monthly phases of the moon and tides, the seasons—seedtime and harvest, war and peace, recession and boom—and sleeping and waking all contribute to the validity of this worldview. Once every 93,408 years, our entire solar system completes one full cycle, like a cosmic clock resetting itself to zero."

My Reflections

The professor's second point sparked my thoughts. God had certainly established repeating cycles. He created a seven-day cycle, marked by the Sabbath. He instituted the seven-year rest for the land and the fifty-year cycle of new beginnings, called Jubilee. The Hebrew word *et* (a particular time, season, age, occasion, or period of time) applies to this view. King Solomon used the word *et* to describe these cyclical patterns in history.

To everything there is a season, a time [et] for every purpose under heaven: a
time to be born, and a time to die; a time to plant, and a time to pluck what
is planted; a time to kill, and a time to heal; a time to break down, and a time
to build up; a time to weep, and a time to laugh; a time to mourn, and a time
to dance; a time to cast away stones, and a time to gather stones; a time to
embrace, and a time to refrain from embracing; a time to gain, and a time to
lose; a time to keep, and a time to throw away; a time to tear, and a time to
sew; a time to keep silence, and a time to speak; a time to love, and a time to
hate; a time of war, and a time of peace. (Ecclesiastes 3:1–8)

According to Solomon, everything in the world keeps reoccurring in cycles.

Even economic cycles are evident in history. A Russian economist, Nikolai
Kondratiev, studied the nineteenth century and concluded that the biblical rule
of the fifty-year cycle did indeed hold up. He found that periods of economic
prosperity appear to happen in cycles of twenty-five or fifty years.[2]

God also thinks in generational cycles. He is the God of Abraham, Isaac, and
Jacob. It took God forty years to cleanse Israel of a disobedient generation that
refused to enter into the Promised Land.

For I, the LORD *your God, am a jealous God, visiting the iniquity of the*
fathers upon the children to the third and fourth generations of those who hate
Me, but showing mercy to thousands, to those who love Me and keep My com-
mandments. (Exodus 20:5–6)

The pessimistic cyclical paradigm postulates that history repeats itself in an
incessant, perpetual circular motion in which we are prisoners in a never-ending
cycle, condemned to repeat the mistakes of the past and succumb to the sins of
our fathers. The warning Paul gave Timothy centuries ago is just as fitting for our
own generation.

But know this, that in the last days perilous times will come: for men will be
lovers of themselves, lovers of money, boasters, proud, blasphemers, disobedi-
ent to parents, unthankful, unholy, unloving, unforgiving, slanderers, without
self-control, brutal, despisers of good, traitors, headstrong, haughty, lovers of
pleasure rather than lovers of God, having a form of godliness but denying its
power...always ***learning and never able to come to the knowledge of the***
truth. (2 Timothy 3:1–5, 7, emphasis added)

Despite its cynical portrayal of life, an awareness of cyclical living is an absolute necessity in order to give stability and regularity to our existence. Our ability to recognize times and seasons that continue to recur is imperative!

A Slinky Viewpoint

The professor's movement instantly elicited my curiosity. Like every other student, my attention was riveted to his actions as he reached beneath the oak podium and lifted out a small, rectangular cardboard box. With a mischievous smile, he opened the container, removed a coiled object, and proceeded to dangle it over the edge of the lectern. It sprang to life, shimmering and bobbing up and down with a wiggling motion, like a hollow metallic snake.

"Welcome to slinky world," he said. "History can be likened to an imaginary slinky pushed off the top of a staircase. Its coiled length extends and compresses in sequential stages as it travels the entire staircase, finally completing its journey at the bottom. Even though it is a continuous, self-contained unit of circles, it is traveling though time and space by adjusting its cycles to the environment and the forces acting upon it.

"Historians call this the *spiral paradigm*. It combines both the linear pattern and the cyclical pattern into one conceptual framework of time. Although history is inclined to repeat itself, there is a forward progression. It is not just going in circles. Each successive repetition may vary in intensity or duration, but it is progressively propelling mankind toward the ultimate culmination of time, as we understand it. This view assumes that there is a beginning and an ending, not just a continually repeating cycle of events. Each occurring cycle serves as a *season* in the linear progression of time that is propelling mankind forward into the future."

An Example from Egypt

Immediately, I thought of an example from the Bible. It's found in chapter 41 of Genesis. Pharaoh searched for someone who could interpret his dreams. In the first dream, he saw seven fat cows and seven lean cows. The ugly, gaunt cows ate up the fine-looking fat cows. In the second dream, seven heads of grain came up on one stalk, plump and good. Then, seven thin heads blighted by the east wind sprang up. The seven thin heads devoured the plump, full heads. The Egyptian magicians couldn't interpret these dreams, and so Joseph was summoned from his prison cell into the presence of the mightiest ruler in the world to interpret the dream. Joseph had a "master's degree" in dream interpretation.

"What does this mean?" Pharaoh asked.

Joseph's response was insightful. "It is not me. God will give Pharaoh an answer of peace. There will be seven years of plenty and seven years of famine. You must store up the grain in the fat years to provide food for the lean years." (See Genesis 41:16, 25–36.)

Joseph knew that the cycles that were coming in Egypt were yet-to-be-written chapters in his own future. Could they be the catalyst leading toward the fulfillment of his personal dreams? Looking back through the eyes of history, we know that the answer is yes. He was being positioned to become second in command and, ultimately, the one who would preserve his family—God's chosen people, Israel—during the coming famine. These cycles of abundance and famine were taking him somewhere!

"Who is wise? One who can tell what will be hatched from the egg that has been laid. Not he who can see the future—that is a prophet. Wisdom is seeing tomorrow's consequences of today's events."[3] How encouraging it is to know that history does far more than repeat itself! It is leading somewhere.

Time Surfing

Transitioning from traditional frameworks to contemporary ones, the professor flicked his hair off of his glasses and shifted the focus of his lecture to a new genre of individuals who had changed the way we analyze history.

"Now that we have examined some of the traditional paradigms used to interpret the past, let's consider some modern ones that examine history with the specific goal of predicting the future.

"The first one is called the *wave theory*. In this paradigm, historical events are interpreted in the context of some overarching influence or cultural focus that encompasses all of society. The strength of this force is called a *wave of influence*. As time progresses and cultures and nations develop, successive waves of influence sweep across an entire society, changing its character dramatically. The ability to predict the next wave and its impact upon society has become a science in itself.

"Pioneer futurists Alvin and Heidi Toffler launched the discipline of futurism with their books *Future Shock* in 1970 and *The Third Wave* in 1980.[4] They devised a historical paradigm that has become a standard for analyzing the past and present and predicting the future. They dared to ask questions nobody else thought of. The answers they arrived at have fundamentally redefined our method of making sense of our world.

"In their book *The Third Wave*, they describe three types of societies, each one based on the concept of 'waves'—each wave pushes the older societies and cultures aside. The first wave is the Agricultural Revolution, which replaced nomadic hunting and gathering. The second wave is the Industrial Revolution, occurring from the late 1600s through the mid-1900s. The main components of this second wave are the nuclear family, the factory-type education system, and the corporation.

"Toffler describes the second-wave society as industrial and based on mass production, mass distribution, mass consumption, mass education, mass media, mass recreation, mass entertainment, and weapons of mass destruction. If you combine those things with standardization, centralization, concentration, and synchronization, you wind up with the style of organization we call bureaucracy."

The professor commented, "Since the late 1950s, most countries have been moving away from a second-wave society into a third-wave, post-industrial society. Toffler describes this era as the 'Information Age.' Diversity, knowledge-based production, space exploration, electronics, globalization, and scientific technology will transform our world. In this milieu of rapidly increasing knowledge, the acceleration of information and change will inundate us. He predicts that the future lies in outer space, human cloning will become a reality, and the modern office will be paperless.

"This husband-and-wife team of global forecasters has established the basic viewpoint that there can be no economic transformation without a corresponding upheaval in our social, political, and cultural institutions and values. They suggest that change is nonlinear and can go backward, forward, and sideways; change is the process by which the future invades our lives."

162 _ The Light Giver

California, Here It Comes

"John Naisbitt is another forward-looking theorist," the professor continued, leaning forward over the lectern to emphasize his point. "Like the Tofflers, he helped to revolutionize our thinking about predicting the future. In his ground-breaking book *Megatrends*, he theorizes that the most reliable way to forecast the future is to try to understand the present.

"Naisbitt has popularized the paradigm that societal changes are influenced by *major trends* in the culture. His approach is to detect and observe these trends within society as catalysts and indicators of what is to come. Pop culture and trendsetters in every facet of life influence our ways of thinking and behaving. These trends reach a *tipping point* that suddenly effects sweeping change.[5] His advice to modern leaders is to 'find a parade and get in front of it.' What happens in California, or, for that matter, China, may in fact become the standard for an entire nation or the world in a few short months.

"One commendable, distinctive quality of Naisbitt's viewpoint is his great regard for the value of mankind, and I quote: 'We must learn to balance the material wonders of technology with the spiritual demands of our human race. We have for the first time an economy based on a key resource [information] that is not only renewable, but also self-governing. Running out of it is not a problem, but drowning in it is.'[6]"

Class Dismissed

"See you next week," the professor announced, placing his lecture notes in his briefcase. "Make sure you complete the assigned reading on your syllabus before our next session."

The class stampeded like cattle at the sound of a gunshot, bolting for the doors and the cavernous cathedral commons room beyond. *Already?* I thought as I stuffed my notebook back inside my briefcase. I grabbed my coat and followed the crowd, feeling somewhat perplexed by the various historical paradigms I had just been given. *Which one is the most accurate?* I wondered.

"Well," I muttered, "the professor just said that running out of information is not the problem; drowning in it is."

One last thought crossed my mind as I stepped up to the roaring fireplace to warm my hands before making a mad dash back to the car through the bitter cold air typical of Pittsburgh in February. *I wonder which paradigm the sons of Issachar would have espoused if they had been teaching this class? Perhaps they possessed one that we haven't considered yet! After all, they were gifted experts. They understood the times!*

I gazed at the shimmering, golden fire. It had a life of its own. The flames danced before me, while the crackling logs shot glowing, white-hot sparks into the air. Boiling sap dripped onto the red-hot coals underneath the grate and sizzled, emitting a pine scent no artificial candle could ever duplicate perfectly. *I could stay here all day*, I thought, with passionate desire, but entertaining the idea didn't persuade me.

"Better get going," I finally acknowledged to the roaring fireplace, as I shivered in anticipation of the frightful conditions outside.

17

A THEOLOGY OF TIME

I braced myself for what lay beyond the revolving door. "I feel more like a dogsled driver than a historian," I grumbled as I stepped into the pie-slice-shaped space and pushed hard against the glass panel. The centrifugal force thrust me out into a teeth-gritting wonderland of white. Enormous snowflakes swirled around me, and I was instantly devoured by the howling blizzard. The wind sweeping around the Cathedral of Learning sounded like a pack of snarling wolves in pursuit of what little body heat I was able to generate inside my pleated, goose-down parka.

Traffic was at a standstill in the rapidly accumulating snow. The signal light at the corner emitted a surreal, alternating red-and-green post-Christmas glow as it penetrated the snow-laden atmosphere. Clutching my briefcase tightly, I reached up with my other hand to secure the hood of my coat more tightly around my face as I trudged toward the car, a mile away. *It will no doubt be buried in snow when I get there*, I admitted.

From my point of view, cloistered like a monk inside my hooded parka, the world outside seemed more like shadow than substance, a world of guesses rather than clarity. A silence accompanies a heavy snowfall that provokes introspection and wonder. It is an invitation to think beyond the obvious, to peer into the unknown and search the silence for a mystical viewpoint that takes us beyond our human limitations, into a realm of imagination and belief in the unseen. My thoughts wandered into this spiritual landscape of exploration and discovery. *I wonder how God views history*, I thought to myself. *Is there a "theology of time" revealed in the Bible?*

From Here to Eternity

Consider God's great plan of redemption, I theorized. *That's a good place to start. I'll call it the "redemption paradigm."*

We can frame all of history in relation to God's plan of salvation. It consists of three events: creation, Christ (the dividing line), and culmination.[1] Before time existed, there was *eternity past*. Out of the nothingness of pre-creation, God formed the time/space cosmos in which we exist. From the beginning of the creation of the cosmos and, specifically, the earth, time relentlessly progressed toward a single event: the birth of Christ. This event radically redefined history. Since His birth, we have been steadily moving toward the last chapter of time.

This paradigm of history is based on *divine intention* and presupposes a *Creator*. All things, including time itself, were created by God for a divine purpose. Christ existed at the beginning.

He is the image of the invisible God, the firstborn over all creation. For by Him all things were created that are in heaven and that are on the earth, visible and invisible, whether thrones or dominions or principalities or powers. All things were created through Him and for Him. (Colossians 1:15–16)

Mankind was created in God's image for companionship with Him. Our intrinsic purpose is intimacy with our Creator.[2] That communion was destroyed by Adam and Eve's disobedience and sin. God has been acting to restore communion with His creation ever since. History is therefore redemptive in nature. Think about it! Time and ancient history steadily moved toward a *kairos* moment.

Kairos is a Greek word that describes the right time or opportune moment for something unique and special to occur. The term is used to identify the action of God as a defining moment in life. It is God's intervention in the affairs of men, individually or corporately. It is a grace event, a divine appointment, or an encounter that manifests God's will and intentions and changes the course of history. We distinguish such miraculous moments by recognizing that the circumstances, resources, and occurrences are beyond human capability, resources, and wisdom to produce or achieve.

The birth, life, death, and resurrection of Jesus Christ, God's only Son, are *kairos* moments. The birth of Christ was the decisive *turning point*, dividing time into two parameters, B.C. (before Christ) and A.D. (*anno domini*, in the year of our Lord). Recently, secular historians have attempted to alter this long-accepted framework of history. They have tried to redefine the paradigm, saying we ought to divide time using nonreligious terms—*ancient* and *common*—instead of using the birth of Christ as a reference point. These historians propose that we use instead B.C.E. (before the Common Era) and C.E. (Common Era), thereby rendering God of no consequence. This presents a problem.

The suggested nomenclature attempts to interpret all events as occurring either before the Common Era or in the Common Era. How, then, does one determine which date establishes the demarcation between common and ancient? And how does one do away with the historical fact that Jesus Christ has always been the divine delineation of history? Historians did not determine that; God decided it, and we acknowledged it. The truth cannot be erased; all of history moves from the garden of Eden to the life of a single individual, Jesus Christ of Nazareth. Everything changed the moment He showed up.

Since the Christ event, modern history has been hurtling toward its conclusion—the *resurrection* of the living and the dead and *eternal judgment*. (See 1 Corinthians 15.)

> *For the Lord Himself will descend from heaven with a shout, with the voice of an archangel, and with the trumpet of God. And the dead in Christ will rise first. Then we who are alive and remain shall be caught up together with them in the clouds to meet the Lord in the air. And thus we shall always be with the Lord.* (1 Thessalonians 4:16–17)

We are steadily moving forward toward the final determination of God's judgment. "*It is appointed for men to die once, but after this the judgment*" (Hebrews 9:27; see also Romans 14:10). When this final judgment occurs, time itself will cease, and the history of mankind as we know it will end.

The Clash of Kingdoms

A blistering blast of freezing wind pushed me sideways as I trudged across the snow-covered campus lawn toward Heinz Chapel. *It's still a long way to the car,*

I lamented, as a brave, aerodynamically challenged starling flew past, only a few feet away from me, and landed on a slender, bare branch. *Not a very good choice*, I thought, watching the little creature cling with a viselike grip to its precarious perch as the frozen branch crackled and swayed in the blizzard. The contrasting, dreamlike picture of this small, fragile black creature against the vast, daunting white landscape thrust me back into the philosophical world of contrasts between darkness and light, good and evil.

There is another way to frame history, I thought. *The Bible says that the entire human race is engaged in a spiritual battle between darkness and light, good and evil, and that the stakes are life or death. We can certainly view history in this context. This clash of kingdoms has existed since the beginning of time and will no doubt continue until time ceases. I'll call this framework of history the "kingdom paradigm."*

History can be interpreted within the context of a continual war between three kingdoms: the kingdom of God, the kingdom of Satan, and the kingdom of self.[3] These three forces are engaged in an intense and bitter battle for the eternal destiny of the souls of mankind. In this struggle, *self* is overcome only through full surrender to *God*.

Engagement with the forces of Satan's kingdom is experienced in both the natural and spiritual dimensions. Our weapons are spiritual in nature, and the combatants are angelic, demonic, and human. (See 2 Corinthians 10:4–5; Ephesians 6:10–18.) Rank and sphere of human, angelic, and demonic authority are conferred by God or Satan and extend to nations and continents. (See Daniel 10:10–21.) Being sure of our identity, authority, and security in Christ is paramount if we are to win this battle. *"We are more than conquerors through Him who loved us"* (Romans 8:37).

We can also identify three *time* dimensions to the kingdom of God: past, present, and future. The kingdom *was*, the kingdom *is*, and the kingdom *will come*. The kingdom *was* until the Old Testament prophets and their prophecies were fulfilled. John the Baptist was the last to function in the capacity of an Old Testament prophet. He *"came preaching in the wilderness of Judea, and saying, 'Repent, for the kingdom of heaven is at hand!'"* (Matthew 3:1–2). As he preached, John said, *"There comes One after me who is mightier than I, whose sandal strap I am not worthy to stoop down and loose. I indeed baptized you with water, but He will baptize you with the Holy Spirit"* (Mark 1:7–8). John identified and introduced the

King of Kings. He humbly acknowledged, *"He must increase, but I must decrease"* (John 3:30).

Jesus preached one specific message—the gospel of the kingdom. It is the declaration of the good news of God's government. *"Jesus went about all Galilee, teaching in their synagogues, preaching the gospel of the kingdom, and healing all kinds of sickness and all kinds of disease among the people"* (Matthew 4:23). He didn't say that the kingdom "was"; he declared, *"Repent, for the kingdom of heaven is at hand"* (Matthew 4:17). When Jesus had been falsely accused of heresy and sedition, Pilate asked him directly, *"Are You the king of the Jews?"* and Jesus replied, *"It is as you say"* (Matthew 27:11). Consequently and appropriately, Jesus was crucified with a sign nailed to His cross that read, *"This is Jesus the King of the Jews"* (Matthew 27:37).

But Jesus also said, *"In this manner, therefore, pray: Our Father in heaven, hallowed be Your name.* **Your kingdom come.** *Your will be done on earth as it is in heaven"* (Matthew 6:9).

Your kingdom *what?* Come? But I thought it was already here!

"Your will be done on earth as it is in heaven." How can this be?

It's simple! Our responsibility is to call down from out of the throne room of God His will and purpose so that they will be manifested on earth. We are called to initiate and cooperate with His divine mandate and His strategy for victory.

Our future is determined and dictated by our willingness to call into this world the ultimate intentions and strategies of God and to activate them against the forces of darkness and our own selfish will, which we constantly battle as long as we inhabit this body of flesh. (See Romans 7:13–25; 8.) Jesus' instructions confirm the Old Testament mandate. Ages ago, God's people were given this promise:

> *If My people who are called by My name will humble themselves, and pray and seek My face, and turn from their wicked ways, then I will hear from heaven, and will forgive their sin and heal their land.* (2 Chronicles 7:14)

When we pray, God acts!

From Genesis to Revelation, from the garden of Eden to the Isle of Patmos, *history is interpreted within the framework of war.* It is God's ongoing process of sifting and shaking with one ultimate goal—the purification of human beings, as well as all of creation, and their restoration to their original state. We are a holy nation, the willing subjects of King Jesus. We delight to do His will and obey His commands. We are God's army.

To whom will we give our allegiance, our worship, and our hearts?

See that you do not refuse Him who speaks. For if they did not escape who refused Him who spoke on earth, much more shall we not escape if we turn away from Him who speaks from heaven, whose voice then shook the earth; but now He has promised, saying, "Yet once more I shake not only the earth, but also heaven." Now this, "Yet once more," indicates the removal of those things that are being shaken, as of things that are made, that the things which cannot be shaken may remain. Therefore, since we are receiving a kingdom which cannot be shaken, let us have grace, by which we may serve God acceptably with reverence and godly fear. For our God is a consuming fire.
(Hebrews 12:25–29)

God has already revealed what the future holds. *"The kingdoms of this world have become the kingdoms of our Lord and of His Christ, and He shall reign forever and ever!"* (Revelation 11:15). There is only one government that cannot be shaken—the kingdom of God—and one Person who never changes—Jesus Christ the King. "The kingdom of God is God's total answer to man's total need."[4]

Jesus said, *"The kingdom of God is within you"* (Luke 17:21). The laws of God's government are inscribed upon our hearts and imbedded in our souls. The kingdom of God is our homeland!

Back to the Future

I leaned into the howling wind, squinting to see just a few feet ahead of me. The snow clinging to my hooded parka and briefcase had transformed me into an abominable snowman. Ice encrusted my eyelashes, and with each breath I took, I created a cloud of condensation.

My hands are frozen, I groaned silently. *These calfskin driving gloves don't provide much warmth.* Thoughts of the roaring fire back in the Cathedral of Learning provided little comfort. *I'll be at the car soon,* I encouraged myself, and I retreated deeper into my contemplative world to find refuge from the world around me, nearly obliterated by the falling snow.

"God's total answer to man's total need," I reiterated. "We have surely made a mess of things. Somehow, we need to get back to the homeland where we started from." And then, it struck me. "Wait a minute! Isn't that what God has been doing all along? He's restoring us back to our original condition! We are going back to the future!"

We have fallen a long way from our original innocence and purity in the garden of Eden. Our hearts are desperately wicked. We have desecrated and destroyed life, and our stewardship of ourselves and our environment is atrocious. But God is up to something! His *redemptive strategy* is being fulfilled. The Christ event is working! The kingdom of God is *coming*! God is *restoring* everything, even creation itself! Paul described the eager anticipation of creation for this very event.

> *For I consider that the sufferings of this present time are not worthy to be compared with the glory which shall be revealed in us. For the earnest expectation of the creation eagerly waits for the revealing of the sons of God.*
>
> (Romans 8:18–19)

A careful look at history indicates this ongoing process of restoration. I'll call it the *restoration paradigm*. The Bible clearly shows that Father God is restoring mankind to Himself. A primary example is God's chosen people, Israel. Jacob's offspring were forced into slavery in Egypt. God sent Moses to deliver them from bondage and lead them to the Promised Land. Succeeding generations have been scattered abroad throughout the earth in the Diaspora. Surviving persecution and diabolical attempts to torture and annihilate them, they have not only endured but prospered. A remnant has returned to their restored homeland, the nation of Israel. When the time of the Gentiles is fulfilled (see Romans 11:25–26), God will remove the blinders from Israel's eyes and restore them back to Himself through Jeshua, the Messiah. Every Gentile believer is grafted into Israel and is the benefactor of God's redemption and restoration. (See Romans 11.)

Another example of the restoration paradigm is God's restoration of the church. If we trace church history from the day of its inception at Pentecost to the present time, we discover that the church has undergone a figurative life, death, and resurrection process. From Pentecost to persecution to political and social correctness, the church transitioned in a few centuries from a people who turned the world upside down by Holy Spirit power and zeal to an institution of lukewarm faith and overall ineffectiveness. In the fourth century, politics and religion choked the church of its spiritual life and influence. The ensuing Dark Ages were characterized by corruption, greed, and a dearth of spirituality. The Reformation sparked a spiritual awakening that restored the priesthood back to the people. The evangelical movement spread the gospel around the world through missions and evangelism. The Pentecostal and charismatic movements reintroduced the church to the power of the Holy Spirit and the gifts of the Spirit.

This process of restoration continues today. The emergence of apostles, prophets, evangelists, pastors, and teachers is a clear sign that we are returning to our foundations. Make no mistake, the church is alive and well on planet earth, and its greatest days are ahead. The grave clothes of religion are coming off! Man-made theories and philosophies are crashing to the ground. The bride of Christ is rising without spot or wrinkle to greet the coming Bridegroom.

Jesus used a basic principle of agriculture to teach this spiritual truth. *"Most assuredly, I say unto you, unless a grain of wheat falls into the ground and dies, it remains alone; but if it dies, it produces much grain"* (John 12:24). Just as Jesus died and rose again from the dead, so His spiritual body, the church, has undergone "death," in a sense, and is being raised back to life from centuries of tepid indifference and ineffectiveness. The body of Christ is returning to her roots and is springing up into new life out of the soil of rediscovered intimacy with God. All of creation has been waiting for this manifestation of the sons of God.

The dry bones in the valley of dead religion are being resuscitated by the breath of the Holy Spirit. The army of God is shaking off its grave clothes. The final chapter of history is about to unfold. Millions of Holy Spirit-empowered men, women, and children are about to change the course of the future and prepare the way for the return of the King![5]

The Pendulum Swings

There it is, at last! I thought with cautious relief. *It looks more like an igloo than a car. I've got some work to do before there will be any relief from this storm. I sure hope that the door isn't completely frozen shut.*

I fumbled for my key beneath my heavy parka and quickly inserted it into the lock. After several attempts, the door finally broke free from the coating of ice. I tossed my briefcase across to the passenger's seat and slid onto the frigid leather upholstery. It felt like frozen sheet metal and crackled like crumpling plastic cellophane.

"Ah, yes!" I sighed when the engine sprang to life with the first turn of the key in the ignition. I cranked the heater on full blast, and cold air cascaded into the car as if straight from the North Pole. "I'm out of here!" I shouted, grabbing the ice scraper and sliding back out into the arctic winter.

More than eight inches of snow had accumulated on the car, and there appeared to be no sign that the storm was abating. *This Pittsburgh weather can quickly change from one extreme to the other*, I affirmed as I brushed the snow in one great sweeping motion from the driver's side of the roof. It exploded into the wind, raising a cloud of white crystals that immediately blew back into my face like flour from a broken sack. "Well, dummy," I groaned, "next time, stand upwind."

It took me ten minutes to clear the snow off of the car. I wrested the wipers free from their frozen attachment to the windshield and banged them against the glass to remove the remaining ice from the blades. "Finished at last!" I cheered, and yanked the door open. The warm air inside made my face tingle, and water dripped down my cheeks from the thawing ice on my eyelashes.

Better turn the wipers on before they freeze to the glass again, I thought, reaching for the switch. They sprang into action, squeaking back and forth across the windshield. I sat, mesmerized by the oscillating wipers, watching the snow fall on the city like an Eskimo peering out of his shelter.

"W-w-well, Lord," I stammered, still trembling from the frigid weather, "I sure hope all this reflection about the theology of time will help me to see things from Your perspective." The words instantly transported me back into my contemplative world for one last visit. In an instant, a thought occurred to me. *History can be likened to these windshield wipers! It moves from one extreme to the other.*

Society moves back and forth like a pendulum in a clock. We can clearly detect these alternating extremes. Let's call it the *pendulum paradigm*. Applying this frame of reference, we interpret a trend as the consequence of various forces of opinion, behaviors, or influences in a society that push beyond cultural norms and accepted limits. A *countermovement* reacts to offset this excess, thereby pushing society in the opposite direction. The limitations of movement in each direction are determined by what the society will tolerate.

The tension created by this process of societal hypotheses and antitheses forces the culture to attempt to redefine itself and arrive at a new theory of acceptable behavior. Often, a society will seek a balance between opposing factors. Without a compromise, the society remains in tension. If the stress of these forces of action and reaction remains unresolved, open conflict will result. The final outcomes of unresolved conflict within a society are mental disorders, disease, sickness, anomie, total rebellion, civil war, and, ultimately, death. A degree of stress is a necessity of life, but if it becomes extreme and remains unresolved, it can be deadly.

All of creation is held in the balance of creative tension. The planets traverse the solar system within a field of gravitational forces that keep them from colliding. The human body also requires tension and relaxation in order to function. The give-and-take of muscles relaxing and contracting is actually what enables us to move. A sailboat cannot move smoothly through the water unless it is powered by the tension of the wind in its sails. Without that stress, the sails are useless.

The principle of creative tension can be applied to every aspect of life. Stress within nations, economies, governments, organizations, families, individuals, and even weather patterns can be beneficial or destructive. When the pressure differential grows to an extreme, a storm is created, and it lasts until the pressure is resolved. In the case of weather, a low-pressure system creates a vacuum, and everything around it rushes toward it to fill the void and restore balance to the atmosphere. If it is serious enough, the perfect storm is created.

The same is true for a person, organization, or society. Extremes are catalysts for conflict. I've been through enough "church wars" to know that this is true. Seeking a balance is a good thing, as long as we do not compromise our core beliefs. Efforts to relieve pressure should never cost us the denial of our faith.

Imbalance is what causes blizzards, I concluded. *I could sit here in this car and wait long enough for the weather to balance itself, and this blizzard will stop. But that may take a while.*

"I will not succumb to the dictates of a blizzard in Pittsburgh," I declared. "If anyone is going to push the limits, I am!"

I released the parking brake, switched the headlights on, and adjusted the heater to keep the windshield defrosted. The car creaked and groaned, as if suffering from arthritis, as it broke free from the icy grip of the parking space. I headed down Fifth Avenue, past the barely visible Cathedral of Learning. Traffic was almost nonexistent in Oakland. A few brave adventurers dared to traverse the snow-covered streets. A student appeared on the sidewalk, crowned with a black and gold Steelers dude hat. The weight of his textbook-laden backpack helped to anchor him in the wind. I turned left onto the Boulevard of the Allies and coasted slowly past Isaly's Dairy Store, where my dad used to take me as a kid to order towering, skyscraper-shaped ice-cream cones and Isaly's famous chipped-chopped ham sandwiches. I cautiously eased downhill onto the Parkway East access ramp.

Not so bad, I thought. *I'll be home soon.* I increased my speed, pulled onto the expressway, and merged with the rush-hour traffic. Three minutes later, I came to a near standstill in the notorious bumper-to-bumper traffic creeping toward the Squirrel Hill Tunnel. *Guess it'll be a while,* I thought, realizing I might not be home for hours. *At least I'm not still sitting back on campus in my parked car waiting for this blizzard to end.*

18

THE TRACK OF TIME

I t's really good to be home," I shouted, stomping the snow from my shoes by the front door. A column of vapor rose from the boiling pot of chili on the kitchen stove like steam from a bubbling volcano. "Just what I need, babe!" I declared, savoring the wonderful aroma of my favorite winter concoction of spicy, reddish-brown sauce, the best ground sirloin, fresh vegetables, a select variety of beans, and some other secret ingredients on the recipe card, which is locked in the family safe for future generations of Fifes.

I unzipped my parka and threw it over the heavily laden hall clothes tree, which I had inherited from my parents. The faithful wooden sentry was slightly bowed from decades of duty, having stood guard in the hallway of my childhood home for as far back as I can remember. It now served as a beloved reminder of what my mom had always shouted from the kitchen when I got home: "Be sure to hang up your coat, son!"

The warmth of our family table, and that of our bowls filled to the brim with steaming hot chili, was especially welcome as the storm continued to rage out-side. "How was your first day of class, hon?" my wife asked.

"Very interesting," I replied. "My head is still spinning. I'm intrigued by the many theoretical frameworks of history that the professor described, but even more so by my own reflections when I walked back to the car in the snowstorm after class.

"The professor never mentioned the Christian viewpoint, but then, why would he? There's a dramatic difference between the secular and the religious paradigms. I know that I should really seek God's final opinion regarding this whole issue of time and history. No textbook or professor can match God's thoughts on the matter. I'm eager to get into His presence."

"Why don't you go upstairs after dinner?" she asked with an encouraging smile. "I'll clean up."

She loves it when I spend time alone with God, I reflected after dinner as I ascended the stairway to my private getaway on the second floor. *She sees firsthand what a positive transformation it makes in my life. And it's true,* I affirmed. *The quality of my spiritual life is directly proportional to the length of time that I spend in God's presence in the secret place.*

I closed the door and locked it, then felt my way along the wall in the darkness toward the lamp next to my chair. With a single pull of the chain, light burst into the room and cascaded out through the window to challenge the black midwinter night beyond it. Snowflakes fell lazily outside. The major part of the storm had passed. I settled comfortably into my blue leather La-Z-Boy and reached for my journal and pen on the end table. *Quite a change from a few hours ago,* I sighed as I surrendered to the renewing peacefulness of my secret place. I sat there for some time, embracing the silence and quieting my thoughts.

A Vision of Time

"I love Your presence, Lord. Just being here with You is life giving. What do You want to say to me tonight, Jesus?" I asked.

His response was immediate. A picture spontaneously flashed upon the screen of my mind. The exhilarating vision unfolded like a scene in an action movie. I was standing on the very front of a moving diesel locomotive. I couldn't see the engine behind me, but I could feel its enormous, surging, resonating power vibrating though my body. My entire being was energized. There was no way to diminish the awesome strength of this engine or escape its forward momentum. I intuitively sensed that it represented the power of the Holy Spirit pushing me along the track.

"This is some ride!" I shouted above the roar of the engine. I felt like a hood ornament on a speeding limousine. Wind whipped past my face. My hair flew in every direction. Moisture from my eyes flowed down my cheeks in a steady stream as the locomotive sped forward, rocking back and forth from side to side. The forward speed was so great that I was plastered against the cold steel nose of the engine. There was nothing between me and the tracks a few feet below; no safety rail to hold on to and no escape from becoming a human projectile if the train should stop suddenly. A quick glance down at the railroad ties speeding by beneath me instantly made me dizzy.

The surrounding terrain I was traveling past was completely flat. There were no trees or vegetation visible in any direction, only brown soil. The unidentifiable landscape reminded me of the American plains in a drought: featureless, level, and limitless, with no discernable horizon except for the border between land and sky, miles away. Every once in a while, a black-and-white striped railroad signal arm appeared along the side of the tracks and whizzed by in a flash, with no comprehensible meaning to me.

Dream Works' computerized, digital magic couldn't duplicate this ride, I thought. *This is no imaginary fantasy scene from* The Polar Express. *It's something far more powerful and purposeful.* "Lord, why are You showing me this?" I asked in wonder. "What does this mean? What could You possibly be saying, Jesus?"

"I want to talk to you about time," He responded—not audibly, but Spirit to spirit.

"Time?" I replied. "What can this vision possibly have to do with time?"

I've Been Living on the Railroad

"Let Me explain," He continued. "I want you to focus your attention on the left rail of the track. I laid this rail Myself. I know where it begins and where it ends. This part of the track represents *chronological* time.

"What you are seeing right now in this vision," He said, pointing at a specific place on the rail, "is this actual moment in time that we are spending together."

He explained further, "Every person whom I have created travels upon this track of time. Each individual is assigned a specific distance to traverse. This distance is his or her lifespan, from birth to death. Some will live longer and travel further than others, but there is only one track for all people. You are living your life on this rail of time, along with everyone else who is a part of your generation. History is the story that people tell who have experienced this journey of life.

"Behind you, in the past, there is a location on the rail of time that marks the moment when you were born. Up ahead is the station where your life on earth will end. This is your life, son. Most of it is behind you now, but there is still a distance left to travel. You have been given the gift of life. Live it wisely."

Every human being travels along this track of time, I pondered. *God laid this rail!* A sea of faces raced through my mind. Earth's entire population, from creation to this moment in chronological time—they all had made their journey along this track. Some finished their course millennia ago; others were just beginning their journey.

Regardless of our age, we are bound by the rules of the track, I realized. *Time waits for no one! Motion is constant and relentless, and we are given only so much track to travel. The rail is the chronology of our lifetime journey, and history is the travel journal of life's passengers. For those who keep "track" of time, it is the documentation of mankind from beginning to end.*

Don't Look Back

The tone of the Lord's voice changed dramatically as He delivered a clear warning: "Son," He said, "as you move along the track of time, don't look back!

"You see, some people's lives are full of regret. 'I should've,' 'I could've,' 'If only I would've,' they say. What's behind you is over and done with. You can't go back and change things in the past. I do not want you to live in constant regret! Regrets will cause you to be frozen in time, and you will not be able to move on. Your life and your future will be wasted if you spend them brooding over the past.

"Resentment or unwillingness to forgive yourself and others will harden your heart. The resulting bitterness will poison your life. Don't allow your past failures and wounds to paralyze you. Surrender your past to Me. Let Me take your failures and disappointments. Forgive those who have hurt you and let you down. Lay each day's burdens at My feet, and don't take them back again. This way, you can possess your future without the regrets of the past crippling you. Don't you know how much I love you? There is still much for you to accomplish for Me in the years ahead. Don't let the past keep you from fulfilling your destiny."

He knows us so well, I marveled. *We should not tie ourselves to our history; we must tie ourselves to our potential. It is important to travel light on the track of time. We need to let go of our past and surrender it to Him forever.*

Paul set a great example for all of us to emulate. He wrote,

Not that I have already attained, or am already perfected; but I press on, that I may lay hold of that for which Christ Jesus has also laid hold of me. Brethren, I do not count myself to have apprehended; but one thing I do, forgetting those things which are behind and reaching forward to those things which are ahead, I press toward the goal for the prize of the upward call of God in Christ Jesus. (Philippians 3:12–14)

Stay on Track

The Lord spoke again: "Now I want you to turn your attention to the right rail."

Obediently, I looked down at the right rail and slowly raised my head to trace its linear course into the distance. I was terrified by what I saw. "Lord, please help! I'm in real trouble!" I shouted in fear and total shock. "This is *really* not good! I'm headed for destruction unless You do something quickly."

An inevitable disaster was waiting to happen. Several hundred feet down the track, the right rail gradually began to bend to the right, away from the left rail. Not only did the two rails cease to maintain their parallel equidistance; the separation increased with distance until the right rail went off in an almost perpendicular direction.

"Lord," I pleaded again, "this is not good." Impending tragedy assaulted my mind. "Lord, the track gauge is there for a reason. It must be maintained for the train to stay on the track and reach its destination. I don't understand why You would let this happen, Lord. Why does the right track veer away from the left? There must be an explanation. You laid these rails," I said, my tone accusatory.

"That's right, I did," He replied, understanding my dismay. "Listen carefully. The right rail represents My will. My will keeps you moving safely along the track of time. It's not My nature to impose My will upon you. It is your responsibility to accept and embrace My will and welcome it into your life.

"That is why I have instructed you to pray, '*Thy kingdom come. Thy will be done in earth, as it is in heaven.*' This is not some generic request to cover the entire world. It is a petition for personal direction. It must issue from a heart that is yielded to Me. This is the genuine desire of a submitted servant. When you embrace and activate My will in your life at any given moment, you are maintaining the gauge of the track and insuring your progress in life's journey.

"The rail of My will presses you against the rail of time and keeps you from becoming derailed. My perfect will enables you to live productively and successfully and progress along the track of time. If you reject My will, you'll eventually get derailed. That's why it's important every day for you to seek Me and ask Me for direction. You must desire to do My will."

"Jesus, I really do want Your kingdom to come into my circumstances. I want to live my life as Your servant. Show me Your will every day," I prayed, knowing that He knew my heart better than I did.

Supernatural Connections

"There's one more thing," Jesus said. "Notice the railroad ties passing beneath your feet. They serve a very important function. These ties represent *kairos* moments. They are occurrences that connect the rail of My will with the rail of time. When you experience one of these connections, it is a supernatural event.

"You will meet somebody that you never knew before. Recognize that I arranged it. That person is a gift from Me to enlarge your world and introduce you to a whole new dimension of experience, fruitfulness, and influence.

"I love you, son. I want to do things through you that you could never accomplish by yourself. At times, what I ask you to do for Me, you won't have the power to produce, the intelligence to figure out, or the ability to perform. But do not be anxious. I will grant you My unmerited favor. I will send people and resources into your life to help you get the job done. I will set *divine appointments* that connect you with My supernatural plans and provisions. I will also use you to bless others in the same way.

"When a *kairos* event occurs, it is a window of opportunity. Unless you are consciously looking for these supernatural occasions, they will slip by unnoticed. Once these moments pass by, they may be lost forever. Be alert! Realize that every person you meet or circumstance that arises could be a divine appointment that I arrange to catapult you beyond your limitations. Live your life with this in mind."

The Lord then emphasized the importance of all that He had taught me. "I want you to know that in the coming years, the frequency of these *kairos* moments is going to dramatically increase. I want you to be alert and sensitive to My Spirit's leading. Do not quench or ignore the still, small voice or the impressions that I make upon your spirit."

"I realize how important this is, Lord," I replied. "Jesus, help me to be sensitive to the leading of Your Holy Spirit. I never want to miss a *kairos* opportunity. Open my spiritual eyes to see Your hand at work in my life. Give me the courage to seize the opportunities You provide. And, Lord, please use me as a blessing in the lives of others."

The Revelation of History

I must record the vision, I thought, as His presence lifted and the picture of the track faded. *This revelation about history from the secret place is so important that the church must have it.*

I drew an illustration of the railroad tracks at the top of the blank page of my journal and entered the appropriate nomenclature: "Left Rail: Chronological Time; Right Rail: God's Will; Railroad Ties: *Kairos* Moments." Then, I described the vision, accurately recounting my experience and conversation with the Lord in detail. When I had finished filling several pages, I turned back to the drawing and printed a title at the top of the page: "The Track of Time Paradigm."

Be Alert!

I believe we're living in a time of great favor as God's people. The intersections of God's kingdom purposes with the affairs of mankind are occurring with increasing rapidity. We are fast approaching the end of the track of time. We must be obedient to the King!

Be alert! When God brings a divine opportunity, seize it. Enter into it. Possess it. Own it. We are His agents. We are kingdom bringers—intercessors who are constantly praying His will into this time/space world.

There is so much more to history than a printed page from the journal of life. History is made when God intersects time with His will and His power. As Daniel Webster put it, "History is God's providence in human affairs." We are all a part of that amazing interaction—the Spirit of God interacting with the spirit of man. We are either on God's side or against Him. That decision will determine how well we travel along this track of time called life until our own journey ends.

19

WHAT TIME IS IT?

Our search to understand light and its intrinsic relationship with time led us to examine the nature of history. We have exposed the various philosophical lenses through which people have viewed and interpreted time and its historical significance. We have also discovered that historians use frameworks to explain observable patterns of the past in the hope that identifying these paradigms will give us a clue concerning the future. We have identified some contemporary trends and theories postulated by futurists seeking to foretell what is coming and how the future will look. Their predictions are widely sought after by leaders in such areas as business, industry, economics, politics, and religion.

While all of this information is helpful, it is inadequate. The most significant opinion is not what mankind observes or how we frame time and interpret history. We must seek the Light Giver and Timekeeper of the cosmos for understanding and insight. We must consult the Creator. He speaks by the Holy Spirit, through visions, dreams, and prophecy, to those who will seek Him. The vision of the track of time is an example. God created time, and He alone knows when it will end. God is active in history and in the affairs of mankind. In light of this fact, there is one more topic we must examine. We need to look at what God says in His written Word—the Bible—regarding specific kinds of times and seasons.

The question is, "What time is it?" Let's begin by considering how one person answered that question. The scene is set in a small country church, with a typical white steeple, somewhere in rural America.

Rip Van Winkle in Church

The late August heat had raised the temperature of the little clapboard church to an unbearable level. There were no shade trees to cool the small, white building, and phantom waves of shimmering air rose from the black, shingled roof in the relentless noonday sun. Inside, the scent of warped, dried oak mingled with human perspiration to create a rancid stew of discomfort. The plain wooden pews, like an oven rack under a broiler, were no refuge from the scorching heat. In desperation, the sleepy congregation waved their bulletins back and forth in a feeble attempt to get some relief, trying not to disturb the preacher as he drew near to the crescendo climax of his sermon.

Sitting on the next-to-the-last pew, one of the hardworking, devout farmers in the community had surrendered after a valiant struggle to stay awake and had finally succumbed to the heat. He was sound asleep.

The pastor began to drive home the main point of his message. In ever increasing volume, he proclaimed, "Heaven's clock is winding down. The time of Christ's appearing is near. This could be the final hour!" Wiping the sweat from his brow with an already soaked white towel, he shouted at the top of his voice, with all of the strength he could muster, "What time is it?"

The farmer awoke from his sleep at that instant, startled back into the real world. Immediately he looked at his watch and then shouted back at the preacher, "It's five minutes to twelve, Reverend!"

The farmer's response is typical of most of us. If you want to know the time, simply look at your watch. It's a perfunctory act that we perform hundreds of times every week. But the answer the preacher wanted was not a specific hour and minute. The time he was referring to cannot be determined by a wristwatch or a calendar. Discerning this kind of time requires spiritual insight. The faithful preacher was seeking to warn his flock that they were at the end of the age. If anyone there was to have an understanding of the times and seasons, the farmer would have been a good bet, but, alas, he had fallen asleep. Not only had he missed the message, but when he woke up, he responded impulsively.

Jesus spoke about this in the parable of the ten virgins.

Then the kingdom of heaven shall be likened to ten virgins who took their lamps and went out to meet the bridegroom. Now five of them were wise, and five were foolish. Those who were foolish took their lamps and took no oil with them, but the wise took oil in their vessels with their lamps. But while the bridegroom was delayed, they all slumbered and slept. And at midnight a cry was heard: "Behold, the bridegroom is coming; go out to meet him!" Then all those virgins arose and trimmed their lamps. And the foolish said to the wise, "Give us some of your oil, for our lamps are going out." But the wise answered, saying, "No, lest there should not be enough for us and you; but go rather to those who sell, and buy for yourselves." And while they went to buy, the bridegroom came, and those who were ready went in with him to the wedding; and the door was shut. Afterward the other virgins came also, saying, "Lord, Lord, open to us!" But he answered and said, "Assuredly, I say to you, I do not know you." Watch therefore, for you know neither the day nor the hour in which the Son of Man is coming.   (Matthew 25:1–13)

Timing Is Everything!

The warning is clear. We may not know the specific day or the exact hour, but it is crucial that we know the season we are living in. Not knowing can be disastrous. Timing is everything!

This truth brought Jesus to tears because the entire city of Jerusalem didn't have a clue what time it was.

Now as He drew near, He saw the city and wept over it, saying, "If you had known, even you, especially in this your day, the things that make for your peace! But now they are hidden from your eyes. For days will come upon you when your enemies will build an embankment around you, surround you and close you in on every side, and level you, and your children within you, to the ground; and they will not leave in you one stone upon another, because you did not know the time of your visitation."   (Luke 19:41–44)

It was Jerusalem's *"time of...visitation."* This was a specific period in history determined by God, which clearly revealed and defined what He was up to. The Bible identifies and refers to a number of distinct spiritual seasons that define a specific window of time in which God issues a warning of judgment or provides an opportunity. God operates within these distinct periods to accomplish His will and purpose. In fact, God often waits for a particular season to arrive, and then He springs into action to accomplish and fulfill His plan. It is important that we identify these spiritual seasons.

The Fullness of Time

The Bible tells us that creation was a process. On the sixth day, "*God saw everything that He had made, and indeed it was very good. So the evening and the morning were the sixth day. Thus the heavens and the earth, and all of the host of them, were finished*" (Genesis 1:31–2:1).

On the seventh day,

God ended His work which He had done, and He rested on the seventh day from all His work which He had done. Then God blessed the seventh day and sanctified it, because in it He rested from all His work which God had created and made.   (Genesis 2:2–3)

The process of creation was finished.

The number seven symbolizes completeness, fullness, and perfection. This number is used more than any other number in the Bible except for the number one.[1] There were seven days in creation. The priests were consecrated for seven days. Israel marched around Jericho seven times on the seventh day. There are seven feasts and seven branches on the lampstand. Even the Holy Spirit is described as the sevenfold Spirit of God.

Many things in our environment reveal the number seven. Snowflakes and frost on a window reflect patterns of seven. The human body renews itself every seven years. Our very bone structure reflects completeness with seven bones in the face, neck, and ankle and seven holes in the head. Our music is based on the mathematics of the number seven. All of the symphonies and all of the melodies ever composed are built on a scale of seven notes. Composers use a variation of these same seven notes, with sharp and flat pitches and at different octaves. God, the Creator of music, designed it with perfect fullness.

The Bible refers to the "fullness of time" as a period when things are complete or fully ready. All preparation ceases. There is nothing more to do. It is time to rest and enter into the purpose for which the season was designed. The Son of God provides us with a perfect example. Jesus was born in the "fullness of time."

> *And it came to pass in those days that a decree went out from Caesar Augustus that all the world should be registered....So all went to be registered, everyone to his own city. Joseph also went up from Galilee, out of the city of Nazareth, into Judea, to the city of David, which is called Bethlehem, because he was of the house and lineage of David, to be registered with Mary, his betrothed wife, who was with child. So it was, that while they were there, the **days were completed** for her to be delivered.* (Luke 2:1, 3–6, emphasis added)

Everything was ready! God had prepared the stage for Jesus' appearing. The Roman Empire was in place, with its common language and modern roadways. Mary was chosen to bear the Son of God. The Holy Spirit moved into action. The days were completed—it was the "fullness of time"—and *"she brought forth her firstborn Son, and wrapped Him in swaddling cloths, and laid Him in a manger"* (Luke 2:7). The angels delivered the message, and the shepherds responded. Wise men knew the season. They came from the East because it was "time"! Even the stars were signaling it. It was the fullness of time for Jesus to come to Earth.

No other time would do. It took millennia for God to prepare things for the perfect entrance of His Son into human affairs. This was the moment that all of creation had been waiting for. It was perfect.

> *But when the **fullness of the time** had come, God sent forth His Son, born of a woman, born under the law, to redeem those who were under the law, that we might receive the adoption as sons. And because you are sons, God has sent forth the Spirit of His Son into your hearts, crying out, "Abba, Father!" Therefore you are no longer a slave but a son, and if a son, then an heir of God through Christ.* (Galatians 4:4–7, emphasis added)

The Gentiles and Israel

Paul explained that you and I are living in a season of preparation as God moves upon the hearts of Gentiles with the power of the gospel. Even though Israel rejected Jesus as the Messiah, their rejection is not final. He wrote,

For I do not desire, brethren, that you should be ignorant of this mystery, lest you should be wise in your own opinion, that blindness in part has happened to Israel until the fullness of the Gentiles has come in. And so all Israel will be saved, as it is written: "The Deliverer will come out of Zion, and He will turn away ungodliness from Jacob; for this is My covenant with them, when I take away their sins."   (Romans 11:25–27)

We are living in the season right now in which God is reaching out to the Gentile nations with the good news of His kingdom and the saving power of Jesus Christ the Lord. This season will come to an end. When it is finished, completed, and perfect, the blinders will be removed from the eyes of the Jews. What a glorious day it will be when all of Israel will see that Jesus is the Messiah.

A Work in Progress

God is not impatient. He will not be forced to act prematurely. He is never late. He is always on time! He is actively involved in the process of completion. What is true for Jesus, the Gentiles, and Israel is also true in your circumstances. Whatever is going on in your life, rest assured that God is involved. You may want the answer or the solution quickly. You may grumble and complain about the circumstances. But, remember—what God does is perfect, and He is in the process of perfecting you and me. In the fullness of time, this season will come to an end. God is up to something in our lives. He is transforming us into His image.

Due Season

The Bible identifies another specific time frame: "due season." We often think of due season as a particular date, such as April 15, when our income taxes are due, or the day in the month when the mortgage or rent is owed. Due season is a clear indication that something owed must be paid or something planted must be harvested because it has come to maturity or ripened. It is a call to action. Due season demands a response. Something that is hoped for or worked toward must be forthcoming.

It was due season when Jesus died on the cross. Paul wrote,

Now hope does not disappoint, because the love of God has been poured out in our hearts by the Holy Spirit who was given to us. For when we were still

*without strength, in **due time** Christ died for the ungodly.*
(Romans 5:5–6, emphasis added)

The debt of mankind's sin was fully paid on that very day. The bill came due, and Jesus paid it on our behalf!

There is a due season for all of the seeds you plant.

*Do not be deceived, God is not mocked; for whatever a man sows, that he will also reap. For he who sows to his flesh will of the flesh reap corruption, but he who sows to the Spirit will of the Spirit reap everlasting life. And let us not grow weary while doing good, for in **due season** we shall reap if we do not lose heart. Therefore, as we have opportunity, let us do good to all, especially to those who are of the household of faith.*   (Galatians 6:7–10, emphasis added)

One thing we can be sure of: due season inevitably comes. It may be tomorrow or many days from now, but when it comes, all that we have worked for, hoped for, and prayed for will be forthcoming. Solomon, one of the wisest men in history, wrote, "*Cast your bread upon the waters, for you will find it after many days*" (Ecclesiastes 11:1).

The apostle Peter understood this principle. He encouraged the ambitious younger generation of his day with this advice:

Likewise you younger people, submit yourselves to your elders. Yes, all of you be submissive to one another, and be clothed with humility, for "God resists the proud, but gives grace to the humble." Therefore humble yourselves under the mighty hand of God, that He may exalt you in due time, casting all your care upon Him, for He cares for you.   (1 Peter 5:5–7)

There comes a time when we should expect a return for the prayers and seeds we have sown. Don't miss your due season! God has promised a harvest for you. It is a biblical principle. But beware—the harvest will have the same nature as the seeds you have sown.

Coming to Pass

There are distinct events or moments that herald the *changing* of the spiritual seasons and become clearly identifiable delineations. The Bible refers to these spaces as periods when things "come to pass."

One such event occurred in Joshua's life.

After the death of Moses the servant of the LORD, *it* **came to pass** *that the* LORD *spoke to Joshua the son of Nun, Moses' assistant, saying: "Moses My servant is dead. Now therefore, arise, go over this Jordan, you and all this people, to the land which I am giving to them; the children of Israel."*

(Joshua 1:1–2, emphasis added)

Luke, the historian, also described the events immediately preceding Jesus' birth as a "coming to pass" experience: *"And it* **came to pass** *in those days that a decree went out from Caesar Augustus…"* (Luke 2:1, emphasis added).

Jesus warns us to pay close attention and watch for these "coming to pass" moments.

Then He spoke to them a parable: "Look at the fig tree, and all the trees. When they are already budding, you see and know for yourselves that summer is now near. So you also, when you see these things happening [coming to pass], *know that the kingdom of God is near."*   (Luke 21:29–31)

God declares,

I am the LORD, *that is My name; and My glory I will not give to another, nor My praise to carved images. Behold, the former things have* **come to pass**, *and new things I declare; before they spring forth I tell you of them."*

(Isaiah 42:8–9, emphasis added)

The lyrics from one of King David's songs capture the joy of knowing that things will come to pass.

Sing praise to the LORD, *you saints of His, and give thanks at the remembrance of His holy name. For His anger is but for a moment, His favor is for life; weeping may endure for a night, but joy comes in the morning.*

(Psalm 30:4–5)

Things happen, good and bad. In the course of events, seasons come and go. There are times when we can persevere, despite difficulties, because we know that our experience is temporary, even though it has eternal significance. When it is behind us, however, we rejoice and declare, "It came to pass!"

Perilous Times

We are living in the last days. All of the prophetic indicators clearly reveal this fact. The Bible refers to this period as *"perilous times"*:

But know this, that in the last days perilous times will come: for men will be lovers of themselves, lovers of money, boasters, proud, blasphemers, disobedient to parents, unthankful, unholy, unloving, unforgiving, slanderers, without self-control, brutal, despisers of good, traitors, headstrong, haughty, lovers of pleasure rather than lovers of God, having a form of godliness but denying its power. And from such people turn away! (2 Timothy 3:1–5)

Narcissistic, greedy, prideful, undisciplined, evil, violent—all of these adjectives are a perfect generalization of our society and our world. These are perilous times, indeed, and we are warned to navigate through them with extreme caution. We are instructed to be in the world but not of it. (See John 17:15–18.) However, turning away from these things is not enough. We must turn to God, the author and finisher of our faith. (See Hebrews 12:2.) We must be led by the Holy Spirit and walk in the power of the Spirit, not by the dictates of dead religion or societal pressure.

We cannot avoid perilous times. What we can do is redeem them, as Paul instructed us: *"See then that you walk circumspectly, not as fools but as wise, redeeming the time, because the days are evil. Therefore do not be unwise, but understand what the will of the Lord is"* (Ephesians 5:15–17).

Opportune Time

The opportunity of a lifetime must be seized in the lifetime of the opportunity. Jesus understood this truth, and when the opportunity to heal a blind man presented itself, He acted swiftly. He explained His behavior by saying, *"I must work the works of Him who sent Me while it is day; the night is coming when no one can work. As long as I am in the world, I am the light of the world"* (John 9:4). There is "nowness" to opportunity! Paul encouraged us, saying, *"Behold, now is the accepted time; behold, now is the day of salvation"* (2 Corinthians 6:2).

Chaos is the womb of opportunity and creativity. The chaotic, evil nature of current events is an incredible opportunity for us to be light and salt in the earth as we bear witness to the love and mercy of Jesus Christ. Perilous times provide an environment that ripens the harvest. When the harvest comes, there is a window of opportunity in which it must be gathered. Urgency is the appropriate disposition. *"The harvest truly is plentiful, but the laborers are few. Therefore pray the Lord of the harvest to send out laborers into His harvest"* (Matthew 9:37–38).

Opportunity usually doesn't advertise itself. It shows up suddenly and may remain for only a brief moment or season. It must be seized. But fear often paralyzes us, rendering us unable to act. Courage is the answer. Fear is emotional, but courage is rational and based on God's faithfulness and the truth of His Word. For example, every member of Saul's army, including Saul himself, was afraid to face the giant Goliath. (See 1 Samuel 17.) The entire army had an opportunity but lacked the courage. David seized the occasion, and it launched him into his destiny. In a single moment, his candidacy for kingship was affirmed, and he became a wealthy man.

Don't allow opportunity to pass you by. Take courage! God is on your side.

Not Yet

Some of the most difficult times in life are those "in-between times," when we are not yet where we want to be. We know there is a feast and that we are invited, but we haven't been given permission to go yet. What's even worse, others are entering into the party, and all we can do is watch. Jesus knew just how we feel when He said, *"My time has not yet come, but your time is always ready. The world cannot hate you, but it hates Me because I testify of it that its works are evil. You go up to this feast. I am not yet going up to this feast, for my time has not yet fully come"* (John 7:6–8). Jesus had to wait until His time had fully come. That time was in the Father's hands.

When God says, "Not yet," we feel like a runner poised for the race, waiting for the starting gun to go off. Everything within us is ready to explode into forward motion. Our muscles are tensed, our heart rate increases, and our adrenaline is pumping. But if we start prematurely, we will be disqualified. We must wait! That is the difficult part.

A friend of mine explains it this way: "When God closes a door, He always opens another one, but it's hell in the hallway." Have you ever been in the hallway? It's dark and confusing. Uncertainty and insecurity creep upon us like a cloak of despair. "God, have You forgotten about me?" we cry out. "Will You ever come to my aid?" we ask with a moan of abandonment. "This is hopeless. I will never see success and victory. I guess my life is over."

Stop it! Have patience, child of God. It is His good pleasure to give you the kingdom. (See Luke 12:32.) When God says, "Not yet," He isn't neglecting you; He is shaping you. Trust His silence as an affirmation of His love. He is at work at the other end of the hallway, and the door is about to open and flood your world with the fresh light of understanding and new opportunities. The season of "not yet" is the hallway to new things, the "in-between" time of life, when we transition from the old things that are passing away into the new things God has planned for us.

An Appointed Time

If you check your calendar, whether it's paper or electronic, you will no doubt find some entries of upcoming appointments. They are important to you; that's why you wrote them down or typed them in. You don't want to forget. Birthdays, anniversaries, meetings, travel plans, vacations—they're all there. But there is one appointment that you forgot to record. Sorry! You can't write this one down, but I guarantee you it is coming. God has already set the date. *"It is appointed for men to die once, but after this the judgment"* (Hebrews 9:27).

"Hold it," you say. "Let's not go there. Do we have to talk about death and judgment?"

We try to avoid these issues. We don't talk about them at the dinner table or at any other time. We face them only when we are forced to do so by our circumstances. Then reality hits us, and this truth becomes inescapable: *"To everything there is a season, a time for every purpose under heaven: a time to be born, and a time to die"* (Ecclesiastes 3:1–2).

Seasons of birth and seasons of death are parts of the cycle of life. Disney captured the essence of this truth in the animated classic *The Lion King*. Somewhere along the process, between the bookends of life and death, we hope to learn how to roar. And so life goes on. Every newborn baby is God's way of saying, "Life is good!"

The Hebrew view of life describes the seasons of a man's journey from birth to death in stages. We are born. We reach manhood at the age of thirteen (bar mitzvah).

Then, we think we can conquer the world—and we attempt to do so. Eventually, we are wounded on the battlefield of life and realize our vulnerability. The following stage—genuine maturity—comes out of being a wounded warrior, and although we have finally grown up, we walk with a limp. At long last, we reach the final stage of real wisdom, when our hair has turned silver (if we still have any) and becomes a "crown of glory." Others seek us for counsel and advice because we have traveled further down the road than they have. And then, all too soon, death comes.

Life assessment ultimately occurs in the presence of God. He calls it judgment: inescapable, ultimate, courtroom-like, before His throne, real judgment. We will give an account of how we stewarded the time He gave us on this earth, and we will be rewarded accordingly. If we have received Jesus Christ as our Lord and Savior, eternity in God's presence is assured. How we spend that eternity will be determined by our stewardship here on this earth. It might not be a bad idea for all of us to consider making a greater investment in the things of heaven now, rather than spending so much on earthly pursuits.

> *Do not lay up for yourselves treasures on earth, where moth and rust destroy and where thieves break in and steal; but lay up for yourselves treasures in heaven, where neither moth nor rust destroys and where thieves do not break in and steal. For where your treasure is, there your heart will be also.*
>
> (Matthew 6:19–21)

> *And behold, I am coming quickly, and My reward is with Me, to give to every one according to his work. I am the Alpha and the Omega, the Beginning and the End, the First and the Last.* (Revelation 22:12–13)

What Time Is It?

"It was the best of times; it was the worst of times." These oft-quoted words, from Charles Dickens's *Tale of Two Cities*, describe accurately the condition of his age. His effort to identify the season he lived in seems like an oxymoron, but it is accurate. It was a time of contradictions and conflicts. We must credit him for having the courage and insight to assess his times, to recognize the season, and to act circumspectly.

What best describes the season you are living in now? Is it the fullness of time? Is it due season? Are things coming to pass? It may be a perilous season, and your greatest opportunities are right in front of you. Or perhaps God has said, "Not yet!" Do you understand the times? Do you know the appropriate action to take? The sons of Issachar understood the times and knew what men should do. How about you?

One key to anticipating the future is accurately reading both past and present by seeing things from God's perspective. First, you must recognize the external events that will affect your life, and then you must interpret those events without the interference of emotions or ego.

Look backward to see your future. Cicero wrote, "It was ordained at the beginning of the world that certain signs should prefigure certain events." Learn to perceive clues in history and current events that foreshadow the future. If things are changing, it is because they are being acted upon by some force. Find that force, recognize it, and determine how it is likely to behave. Will it continue, strengthen, or weaken? In other words, before looking forward, look backward. When you are able to determine cycles and trends, it means you are equipped to make wise decisions and position yourself for increase and success.[2]

Paul encouraged us with these words:

Now He who searches the hearts knows what the mind of the Spirit is, because He makes intercession for the saints according to the will of God. And we know that all things work together for good to those who love God, to those who are the called according to His purpose.   (Romans 8:27–28)

Perhaps the words of Kathryn Kuhlman express it best: "As long as God is still on His throne and hears and answers prayer, everything will come out all right!"[3] She was not advocating a blind trust, though. She was challenging us to pray as we discern the times, see what God is up to, know what time it is, and cooperate with His plans.

God's will is being worked out in this world! The times and seasons reveal it. We are Spirit-led history makers and changers who are called to pursue His purpose and impact society for His kingdom. The next time someone asks you, "What time is it?" don't look at your watch. Tell the truth about the age we are living in and what God is up to. Point to the Source of wisdom.

PART FOUR

THE SOURCE OF WISDOM

"He will be the sure foundation for your times, a rich store of salvation and wisdom and knowledge; the fear of the LORD is the key to this treasure."
—Isaiah 33:6 (NIV)

20

THE WISDOM SEEKERS

Get wisdom!…Wisdom is the principal thing; therefore get wisdom. And in all your getting, get understanding" (Proverbs 4:5, 7). This is the advice of a king. And not just any king—Solomon was one of the wealthiest, most powerful, most influential potentates in the world. What made him so great? His desire and pursuit of wisdom! He valued knowledge and understanding above all other things.

One night, the Lord appeared to Solomon in a dream and said, "Ask! What shall I give you?" (1 Kings 3:5).

As Solomon pondered the question, he reflected on his human condition:

Now, O LORD my God, You have made Your servant king instead of my father David, but I am a little child; I do not know how to go out or come in. And Your servant is in the midst of Your people whom You have chosen, a great people, too numerous to be numbered or counted. Therefore give to Your servant an understanding heart to judge Your people, that I may discern between good and evil. For who is able to judge this great people of Yours?
(1 Kings 3:7–9)

It pleased the Lord that Solomon made this unselfish request. (See 1 Kings 3:10.) He replied,

Because you have asked this thing, and have not asked long life for yourself,
nor have asked riches for yourself, nor have asked the life of your enemies,
but have asked for yourself understanding to discern justice, behold, I have
done according to your words; see, I have given you a wise and understanding
heart, so that there has not been anyone like you before you, nor shall any like
you arise after you. And I have also given you what you have not asked: both
riches and honor, so that there shall not be anyone like you among the kings
all your days.   (1 Kings 3:11–13)

Solomon spent his life pursuing knowledge and wisdom. He invited people from all over the world to appear in his royal court and recorded many of their insights in a book that remains to this very day the hallmark of good judgment. It is called *"The proverbs of Solomon the son of David, king of Israel"* (Proverbs 1:1).

We would do well to heed the king's advice, for *"he who gets wisdom loves his own soul; he who keeps understanding will find good"* (Proverbs 19:8).

Wisdom is the principal thing; therefore get wisdom. And in all your getting,
get understanding. Exalt her, and she will promote you; she will bring you
honor, when you embrace her. She will place on your head an ornament of
grace; a crown of glory she will deliver to you.   (Proverbs 4:7–9)

The Urim and the Thummim

Solomon is just one individual in the long line of Jacob's offspring who sought wisdom. His significance lies in the fact that he went to the right source: God. Long before Solomon, at the very beginning of Israel's nationhood, the Almighty provided a means for obtaining wisdom. He instructed Moses to supply the high priest with a device that would give him the ability to access and determine the wisdom of God.

And you shall put in the breastplate of judgment the Urim and the Thummim,
and they shall be over Aaron's heart when he goes in before the LORD. So
Aaron shall bear the judgment of the children of Israel over his heart before
the LORD continually.   (Exodus 28:30)

Inside the breastplate of judgment, which rested over the heart of the high priest, there was a small pouch containing two stones that could not be distinguished from each other by touch. These stones were used to obtain messages from God. The manner in which the high priest performed this act is unexplained in the Scriptures, but we know that he was able to determine God's response to the questions posed by leaders of the nation based on which stone he pulled out of the pouch. (See Numbers 27:21; 1 Samuel 14:41–42; 28:6.)

Urim and *Thummim* literally mean "Lights and Perfections."[1] Amazing! From the foundation of Israel, wisdom was sought from the Light Giver, and His instructions and revelation were perfect. Each time the priest pulled out a stone from the pouch over his heart, the will of Yahweh was revealed. This was no dutiful, mechanical action on the priest's part. At critical times, God's wisdom was sought with the survival of the nation hanging in the balance. It was life or death, justice and truth, but it was always a heart issue for the priest and a necessity for leadership. God's response was never questioned or doubted. Wisdom came forth from the Almighty. The priest, the leadership, and the people recognized and acknowledged that God spoke in this fashion through the stones of light, and they acted on His wise counsel.

Prophets replaced the Urim and the Thummim after the time of David, and when the Jewish exiles returned from Babylon, the stones of discernment were a distant memory. But the principle remained—if you need wisdom, "Ask of God." (See 1 Samuel 23:2, 9–12.)

Millennia later, the apostle Peter led the disciples in an "Urim and Thummim moment." Peter stood up in the midst of the disciples and confronted them with the need to make a decision—someone to take the place that Judas had vacated. He quoted the sacred text: *"Let his days be few, and let another take his office"* (Psalm 109:8).

Two men were chosen from among all of those who had followed Jesus since John's baptism and who had personally witnessed His resurrection: Joseph, called Barsabas, who was surnamed Justus, and Matthias.

> *And they prayed and said, "You, O Lord, who know the hearts of all, show which of these two You have chosen to take part in this ministry and apostleship from which Judas by transgression fell, that he might go to his own place." And they cast their lots, and the lot fell on Matthias. And he was numbered with the eleven apostles.*   (Acts 1:24–26)

We don't know what the vote actually was. Could it have been unanimous? What we do know is that about one hundred and twenty people took part in casting lots. Each one had to seek the Lord for wisdom and direction. It was a heart matter, not an issue of personality or a political decision. God's wisdom was sought. To this day, we believe that God made the choice.

Inside Knowledge

The secret of the Urim and the Thummim is supernatural, divine revelation. The high priest understood this every time he reached into the pouch to obtain the wisdom of God. The light keeper who tended the lampstand within the shadowy recesses of the Holy Place made no pretense, either. He was performing his duty in the presence of the Holy One, and his distinct privilege was to attend to the *Light*. He was illuminated and enlightened with divine revelation. The light keeper was encompassed in the brilliance of God's wisdom, and the Almighty wrote His oracles upon his heart each night. The sons of Issachar were wisdom seekers, as well. They understood the need for divine revelation in order to make wise decisions and live circumspectly.

All of these individuals obtained "inside knowledge." They point us in the right direction. Like they did, we have a desperate need to hear a "Thus saith the Lord"! It immediately lets us know we are receiving divine counsel. The apostle Peter nailed it when he wrote the following:

And so we have the prophetic word confirmed, which you do well to heed as a light that shines in a dark place, until the day dawns and the morning star rises in your hearts; knowing this first, that no prophecy of Scripture is of any private interpretation, for prophecy never came by the will of man, but holy men of God spoke as they were moved by the Holy Spirit. (2 Peter 1:19–21)

Notice that these "*holy men of God*" were enlightened oracles, moved by the Holy Spirit to deliver inside information.

Revelation knowledge, whether it comes from the Scriptures, in the form of a prophetic word, or as a result of tending the lampstand in the secret place, is like a light that shines in a dark place. This light is supernatural. It provides inside information and brings clarification. It is the light of God shining upon our world and our lives. Without this spiritual enlightenment, we are like the blind leading the blind. Ultimately, we will all fall into a ditch.

Both history and time are an enigma when we try to interpret them from an intellectual point of view. No matter how intelligent we may be or how well informed we are, the affairs of man, as reported in the daily news, flash by us in an endless succession of disasters, tragedies, and crimes against humanity, like noise emanating from the Tower of Babel, confused and distorted. History becomes a whirlwind of good or bad news, and we struggle to make sense of it all and discern the big picture. What we need is revelation—inside knowledge from the Light Giver. We need to see time and history from His perspective.

Time Travelers

Our imaginations are tantalized by the thought that time can somehow be transcended—that there just may be a way to go back to the future. Maybe H. G. Wells wasn't a writer of science fiction. Perhaps he was a prophet. Could it really be possible to build a time machine with the ability to transport us into a different age?

Even better, is it possible to transcend time altogether and enter eternity *without dying?* Such an experience would surely raise our awareness and understanding of eternal priorities and perspectives. In the light of such an experience, we could live with an uncommon wisdom that transcends common knowledge. The answer is yes! It is possible!

"How can you be so sure?" you ask.

Because the Bible tells us that there are people who have made the transition from time to eternity. These individuals bent the rules! They traveled through time and space and then returned to tell us about their journeys. No, they are not modern-day astronauts. These individuals comprise an elite group whose intimacy with God qualified them to transcend the common and achieve the uncommon. The state of awareness they obtained in God's presence regarding life and the wisdom to live it could not have been found in any other way.

Enoch was such a time traveler. He did not see death at all, but God took him into heaven. (See Genesis 5:24.) His writings, although not considered to be sacred, have great historical value, especially to Jewish scholars who lived in the centuries leading up to Christ's birth. The books of Enoch are apocalyptic in nature (from the Greek word *apokalupsis*, meaning "revelation" or "disclosure"). He spoke about such subjects as the angels, whom he referred to as the "Watchers," identifying them by name and rank. He recounted the fall of certain evil angels and their intermarriage with the daughters of men. He spoke about the coming judgment of the wicked. His books read like a spiritual travelogue as he recounts his many journeys while being accompanied by God and angels.

Enoch saw the heavens, the future of the world, and the predetermined course of human history. (See Jude 1:14–15.) Long before the flood, the patriarchs, and the great prophets and kings of Israel, Enoch walked with God. In that communion, he plumbed the depths of God's mysteries and secrets and returned with an uncommon wisdom. Enoch walked with God and, in so doing, transcended time and space.

Jesus is the consummate time traveler.

In the beginning was the Word, and the Word was with God, and the Word was God. He was in the beginning with God. All things were made through Him, and without Him nothing was made that was made.…And the Word became flesh and dwelt among us, and we beheld His glory, the glory as of the only begotten of the Father, full of grace and truth. (John 1:1–3, 14)

Jesus brought eternity to earth!

After Jesus' death and resurrection, His disciples watched as

He was taken up, and a cloud received Him out of their sight. And while they looked steadfastly toward heaven as He went up, behold, two men stood by them in white apparel, who also said, "Men of Galilee, why do you stand gazing up into heaven? This same Jesus, who was taken up from you into heaven, will so come in like manner as you saw Him go into heaven." (Acts 1:9–11)

God is able to traverse time at His choosing, and He does so in order to effect His divine plan. He thinks nothing of coming and going in and out of our time/space world from His eternal realm. He also has the power to enable us to do the same.

Moses and Elijah are proof. They are among this amazing group of cosmic "pneumanauts." Moses was denied entrance to Canaan because of his personal failure, so he went up onto the mountain to die. Elijah didn't die; he was taken up into heaven by a whirlwind as a chariot "limo" accompanied him into eternity. But both Moses and Elijah broke the rules—they left and then came back!

A summit was called by the Son of God on the Mount of Transfiguration. Peter, James, and John were invited. Jesus was changed before their very eyes. The light of God encompassed and infused Him. The Light Giver was ablaze with the fullness of His glory and wisdom. In the midst of this light, Moses and Elijah showed up to talk with Jesus. What was said? We don't know. But in that blinding revelation, Jesus' face shone like the sun, and His clothes became as white as the light. He became the Lampstand! These three time travelers were in the *revelation zone*. They supernaturally connected time with eternity, and the fullness of God's wisdom was revealed and affirmed in the midst of their discourse.

Philip the evangelist broke the rules, too. He was instructed by an angel to go toward the south along a road that went down from Jerusalem to Gaza. As he went, an Ethiopian eunuch of great authority who served Candace the queen was reading the prophet Isaiah while he rode in his chariot. Philip preached Christ to him, and he believed and was baptized.

> *Now when they came up out of the water, the Spirit of the Lord caught Philip away, so that the eunuch saw him no more; and he went on his way rejoicing. But Philip was found at Azotus. And passing through, he preached in all the cities till he came to Caesarea.* (Acts 8:39–40)

Philip was transported from one place to another. There was no taxi or caravan. No camel showed up to take him on the journey. He simply disappeared from one location and showed up in another. Wow! In an instant, he just disappeared. The next thing you know, he's in Azotus. How long did it take? Wrong Question! You can't measure eternity by time. How did God do it? By the Spirit! He moved Philip into the transcendent dimension where the laws of time and physics no longer apply. In this eternity hallway, God transported His servant to the place of his next assignment and gave him wisdom regarding how to accomplish it. And guess what? Philip was flesh and blood. So were Enoch, Moses, Elijah, and Jesus.

The "Know" Zone

There is a spiritual dimension that transcends time. It is not bound by the laws of nature or limited by space. I call it the "Know Zone." When God calls you into this dimension, you lose track of earthly things, and time no longer matters. You just "know" you are in His presence, and massive downloads of revelation and wisdom flood your understanding and enlighten your life. You are in the presence of the Light Giver.

The apostle Paul described it this way:

It is doubtless not profitable for me to boast. I will come to visions and revelations of the Lord: I know a man in Christ who fourteen years ago; whether in the body I do not know, or whether out of the body I do not know, God knows; such a one was caught up to the third heaven. And I know such a man; whether in the body or out of the body I do not know, God knows; how he was caught up into Paradise and heard inexpressible words, which it is not lawful for a man to utter. Of such a one I will boast; yet of myself I will not boast, except in my infirmities. For though I might desire to boast, I will not be a fool; for I will speak the truth. But I refrain, lest anyone should think of me above what he sees me to be or hears from me. (2 Corinthians 12:1–6)

Paul affirmed twice that this is not a matter of "in-body" or out-of-body experiences. It is an issue of transcending time and space and suddenly finding yourself in the presence of the eternal One. Was Paul speaking about his own experience? We don't know, but I believe he had firsthand experience. Perhaps he was referring to John the beloved, the great apostle. Paul no doubt knew John and had fellowshipped with him on numerous occasions. John wrote an entire book that holds an honored place at the end of the Bible, the book of Revelation. Listen to his story.

I, John, both your brother and companion in the tribulation and kingdom and patience of Jesus Christ, was on the island that is called Patmos for the word of God and for the testimony of Jesus Christ. I was in the Spirit on the Lord's Day, and I heard behind me a loud voice, as of a trumpet, saying, "I am the Alpha and the Omega, the First and the Last," and, "What you see, write in a book and send it to the seven churches which are in Asia: to Ephesus, to Smyrna, to Pergamos, to Thyatira, to Sardis, to Philadelphia, and to Laodicea." Then I turned to see the voice that spoke with me. And having turned I saw seven golden lampstands, and in the midst of the seven lampstands One like the Son of Man, clothed with a garment down to the feet and girded about the chest with a golden band. His head and hair were white like wool, as white as snow, and His eyes like a flame of fire; His feet were like fine brass, as if refined in a furnace, and His voice as the sound of many waters; He had in His right hand seven stars, out of His mouth went a sharp two-edged sword, and His countenance was like the sun shining in its strength. And when I saw Him, I fell at His feet as dead. But He laid His right hand on me, saying to me, "Do not be afraid; I am the First and the Last. I am He who lives, and was dead, and behold, I am alive forevermore. Amen."

(Revelation 1:9–18)

After these things I looked, and behold, a door standing open in heaven. And the first voice which I heard was like a trumpet speaking with me, saying, "Come up here, and I will show you things which must take place after this." Immediately I was in the Spirit....

(Revelation 4:1–2)

John was in the "know zone." He was *"in the Spirit."* He was in the third heaven. Most important, he was in the presence of God.

The Hidden Treasure

The kind of wisdom that comes through prophetic revelation in the "know zone" is so valuable, it is priceless. *"How much better to get wisdom than gold! And to get understanding is to be chosen rather than silver"* (Proverbs 16:16). Paul referred to it as a hidden treasure that must be searched for at all cost.

For I want you to know what a great conflict I have for you and those in Laodicea, and for as many as have not seen my face in the flesh, that their hearts may be encouraged, being knit together in love, and attaining to all riches of the full assurance of understanding, to the knowledge of the mystery of God, both of the Father and of Christ, in whom are hidden all the treasures of wisdom and knowledge.

(Colossians 2:1–3)

Notice that he said not just a few things but all things! The entire treasure of wisdom and knowledge is hidden in Christ. Every nugget of truth, every insight into history, all of the secrets of creation, and even the knowledge and wisdom to understand the times we live in, are waiting for us to discover in Christ!

James added this exhortation:

If any of you lacks wisdom, let him ask of God, who gives to all liberally and without reproach, and it will be given to him. But let him ask in faith, with no doubting, for he who doubts is like a wave of the sea driven and tossed by the wind. For let not that man suppose that he will receive anything from the Lord; he is a double-minded man, unstable in all his ways. (James 1:5–8)

Is it really that simple?

Yes! Jesus said, *"Ask, and it will be given to you; seek, and you will find; knock, and it will be opened to you. For everyone who asks receives, and he who seeks finds, and to him who knocks it will be opened"* (Matthew 7:7–8). The Light Giver is waiting for you to knock on the door. There is a passageway that leads into His presence. C. S. Lewis knew about it. Let's see what he had to say.

21

THE SECRET PLACE

Lucy paused and stared up at the imposing wardrobe. *There's no where else to go. This is the last resort,* she thought. *This is the perfect place to hide.*

Approaching footsteps in the hallway outside the room forced her to act quickly. With childlike apprehension, she swung open the massive doors. A wave of mothball-scented air cascaded out from the dark interior. Covering her mouth to muffle her choking gasp, she stepped into the shadowy enclosure and pulled the doors shut behind her. She pushed her way past the heavy coats and carefully stored garments, seeking the furthest recesses of the enclosure, where she would be invisible. *At last, I'm safe. I will be the winner of hide-and-seek.* She giggled with glee.

Suddenly, the world outside, beyond the confines of her enclosure, became a distant memory. The intoxicatingly strong scent of pine sap invaded her consciousness. *I recognize that smell,* she acknowledged. Memories of Christmas wreaths, decorated trees, and her home filled with the aroma of the festive season flashed through her mind. Then, an evergreen bough brushed across her face.

"Where am I?" Lucy shouted in amazement. "This is not a closet; it's a doorway into another world. I have crossed over a threshold from one dimension to another."

One more step, and she was through the doorway. She was engulfed in a wonderful, supernatural world. She didn't know anything about it yet, but she was about to find out. In this dimension, good and evil engaged in mortal combat, animals talked, and Aslan ruled.

I have been gone for a very long time, she realized, after spending many hours at Mister Tumnus' house in Narnia. *The tea made me sleepy, and that music was mesmerizing. I must get back to the others.*

She made her way back to the lamppost, with Mister Tumnus' help. Giving a reluctant wave good-bye, she pushed the evergreen boughs aside and pressed back into the passageway, past the garments inside. With a firm shove on the door, daylight from the real world burst into the wardrobe. "But they're both real," she whispered in wonderment, sweeping any doubt from her mind. "I've seen it myself. Narnia is just as real as this world! I must tell the others," she squealed with delight. "I can't wait to show them the world I have discovered beyond the wardrobe." Not once did she consider the possibility that they wouldn't believe her.

"Where have you been?" her brothers and sister asked. "We have been hunting for you for almost an hour."

Lucy was dumbfounded. She had been gone all day, but in real time, it had been only a few minutes. *How could that happen?* she wondered.

"It's just your childish imagination," Edmond said, in response to her account of the wardrobe and the secret doorway. "That's impossible! How could there be another world and a secret passageway that leads to it?"

⌒

C. S. Lewis was a master storyteller and a Christian apologist who profoundly influenced his generation. Lewis revealed his intentions when he wrote, "Any amount of theology can be smuggled into people's minds under the cover of romance without their knowing it."[1]

Lewis understood that we needed to be stretched! Our logical way of dealing with life and reality is inadequate. Although we would not necessarily categorize him as a Christian mystic, he was profoundly persuaded that mysticism is the key to comprehending the unseen. He stated, "Mysticism is, by empirical evidence, the only real contact man has ever had with the unseen. It is therefore the one true religion. One thing common to all mysticisms is the temporary shattering of ordinary spatial and temporal consciousness and our discursive intellect."[2]

Lewis believed that the passageway into God's presence is the mystical experience. Christian mysticism is at the core of Christian spirituality. It is the desire and passion to know God directly—not just through the Scriptures, doctrine, or tradition. It is the absolute conviction that God made us for intimacy with Him and that, through Jesus Christ, that intimacy has been restored.

The Desert Fathers were Christian mystics who sought a God encounter in the wilderness. Monks and nuns entered the confines of a spiritual community in order to seek intimacy with God. Contemporary Christians have the same desire. We cry like David, "*As the deer pants for the water brooks, so pants my soul for You, O God. My soul thirsts for God, for the living God. When shall I come and appear before God?*" (Psalm 42:1–2).

Portals from Time to Eternity

Jacob, the patriarch of Israel, provides us with the best biblical illustration of what Lewis was attempting to explain.

> *Now Jacob went out from Beersheba and went toward Haran. So he came to a certain place and stayed there all night, because the sun had set. And he took one of the stones of that place and put it at his head, and he lay down in that place to sleep. Then he dreamed, and behold, a ladder was set up on the earth, and its top reached to heaven; and there the angels of God were ascending and descending on it. And behold, the LORD stood above it and said: "I am the LORD God of Abraham your father and the God of Isaac; the land on which you lie I will give to you and your descendants. Also your descendants shall be as the dust of the earth; you shall spread abroad to the west and the east, to the north and the south; and in you and in your seed all the families of the earth shall be blessed. Behold, I am with you and will keep you wherever you go, and will bring you back to this land; for I will not leave you until I have done what I have spoken to you." Then Jacob awoke from his sleep and said, "Surely the LORD is in this place, and I did not know it." And he was afraid and said, "How awesome is this place! This is none other than the house of God, and this is the gate of heaven!"*
>
> (Genesis 28:10–17)

Jacob's ordinary spatial and temporal consciousness was shattered by an encounter with God. Like Lucy, he inadvertently discovered a portal from one dimension to another. Lucy was looking for a place to hide; Jacob just wanted a place to sleep. What he thought was simply a spot to bed down for the night became a *doorway* from time to eternity. The commerce of heaven was being conducted in this passageway as angels, the messengers of God and the servants of men, performed their duties as holy couriers delivering the wisdom and direction of God from the strategy room of heaven.

When he awoke, Jacob's perception was forever altered. He had discovered a secret doorway. He had made contact with the unseen God. He had received wisdom and revelation regarding his own future, the future of Israel, and the future of the entire world. He had even been told where his ancestors would live as God deeded to him real estate.

The name of the city where Jacob discovered the supernatural portal between heaven and earth was Luz, which means "light." No coincidence, I'm sure. Jacob renamed it Bethel, "the house of God." (See Genesis 28:19.)

A portal is anyplace where God is accessible. It is a place where intimate God encounters occur. The garden of Eden was such a place. When Abraham and his sons built an altar to God, it was to commemorate a God encounter. The burning bush was a portal. Both the tabernacle in the wilderness and the Holy of Holies were portals where God guaranteed His presence. The Scriptures often refer to these portals as an "open heaven." (See Psalm 78:23–25; Isaiah 24:18; Malachi 3:10; John 1:51; Acts 7:56; Revelation 4:1.) These portals are not necessarily permanent physical places. They may be accessed wherever a believer is seeking God.

The Secret Place

Like Jacob, I inadvertently discovered a secret portal into the presence of Eternity. It was the first day of the year 1999. I had reached a crossroads in my own spiritual journey. Exhausted and spiritually burned out after decades of ministry, I was in desperate need of help. I knew that I could not go on without His presence and guidance. I made my way to my study and locked the door behind me. I removed the phone from the receiver and settled into my chair. *I need a God encounter*, I thought. *Unless You come and manifest Yourself, I quit. I can't do this anymore.* This was not a demand; it was desperation. I had no idea what was about to happen to me.

Tears began to form in the corners of my eyes as I prayed, "Lord, please help me to make the right choices today and in the days to come. Teach me Your ways, Lord, and grace me to be a man after Your own heart. Above all, I desire to hear Your voice and to know Your will and Your ways."

At that moment, something unexplainable happened. A groaning cry stirred deep within me and rose up like a primal scream from the depths of my soul. I believe it had its roots in every previous generation, all the way back to Adam and Eve. It was the cry of loneliness and of a longing for intimacy with God. The words tumbled out of me. They were not the premeditated result of my discursive intellect, as Lewis described it. This was the spontaneous utterance of my heart.

"God," I prayed in complete sincerity, "I want to be like Enoch. I want to walk with You and be Your friend." I wasn't sure why I said it that way, but I knew I meant it with all of my being.

What happened next is forever etched in my memory. God responded! He spoke directly into my spirit. "Son, I have heard your prayer, and I am going to answer it. I am going to come and walk with you, just like I walked with Enoch."

The atmosphere in the room instantly became electrified. The air crystallized before my eyes. It shimmered and glistened like atom-sized diamonds, reflecting the light of God's glory. The weight of His presence was so heavy, I could not lift my head. Tears coursed down my cheeks and fell onto the pages of my journal. Time stood still. For me, it seemed like minutes, but His presence remained for hours. When I finally left the study, the entire day had come and gone. This was the first "Enoch walk" I experienced with the Lord.

Day after day, I hurried to my study to meet with Jesus. Wisdom and revelation poured forth in a steady stream of wondrous insight and understanding. Scriptures that had been puzzling to me despite years of study became understandable as I sat at His feet and listened to the Author explain the text. My spirit, mind, and body were being restored and healed with each passing day.

My study became a place of illumination as I sat in the presence of the Light Giver. I couldn't wait to be with Him. Like Jacob, I could truly say, "Surely, the Lord is in this place. How awesome is this place! This is none other than the house of God." This small room became a portal, a doorway, a sacred space connecting heaven and earth, where angels traveled and Jesus came to walk with me.

Months later, I discovered an explanation for what I had experienced and continue to enjoy.

[Jesus said,] *"And when you pray, you shall not be like the hypocrites. For they love to pray standing in the synagogues and on the corners of the streets, that they may be seen by men. Assuredly, I say to you, they have their reward. But you, when you pray, go into your room, and when you have shut your door, pray to your Father who is in the secret place; and your Father who sees in secret will reward you openly."* (Matthew 6:5–6)

I am living this text, and so can you.

The Doorway to Wisdom

The secret place is real! It is the doorway into God's presence, where He meets with us individually. In this sacred space, God comes to give us wisdom and revelation. In His presence, we receive knowledge and understanding. *There is no substitute for intimacy with God!* A single prophetic word or vision from Jesus can alter the course of our lives and change history. Satan knows this, and he will do everything in his power to keep us from the secret place. Our fleshly desires become obstacles, as well. All of earth and the demonic hordes of hell are pitted against us to keep us from His presence. An event in the life of Jesus and His disciples testifies to this reality:

Then Jesus came with them to a place called Gethsemane, and said to the disciples, "Sit here while I go and pray over there." And He took with Him Peter and the two sons of Zebedee, and He began to be sorrowful and deeply distressed. Then He said to them, "My soul is exceedingly sorrowful, even to death. Stay here and watch with Me." He went a little farther and fell on His face, and prayed, saying, "O My Father, if it is possible, let this cup pass from Me; nevertheless, not as I will, but as You will." Then He came to the disciples and found them asleep, and said to Peter, "What? Could you not watch with Me one hour? Watch and pray, lest you enter into temptation. The spirit indeed is willing, but the flesh is weak." (Matthew 26:36–41)

They were gathered in the secret place. The garden of Gethsemane became a portal between heaven and earth. Jesus and the Father held an intimate conversation. Eternal business was transacted. The Father's wisdom and strategy were affirmed. But the disciples succumbed to the weakness of their flesh. One hour was too long. Certainly, the enemy had a hand in it, as well. No doubt the words of Jesus haunted Peter for a long time: *"Could you not watch with Me one hour?"* How would you answer that question?

We are all subject to fleshly desires and temptations. The pressures and responsibilities of life demand our attention. But there is a way to overcome the things that divert our attention and keep us from the secret place. The Lord spoke to me in a vision one day about these diabolical distractions.

22

DIABOLICAL DISTRACTIONS

God created us with the wonderful ability to perceive our world, but we do not react equally to all of the stimuli bombarding us. We choose what to focus our attention upon; everything else in our environment is blocked out. In a house full of people, a mother will hear her baby's cry above the din of conversation. You are reading at this very moment, but stop for a minute, close your eyes, and attend to the various stimuli around you: the pressure of clothing on your neck or shoulders, the sound of a lawn mower next door, the hum of the refrigerator, or the smell of cookies baking in the oven. If a car should pass by, chances are, you never would have even noticed, had I not changed your level of perception.

Psychologists call the ability to choose what we focus on "selective perception." There are degrees of awareness in which we may be more or less receptive to stimuli in our environment.[1] Perception is determined by our choices. We program ourselves to distinguish all of the signals coming to us. Among the multitude of things clamoring for our attention, we decide what is most important. That's where we focus our attention.

Our attention to any given thing or event is determined by the value we assign to it. Sometimes, our priorities go awry. The things we choose to focus on are of secondary importance, or no importance at all, compared with what we ought to be wholly focused on.

The Main Thing

Stephen Covey, author of *The Seven Habits of Highly Effective People*, followed his blockbuster seller with an equally important book, *First Things First*. In it, he claims that "putting first things first is at the very heart of life."[2] His premise is absolutely correct. But putting "first things first" means more than prioritizing our to-do list. It demands that we evaluate our priorities and make choices regarding what is the most important thing in our lives. Everything else must proceed from that decision.

King David did exactly what Covey suggested—long before Covey wrote his book. David processed everything available to him and weighed his options in terms of importance. He narrowed it all down to the number one, most valuable thing in his life and vowed to make it his primary pursuit. He expressed it like this: "*One thing I have desired of the LORD, that will I seek: that I may dwell in the house of the LORD all the days of my life, to behold the beauty of the LORD, and to inquire in His temple*" (Psalm 27:4).

The presence of God was David's utmost priority. Of equal importance was obtaining wisdom from the Light Giver. He wanted to behold God's beauty, *and* he had some questions to ask of the Almighty. His heart's cry comes across in Psalm 42:1–2: "*As the deer pants for the water brooks, so pants my soul for You, O God. My soul thirsts for God, for the living God. When shall I come and appear before God?*" His passion was God's presence. His source of wisdom was Jehovah. He was a man after God's own heart. (See Acts 13:22.)

Troubled About Many Things

Nothing in this world should take precedence over God's presence in our lives. Regrettably, that is exactly what happens. Once we make the choice to seek His face and are passionate about it, everything seems to be set against us. Even doing good things can take precedence and keep us from Him. Just ask the expert, Martha.

Now it happened as they went that [Jesus] entered a certain village; and a certain woman named Martha welcomed Him into her house. And she had a sister called Mary, who also sat at Jesus' feet and heard His word. But Martha was distracted with much serving, and she approached Him and said, "Lord, do You not care that my sister has left me to serve alone? Therefore tell her to help me." And Jesus answered and said to her, "Martha, Martha, you are worried and troubled about many things. But one thing is needed, and Mary has chosen that good part, which will not be taken away from her."

(Luke 10:38–42)

There's a Martha in most of us. We welcome Jesus into our house and then become preoccupied with everything but Him. It's the Martha in us that says, "I know You're here, God, but I'm really busy. And by the way, I'm doing this for You, You know. Once I get this done, I will take time to sit in Your presence. Why don't You tell those who are sitting at Your feet to come help me?"

I can't tell you how many times I have had to repent and ask God's forgiveness for all of the distractions that have kept me from Him, some of them more an excuse than anything else. The pages of my journal have been marked again and again by my tears of repentance.

One day, after another long period of absence from the secret place, I confessed, "Lord, I'm such a hypocrite. I'm driven into Your presence out of necessity rather than relationship. My life is so full of busyness. God, I need Your help!"

I instantly discerned His familiar voice in my spirit, and I was stunned by His response. "Son, if you are having difficulty getting into the secret place, don't you think that others have the same problem?"

The light went on! "I'm not the only one, am I, Jesus?"

"No," He replied. "I am waiting to spend intimate time with My children, but they seldom come."

Driven to Distraction

"Lord, how can I overcome the constant distractions?" I pleaded.

Instantly, a picture of the wheel from the popular television show *Wheel of Fortune* flashed onto the screen of my mind. The wheel was spinning and clicking away as each wedge-shaped section on the wheel passed by the arrow.

"Where will it stop?" I wondered, as the vision played out like a scene from TV. I knew that the wedges were marked with various amounts of money, and some of them even featured special prizes and awards. But the wheel was spinning too fast for me to read the amounts or items. Gradually it slowed, and I could see the categories clearly. Instead of monetary amounts, each category was identified by a topic. The first one was labeled "Material Possessions." Next to it was "Health Issues." I read each section in amazement: "Money," "People," "Work," "Ministry," "Duties," "Entertainment," "Fantasy," "Worldliness," "Church," and so on.

"Church!" I gasped. "You mean that church can take priority over time with You, Lord?"

He didn't have to answer. I was guilty of that one—and so many more.

Then God spoke again. "Son, this is the way your mind is. The devil comes and spins the wheel. Your attention goes to wherever the wheel stops on each spin. It clicks around until it stops, and that's where your focus goes. The enemy is wreaking havoc with your thoughts and ability to focus. He uses the wheel of distraction."

"That's *exactly* what happens to me, Lord," I acknowledged. "I'm a wheel watcher."

The devil designs the wheel and chooses the exact categories he knows will distract you and me. Do you suppose church could distract us from intimacy with God? Tell me about it! How about judgmental attitudes? Criticism? Boy, the enemy spins the wheel, and when it stops on those—bam! We get into a critical spirit, and guess what happens to our intimate time with the Lord?

Fleshly desires, addictions, sin, perfectionism...listen! If you're a perfectionist, the enemy will make your wheel stop on that wedge all the time. What about success? Failure? Family? Vacations? Hurts? Offenses? Rejection? Acceptance? Popularity? Approval? Self-esteem? Envy? Jealousy? Condemnation? The enemy knows what buttons to push in our lives. Just when we've gotten one issue resolved, he spins the wheel again. Our minds become confused, our spirits troubled. The presence of God is the farthest thing from our attention. We become unproductive and unfulfilled.

The Mind Field

The Lord spoke again and said, "Distraction will always be in your world and in your thoughts. Do you see what a scheming attack the enemy has mounted against you? He comes to steal and to rob you of intimacy with Me. Your mind is the battlefield. He knows that if he can keep you from My presence, he can defeat you, so he spins the wheel of distraction to divert your attention and your focus. If he succeeds, you will become so busy and confused that you can hardly hear My voice.

"Son, I want you to step away from the wheel of distraction. I am not the author of confusion. You must tune in to My Spirit. I'm jealous for you. I have waited and waited like a jilted lover, longing for intimacy with you. The quality of your life is directly proportional to the time you spend in My presence."

The moment Jesus said to me, "Son, I want you to step away from the wheel of distraction," I thought about Mary. Unlike Martha, she made the choice to step away from all the duties and responsibilities that demanded her attention. She knew there were things to be done; she realized that she had responsibilities; she knew the rules of hospitality. But she chose to step away from the wheel of distraction. There is always something demanding our attention and focus. Like Mary, there comes a time in our lives when we must say, "I choose to step away."

Practice Planned Abandonment

I learned this lesson the hard way. I spent three or four days each week mowing the grass on our church property because it needed to be cut, and I had decided that there was no one to cut it but me. One day, as I bumped down the hillside, perched precariously on the yellow seat of my heavy-duty, apple green John Deere, grass flying everywhere and pollen spewing into the air, I had a *Forrest Gump* moment.

Forrest spent day after day just running. He ran everywhere. He wore out his shoes in the process and gathered a lot of devotees who could identify with his running. When asked why he was running, he simply said, "I like to run." He had no cause or agenda; he just kept running. He ran and ran, all across the nation, until, one day, he just stopped in the middle of a highway somewhere in the desert of the great American West. The camera panned in close as Forrest's eyes, glazed over with weariness, stared into the distance. Then he said, "I'm tired! Think I'll go home now."

The camera flashed back to the people who had been running behind him. They stood in the middle of the road, dumbfounded. One of them spoke. "What do we do now?"

That day had come for me. "I'm tired," I said. "Think I'll go home now." And I stopped mowing the twelve-acre lawn for good. Instead, I went home to the secret place. The results were instantaneous. New vitality surged into my spiritual life. Fresh wisdom and revelation flowed from His presence. I was transformed, healed, and set free from past regrets. What to preach was no longer an issue. I had more material than I could use in a lifetime. But, even more important, I was in His presence. We were walking together and talking together each and every day.

There's always something demanding our attention. Even the things we want to avoid can keep us from Him. In her excellent book *Jesus, Life Coach*, Laurie Beth Jones encourages us to practice *planned abandonment*. "Planned abandonment means learning how and when to say no, as well as cultivating the discipline of saying no."[3] Most of us want to serve and please others, but we can't afford to let those desires distract us. There comes a point where we must practice planned abandonment like Mary, and say, "No. I'm not working in the kitchen today. I choose to sit at Jesus' feet." She said no to her sister, to cultural expectations, and to everything inside her that summoned her to duty rather than intimacy with God.

Ticks of the Mind

The apostle Paul said that *"we do not wrestle against flesh and blood, but against principalities, against powers, against the rulers of the darkness of this age, against spiritual hosts of wickedness in the heavenly places"* (Ephesians 6:12).

The battleground is our mind, and Satan knows where to attack us. He knows what will especially annoy, distract, and consume us. As Joyce Meyer so aptly put it,

> He begins by bombarding our mind with a cleverly devised pattern of little nagging thoughts, suspicions, doubts, fears, wonderings, reasoning and theories. He moves slowly and cautiously. He has a strategy for his warfare. He has observed us for a long time. He knows what we like and what we don't like. He knows our insecurities, weaknesses and fears. He knows what bothers us the most.[4]

I liken a distraction to a "tick" in the mind. It fastens itself to our thoughts and sucks the life out of us. Ticks are tenacious. You really have to work at getting them out. When our dog gets a tick, we put Vaseline on the bug to suffocate it and then pull it out with tweezers. That's what we must do when Satan spins the wheel of distraction and it stops on something he knows will attach itself to our thoughts and keep us from spending time with the Lord. We have to suffocate that distraction and get it out of our mind. They are diabolical distractions.

Come Home

Have you been troubled about many things, as Martha was? Are you fed up with the enemy's constant bombardment of distractions? Have you grown weary of man's attempts to figure things out? Do you desire knowledge and understanding that surpass what this world can offer? Then, stop running—you are ready to come home. Make the choice today. Like Mary, choose to sit at Jesus' feet!

Jesus is waiting to give you new life and prophetic revelation. Let me show you the pathway into His presence, the secret to intimacy with Him. He is the Light Giver and the Source of all wisdom. In His light, we see light. (See Psalm 36:9.)

23

THE WAY INTO HIS PRESENCE

Let me tell you about the upper room in my home that I call my secret place. I intentionally designed and decorated this personal space to provide an atmosphere that invites God's presence.

My Own Secret Place

Just inside the door, dominating the wall above my desk and always visible to me when I am writing, is a large painting by Thomas Kinkade. The scene portrays a beautiful spring meadow dappled in sunlight. A small stream cascades over boulders and dances through the meadow among dazzling flowers. The artist painted an empty gazebo in the center that signals a welcoming invitation to come and enjoy the delights of the wonderful garden. But unless you look closely, you miss the most important detail of the painting. Hidden in the shadows at the top left of the picture, a lone figure stands on a pathway leading down toward the meadow. He is clothed in a white robe. It is Jesus! He is watching and waiting for someone to appear. The painting is titled *Pools of Serenity—The Garden of Prayer*. It should come as no surprise to you why I love this painting. It portrays the secret place, and Kinkade is renowned as the "Painter of Light."

On the opposite wall is a stunning portrait of Ezra the Scribe. He is dressed in a royal blue robe. A red headband graces his aged forehead, and a patterned gold sash drapes his shoulders, framing his wizened gray beard with authority. His left hand holds a quill pen to the scroll on the table before him. Over his head, an oil lamp glows, shedding light on the scribe as he records the revelation of God. His expression reflects wisdom and understanding. He is in the "know zone."

The center of my sanctified space is dominated by a rectangular, glass-top coffee table. A glistening silver sword lies crossways, stretching from corner to corner. Its hilt is embellished with two pewter medallions, the lampstand on one side and the ark of the covenant on the other. The Star of David commands the bottom of the gold handle, which is covered in red leather. It is the sword of Solomon.

Positioned next to the sword is a mahogany display box that contains a collection of pens. My favorite is the Goofy pen that my wife, Eunice, gave me as a Christmas gift. I used this pen to write my first three books. It serves as a reminder that my feet are firmly planted in this world, even when I am in the secret place. Like Goofy, I need to remain lighthearted and fun loving. Catty-corner from the display case, a gold inkwell and quill pen stand next to a leather-bound journal. Last but not least, a small, ancient earthen oil lamp sits next to the sword.

Across the room, under the skylights and next to the Amish-built oak book-case, a La-Z-Boy recliner upholstered with supple blue leather faces the sliding glass doors that lead onto the balcony. This balcony, three stories above ground, offers a breathtaking panorama of the entire valley and the Pennsylvania hills in the far distance. Early in the morning, when mist covers the fields, the view is almost surreal. It has an otherworldly, dawn-of-creation, mystical magnetism that inspires meditation.

Next to the chair is a pecan end table holding various navigation instruments—a compass, a telescope, a thermometer, a barometer, an hourglass, and a sundial—all of them reminders of my need to seek God's guidance and wisdom to navigate life's journey.

This upper room is where I meet with Jesus. It is where we talk and take our "Enoch walks." Sitting in my recliner in the midst of His presence, I fill my journal pages with records of wisdom, revelation, and prophetic insight. This is not the only place where God speaks to me, but it is the one place where I know that there is an open heaven and He is waiting for me. It is a portal from time to eternity. It is the place where I can lay my head down like Jacob did and know that there is a ladder to heaven, angels are present, and the flow of revelation never ceases. This is my secret place. I encourage you, if you haven't already done so, to set aside your very own special place where you can close the door and talk intimately with God.

The Vision Continues

The evening of the day on which I had received the vision of the wheel of distraction, I entered the secret place with heightened expectation. I closed the door, retrieved the appropriate pen from its glass case, and lifted my journal from the coffee table. The last shadows of nightfall lengthened across the distant hills outside as I turned on the light and sat down in my prayer chair.

"Jesus, I love You so much," I prayed. "I have come to sit at Your feet. What do You want to say to me tonight?"

I barely had time to open my journal when the vision of an hourglass appeared. I watched the sand slowly flowing down through the narrow opening at its center.

"God, what is this about?" I asked. "What are You saying to me?"

Before He responded, my rational mind kicked in. This is always a temptation we must try to avoid, but on this occasion, I succumbed to it. I began to consider all of the things I had learned about hourglasses.

The hourglass is also called a "sand clock" and a "sand glass," I recalled. Like other timepieces, it needs to be carefully calibrated, or it's useless. It must be fine-tuned so that it measures the correct length of time.

Several factors contribute to its accuracy. The type and quality of sand is a major key. It must have a rate of flow that does not fluctuate. Sand that is too coarse will wear away the glass, eventually making the neck too large. Most important is the ratio of the width of the neck, or the hole in the tube, to the diameter of the sand particles. If the sand particles are the wrong size, they won't pass properly through the narrowest point. The quality of the sand is critical. It must be fine, dry, and consistently formed so that it can flow smoothly.

Pretty amazing that I remember all of this, I thought, congratulating myself. But then I realized how rude I was being.

"Lord, I'm sorry. I'm paying attention to my own musings and not You. Please forgive me. What do You have to say about this hourglass? Does this vision have something to do with the wheel of distraction?"

The Lord began to explain the vision. "Son, do you see how the sand rests above the opening at the center of the hourglass? This is how you must become, settled and focused. Let your thoughts become like fine grains of sand, consistently formed, all bearing down in restful peace toward the focal point. You must calm your thoughts and your spirit and concentrate. Like the sand presses toward the center, focus your thoughts on Me. This is the first step into the spiritual dimension of My presence."

What a contrast, I realized immediately. The dissimilarity between the wheel of distraction and the resting sand in the hour glass is striking.

Spiritual Attention Deficit Disorder

Most people are familiar with ADD—attention deficit disorder, or the inability to remain focused for an extended period of time. I believe that a similar malady occurs in our spiritual lives. I call it SADD (spiritual attention deficit disorder)—the inability to focus on the Lord. It is the frustrating failure to bring yourself to that place where you can wait in His presence long enough to hear Him speak to you.

I don't have ADD, but I do have SADD. In fact, even when I am in a church meeting, there are times when I'll check out, mentally. I may be physically present, but in my mind, I've gone somewhere else.

The apostle Paul suggested a solution to this problem.

For the weapons of our warfare are not carnal but mighty in God for pulling down strongholds, casting down arguments and every high thing that exalts itself against the knowledge of God, bringing every thought into captivity to the obedience of Christ. (2 Corinthians 10:4–5)

Run to His Presence

"How do I bring my thoughts into captivity to You, Jesus?" I asked. "I need to corral my runaway mind."

He offered a solution. "Son, when I'm present, run to My presence; don't run away from it. When the enemy seeks to distract you, deliberately choose to sit at My feet."

I have learned to make this declaration when I am struggling with distractions: "I'm not going to let the devil spin the wheel of distraction and keep me away from Your presence. I'm going to be like the hourglass; I command every one of my thoughts to surrender to Jesus—especially the thoughts the enemy wants me to focus on. I bring them into the captivity of Christ."

Jesus is the Prince of Peace! As long as we are shaking the hourglass, the sand is not going to run through it. It's disturbed; it's distressed. But the minute it calms down and comes to a place of settling and rest, something different happens. There are two indisputable facts we must accept. Number one: there is a God. Number two: you are not God. He can handle the universe, the world, and all of your issues and concerns. Let go!

Stop shaking the hourglass. When we surrender our thoughts to the Prince of Peace and bring them under His sovereign lordship, we become settled down and focused upon Him. In this place of tranquility, we can begin to hear His voice.

Transcendence

When we finally come to a place of rest in Jesus, something shifts. The sand flows from the top of the hourglass to the bottom. Like the sand, we go beyond the physical world, with its time and space restrictions, into the eternal, spiritual dimension where God exists.

The narrowest point of the hourglass is the doorway into this dimension of the Spirit. When our thoughts pass from the top of the hourglass to the bottom, we are transitioning from time to eternity. God is the place of transcendence. We experience an encounter with the eternal One! We begin to comprehend things we never could have known by our human effort. We see history through Jesus' eyes. We learn about ourselves, and we obtain knowledge and wisdom that far exceed the best books, schools, and professors in the entire world.

I believe this is why *time* in the secret place stands still! In a sense, time is an eternal dimension.[1] It is a room surrounded by eternity and is defined within eternity's context. When we experience this supernatural, mystical moment, it is not our imagination! We are not being deceived. This is not some sort of weird, paranormal intersection with the other world. C. S. Lewis affirmed this fact, saying, "I don't regard mystical experience as an illusion. I think it shows that there is a way to go, before death, out of what may be called 'this world.'[2]

More Insight

"This is amazing, Lord," I said, carefully recording our conversation in my journal.

"There is much more for you to learn from this vision," He explained. "I want to take you inside the hourglass."

24

INSIDE THE HOURGLASS

My attention was riveted on the vision of the hourglass. "What do You mean, Lord?" I asked, pondering His words with heightened curiosity. "I understand the significance of quieting my thoughts, but please go on. What is the significance of the inside of the hourglass?"

Jesus directed my attention to the top half of the hourglass. "Son, this hourglass represents the secret place. It is a picture of how you must prepare yourself to welcome My presence. The upper half of the hourglass symbolizes *preparation*."

Immediately, a Scripture came to mind: "*Behold, I stand at the door and knock. If anyone hears My voice and opens the door, I will come in to him and dine with him, and he with Me*" (Revelation 3:20).

"What must I do to welcome You into the room, Lord?" I asked. "How can I open the door?"

"There are three things that I require," Jesus continued. "The first one is solitude. Listen carefully, son, and follow My instructions. When you want to talk with Me, don't act religious and don't try to impress others. It's not about being seen. That may feed your ego, but it won't nurture your soul and spirit. Get focused on Me. You must get away where there are no distractions. I want a secret rendezvous with you, a secret location that others can't invade. I want your undivided attention. You sometimes refer to it as a cave, but I call it the secret place. It must be a closed-door session. No one else is invited. Just Me and you!

"When I wanted to talk to My Father, I always isolated Myself. I sought a private place away from people and interruptions, where We could be alone," Jesus explained.

Solitude

Solitude was a characteristic of Jesus' life. Being alone was extremely important to Him. He loved being with His Father. It was heaven on earth! He was strengthened and encouraged every time He went away by Himself. He needed the Father's wisdom and advice.

The Gospels record many occasions when Jesus left everything and sought solitude so He could talk to the Father and listen to His counsel. The list is impressive:

Then Jesus was led up by the Spirit into the wilderness.   (Matthew 4:1)

Now in the morning, having risen a long while before daylight, He went out and departed to a solitary place; and there He prayed.   (Mark 1:35)

Now when it was day, He departed and went into a deserted place.
(Luke 4:42)

Now it came to pass in those days that He went out to the mountain to pray, and continued all night in prayer to God.   (Luke 6:12)

When Jesus heard it, He departed from there by boat to a deserted place by Himself.   (Matthew 14:13)

So He Himself often withdrew into the wilderness and prayed. (Luke 5:16)

Immediately Jesus made His disciples get into the boat and go before Him to the other side, while He sent the multitudes away. And when He had sent the multitudes away, He went up on the mountain by Himself to pray. Now when evening came, He was alone there.   (Matthew 14:22–23)

Now after six days Jesus took Peter, James, and John his brother, [and] led them up on a high mountain by themselves. (Matthew 17:1)

Then Jesus came with them to a place called Gethsemane, and said to the disciples, "Sit here while I go and pray over there." (Matthew 26:36)

And He was withdrawn from them about a stone's throw, and He knelt down and prayed. (Luke 22:41)

Other Biblical Examples

There are other examples in Scripture of world-changing influencers who sought the solitary place. Moses was tending his father-in-law's sheep on the backside of the desert. In this setting, he saw a flaming bush that was not consumed. He *"turned aside"* and encountered the presence of God. It transformed his life. (See Exodus 3:1–5.)

When Samuel came to anoint a new king in place of Saul, David wasn't at home. The one whom God had chosen was not there. Where was David? Alone on the backside of the desert, tending his father's sheep! (See 1 Samuel 16:11.) In the quiet solitude of the pastures, David worshipped God and spoke to Him.

On his way to Damascus, Paul (when he was still called Saul) was apprehended by the presence of God and was blinded by the encounter. (See Acts 9:1–9.) He became a disciple of Jesus, was baptized, and began to preach. Boy, did he stir up a hornet's nest! The believers had to rescue him and lower him over the city wall at night in a basket. (See Acts 9:22–25.) After he escaped, guess where he went? Straight into the desert! He spent three years in the solitude of the wilderness before he came back to Jerusalem. Paul described his experience in this way:

But I make known to you, brethren, that the gospel which was preached by me is not according to man. For I neither received it from man, nor was I taught it, but it came through the revelation of Jesus Christ. For you have heard of my former conduct in Judaism, how I persecuted the church of God beyond measure and tried to destroy it. And I advanced in Judaism beyond many of my contemporaries in my own nation, being more exceedingly zealous for the traditions of my fathers. But when it pleased God, who separated me from my mother's womb and called me through His grace, to reveal His Son in me, that

I might preach Him among the Gentiles, I did not immediately confer with flesh and blood, nor did I go up to Jerusalem to those who were apostles before me; but I went to Arabia, and returned again to Damascus.

(Galatians 1:11–17)

Paul spent three years in the secret place, walking with the Lord and receiving wisdom and revelation. He returned to Damascus an instructed apostle because the Light Giver had enlightened him. He had attended the school of the Spirit.

Monks and Mystics

Miraculous, life-forming, wisdom-obtaining encounters happen in the wilderness! We call our spiritual mentors from the past the Desert Fathers for a good reason. These early hermits understood this location of extreme solitude to be the place where the greatest revelations of God and highest levels of spiritual maturity are obtained. The word *hermit* (*eremos*) actually means "one that retires from society to live in solitude in the desert."

The desert is the symbol of absolute interiorization, the most extreme form of solitary living. It has always been a metaphor for internalization and overcoming difficulties. In the stark solitude of this treeless, wilderness landscape, there is nothing and no one else. We are alone. We are forced to deal with what's inside. We must face and wrestle with our inner demons. Perhaps that's why we resist the solitude of the wilderness. If we are alone, without the comfort of having other people around us, we have to deal with whatever God shows us about ourselves.

We have such an incredible heritage in the monastic movement. When I was in college, I wrote a paper on monasticism for one of my history classes. I actually did my research in a monastery library in Latrobe, Pennsylvania. For weeks I perused the shelves of long out-of-print books and manuscripts. Their pages were yellowed and smelled musty—a scent that is loved only by librarians and true bibliophiles. There, in that quiet place, amid the aged wisdom that the monks had garnered from God's presence, I learned about the Christian mystics. I discovered priceless truths from their experiences and the knowledge they left behind for us—literally centuries of seeking God and experiencing His presence. In my opinion, the Desert Fathers, monks, and nuns were the charismatics of their age. They sought and tended the fire of the Holy Spirit and encountered God's presence.

St. Andrew, one of the most prominent early mystics, was a hermit who withdrew to the solitude of the desert in order to devote himself entirely to God. He was a forerunner. He blazed a path for his contemporaries. They followed his example because they, too, wanted to encounter the reality of God. The distractions of the world and even the social and political acceptability of Christianity were keeping them from His presence. Carving out their own caves and lonely hermitages, they found God in the desert. His presence was so powerfully manifested among these spiritual pioneers that people came from all over the world to sit at their feet and hear what God would say!

It wasn't long before communities began to grow up around these desert hermitages. The result was cenobitic monasticism, or community life devoted to seeking God. The spiritually devout began to live in communities where solitude was revered and God encounters were considered worthy of a totally dedicated life.

St. Francis of Sales encouraged people entering into meditation, "Mettez-vous en la présence de Dieu"—"Place yourself in the presence of God."[1] We need to observe his admonition. It's that simple. Solitude is being alone, placing ourselves in His presence.

Stillness

"Lord," I spoke, "You said that the top half of the hourglass represents three things. What is the second one?"

The familiar tone of authority I had often heard when my schoolteachers disciplined me was evident in His voice. "It is stillness, son," He replied. "Didn't I say, 'Be still and know that I am God'? Cease your activities and business. Stop trying to solve the problems of the universe, and quit fidgeting. Sit still! If you are troubled and occupied with busywork, then you will not be able to drink of the fresh revelation of My Spirit and commune with Me. My intention is to lead you beside still waters! I will restore your soul as I have promised, but you must be still!"

It instantly occurred to me that this is precisely what Mary did. Mary sat at His feet! She didn't pace around the room or fidget with her hair. Her eyes were fastened on the Savior. She sat at His feet, listening with undivided attention. That's exactly what we need to do—cease our activities and bring our bodies to a place of stillness.

In her book *Solitude and Silence*, Ruth Haley Barton confessed that it took her an entire year to reach a place of being able to just sit before the Lord, open and empty, for ten minutes. A whole year, just to achieve ten minutes of stillness and receptivity! So many people come to me and say, "Well, God doesn't speak to me. I've been seeking Him for a week, and He hasn't said anything." How impatient we are. Be still. Wait! Come to a place of rest!

When Jesus shows up, He often says, "Fear not!" and *"Peace, be still!"* (Mark 4:39). He can even bring stillness to the natural environment. He calmed the raging storms on the Sea of Galilee when He spoke to the wild tempest, *"Peace, be still!"* (Mark 4:39). The wind and the waves obeyed Him. He accomplished two things at once: He stilled the physical environment and He calmed the disciples.

We need to obey Him. He is saying to us, "Peace, be still!" Our inner world and external environment need to come to rest. We must sit at His feet!

Silence

I was still pondering His words about stillness when He spoke again. "The third requirement is silence," He said, still with the sternness of a teacher demanding silence in the classroom.

That makes sense, I thought. *Mary sat at His feet and heard His Word. She wasn't talking; she was listening!*

The prophets understood this divine mandate. They told us how we ought to act in His presence. For example, *"The LORD is in His holy temple. Let all the earth keep silence before Him"* (Habakkuk 2:20). *"Be silent, all flesh, before the LORD"* (Zechariah 2:13). *"Be silent in the presence of the Lord GOD"* (Zephaniah 1:7).

Silence is the womb of intimacy. Language is a projection of our minds. Silence is birthed from the womb of love. We need to quiet our thoughts as well as our world. We must hush the internal dialogue. I call this kind of quietness "receptive silence." For example, there are times during public worship services when my spirit becomes irritated and troubled because I want to get into God's presence, and I need quiet. Why is it that church worship teams don't just shut down sometimes and observe silence? There are moments in intimate worship when we don't need another song so we can finish the set. We need a quiet place; a parenthesis of silence; a breathless, hushed space of just loving Him and listening.

Revelation 8:1 says that *"there was silence in heaven for about half an hour."* Nobody talked, sang, played an instrument, banged cymbals, or shook a tambourine. No one prayed or gave a message in tongues or prophesied. Even the seraphim and the cherubim were speechless. It just got heavenly silent.

Saint Francis said, "Noise is the worst evil after sin." My soul is weakened by confusion and noise, and no noise is as insistent as the one you are trying not to listen to. I've got to have quiet! I love to ride in my car without the radio or CD player on. My grandchildren don't understand, because they crave constant input. I just need quiet. There's something deep in my soul that cries out, "I must find a quiet place where there's peace and I can be alone with God!"

Once I have shut the door to my secret place, I don't need to play worship music anymore. I just want to sit at Jesus' feet in quietness and listen. Silence creates space. In silence and solitude, the soul is able to get a glimpse of eternity.

Sensitivity

The moment I heard Jesus speak, I knew something was different. He directed my attention to the lower part of the hourglass and said with affection in His voice, "This is where I will meet you, son! I promise you. If you follow My instructions and come into a solitary place alone and become silent and still in My presence, I will manifest Myself to you. This is the place where we can enjoy intimate communion. It is an eternal dimension. I will invade time and space so I can be with you."

Something changes when we transition through the neck of the hourglass from the upper to the lower dimension. When we finally overcome distractions and our focus is on Jesus, we are at the entrance to the spiritual realm. Our silence, stillness, and solitude are an invitation He accepts and responds to. At that point, we actually transition into His presence. He manifests Himself. He promises us that if we open the door, He will come in!

Jesus spoke again, with hushed emphasis, His voice almost a whisper: "You must be very sensitive in this dimension. The Holy Spirit is easily grieved, and our communion can be violated and interrupted.

Paul's admonition to the Christians in Ephesus and Thessalonica immediately flashed into my mind: *"Do not grieve the Holy Spirit of God, by whom you were sealed for the day of redemption"* (Ephesians 4:30). *"Do not quench the Spirit"* (1 Thessalonians 5:19).

We must learn to adjust to God and not expect Him to adjust to us. R. T. Kendall shared a perfect illustration in the story of Sandy and Bernice, a missionary couple living in Jerusalem. They noticed that a dove was nesting in the eaves of their house. Sandy recognized an unsettling pattern in the dove's behavior. Every time a door slammed, they raised their voices, or there was another type of loud noise, the dove would be disturbed and flutter off, often not returning for some time.

"I'm afraid the dove will fly away and never come back," Bernice said.

"Well," said Sandy, "either the dove will adjust its behavior to us, or, if we really want to make sure we never lose him, we will have to adjust our behavior to the dove."[2] The lesson is obvious. Sensitivity is paramount. The Puritans often said, "The Spirit comes by foot but leaves by horseback." He is easily grieved.

Listen Before You Speak

Jesus continued, "There are so many things I want to say to you, but you can't listen while you're talking. I will guide you into all truth and tell you about things to come. I will reveal My secrets to you. But you must listen first." (See John 16:12–15.)

Communication is one of the most important skills in life.[3] Our problem is that we don't listen carefully with the intention of understanding what we are hearing. While someone else is speaking to us, we are formulating what we will say in response. And we treat God the same way.

The Rule of Saint Benedict, a handbook of guiding principles for ancient monks and contemporary seekers of God in all walks of life, gives us good advice. Saint Benedict opens his instructions with a simple rule for all of us to live by: "Listen, my son." That's it! Listen!

Wait until God speaks. Don't put words in His mouth. God's silence is holy ground! He waits until He has our attention. No amount of our clamoring, impertinent chatter will help. When He does speak, it is often so softly that if we are not listening closely, we won't hear His voice. The great prophet Elijah learned this lesson after many years of ministry. He expected God to speak in a spectacular, surround-sound kind of way. Instead, this is what he heard:

And behold, the LORD passed by, and a great and strong wind tore into the mountains and broke the rocks in pieces before the LORD, but the LORD was

not in the wind; and after the wind an earthquake, but the LORD *was not in
the earthquake; and after the earthquake a fire, but the* LORD *was not in the
fire; and after the fire a still small voice.*   (1 Kings 19:11–12)

It's God we're talking about here, not some casual acquaintance. He is the
Creator of the universe and the Giver of life. When we are in His presence, we
need to listen deeply. Take a lesson from the little boy Samuel. He had difficulty
recognizing God's voice. Finally, after God had tried for the third time to get his
attention, Samuel responded, *"Speak, for Your servant hears"* (1 Samuel 3:10). We
need to say, like Samuel, "Speak, Lord, for Your servant is listening."

Stay

The top of the hourglass represents time as we know it, but when we transition to the lower level, time seems to stand still. In this incredible place of intimacy and revelation, we no longer care about keeping track of the passing minutes and hours. We are in the presence of eternity, and we just want to stay as
long as possible.

When I'm in the presence of God in the secret place, I don't leave until He
tells me that the conversation is over and I can go. If it means staying all day, I
stay. I don't set a limit on how much time I am going to spend in His presence. I
stay as long as He stays. I know this isn't always feasible, especially for those who
have a job that requires them to work certain hours, or for those who have children to tend to. But we need to set aside space in our schedules, whenever possible, to spend extended periods of time—even the entire day, if necessary—with
Him. Regular spiritual retreats are one way to do this.

On one particular day, I went into my secret place at nine in the morning and
didn't come out until six that evening. The minutes and hours flew by as I walked
with Jesus like Enoch. I had no awareness of passing time. I didn't go to the bath-
room, I didn't eat anything, I didn't drink anything; I just sat in His presence. I
stayed and stayed. I did not leave until I sensed the Holy Spirit lift and give me
permission to go. I didn't say, "Lord, I've got things to do. I must leave." I waited.

When I looked at my watch after an entire day in the presence of Jesus, I
was astounded. Eight or nine hours seemed like twenty minutes. An entire day
had flashed by in what felt like a few seconds. In this sequestered, time-insu-
lated atmosphere of the secret place, book-length revelations flow freely. Moses

experienced this in the context of forty days and nights in God's presence on Mount Sinai.

Take a lesson from Joshua.

Moses took his tent and pitched it outside the camp, far from the camp, and called it the tabernacle of meeting. And it came to pass that everyone who sought the LORD went out to the tabernacle of meeting which was outside the camp. So it was, whenever Moses went out to the tabernacle, that all the people rose, and each man stood at his tent door and watched Moses until he had gone into the tabernacle. And it came to pass, when Moses entered the tabernacle, that the pillar of cloud descended and stood at the door of the tabernacle, and the LORD talked with Moses. All the people saw the pillar of cloud standing at the tabernacle door, and all the people rose and worshipped, each man in his tent door. So the LORD spoke to Moses face to face, as a man speaks to his friend. And he would return to the camp, but his servant Joshua the son of Nun, a young man, did not depart from the tabernacle.

(Exodus 33:7–11)

Joshua stayed in the presence of God. This is no indictment against Moses. No doubt Moses, the seasoned, veteran servant of God, completed his conversation with God. But that was not the case for Joshua. Once God finished talking with Moses, it was his turn. God had some things to say to this soon-to-be leader of Israel. The wisdom and counsel he received in God's presence would serve him well in the coming days.

Remain in God's presence until He releases you. Let God decide when it is time to leave!

The Vision Ends

The Spirit of the Lord lifted, and the vision of the hourglass faded. I jotted a few final thoughts in my journal and then prayed. "Thank You, Lord, for giving me this revelation. Now I understand how the enemy so easily distracts me and keeps me from Your presence."

I studied the diagram of the hourglass I had carefully sketched in my journal. "This is so helpful, Jesus. It is so important to position myself in Your presence and become quiet and still. I love You so much, Jesus. Focusing on Your beauty and love is a joy to me. Help me not to grieve the Holy Spirit. I don't want anything to interrupt our communion. Teach me how to be more sensitive to You, and help me to listen carefully. I can't wait till we can be together again."

I pray that all of you who read this vision will be blessed and encouraged to seek Jesus in the secret place. We need insight and wisdom from the Light Giver that is not of this world.

Here is the sketch of the hourglass I drew in my journal. May it bless you as much as it has blessed me.

Inside the Hourglass

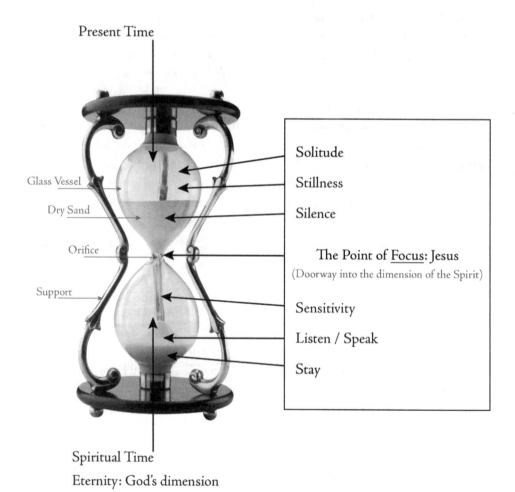

Present Time

Glass Vessel

Dry Sand

Orifice

Support

Solitude

Stillness

Silence

The Point of <u>Focus</u>: Jesus
(Doorway into the dimension of the Spirit)

Sensitivity

Listen / Speak

Stay

Spiritual Time
Eternity: God's dimension

25

NOT OF THIS WORLD

Our journey into the presence of the Light Giver began with a vision deep inside the sacred space of the tabernacle in the wilderness. Little did I realize then that it would culminate with a bus ride back into the seclusion of the desert wilderness of Israel.

Off the Beaten Path

The Jerusalem Road snakes its way up through the stark mountainous wilderness of Israel from the lowest point on Earth, the Dead Sea. It ends in the City of David, perched on a hilltop high above sea level. Thousands of years ago, spiritual pilgrims made this arduous journey on foot or by camel or donkey, if they were wealthy. Their hearts were set on God's presence. They sang their way up through the steep twists and turns of the dusty roadway, braving bandits and robbers. Their songs of ascent (see Psalms 120–134) drifted through the valleys and into the caves of hermits and the tents of Bedouin. Today, the trip is easy. Tourists and spiritual pilgrims travel in air-conditioned buses, sightseeing along the way. Now it takes only a few hours to travel the entire distance from Jericho to Jerusalem.

Our bus driver unexpectedly turned off of the highway somewhere between Jericho and Jerusalem and headed into the mountains on a two-lane road leading up to an out-of-the-way tourist overlook.

I'll be glad to stretch my legs, I thought, *but this hundred-degree afternoon temperature will make sightseeing in the sun a challenge. What could there possibly be to see out here in the middle of nowhere?* I had no idea that what I was about to see would be permanently etched in my memory. I was headed for a *kairos* moment by divine appointment.

I stepped out of the air-conditioned bus into the scorching dry heat of the desert. *Not a tree or shrub in sight,* I observed, licking my dry lips. The panorama was a monotonous, earthen scene of brown hues. Steep mountains surrounded me, and a single, very deep valley came into view as I stepped to the edge of the platform and gripped the metal railing to peer over.

At first, I didn't see it; it blended into the landscape, perfectly camouflaged. I scanned the valley floor and thought, *Well, I've done my duty. It's back on the bus for me. But, wait! What's that?* There was something barely visible on the distant side of the chasm, clinging to the precipitous cliff.

"Oh my goodness!" I blurted out. "It's a monastery. Look! Do you see it?" I asked my wife, who was standing next to me.

"It has been there for thousands of years," the bus driver explained, in response to my exclamation. "The monks have sequestered themselves in this hard-to-reach place where it's absolutely quiet. If you look carefully, you can see a winding path down the face of the mountain. It's the only way into the monastery. Only the bravest, most daring souls venture to go there. It's a rough descent."

I lingered for a long time, gazing down at the ascetic buildings carved into the mountainside. *Imagine the effort it took to construct this place,* I considered. *These buildings are a testimony to their devotion.* I could see in my mind the bruised and calloused hands of the monks tediously laying stone upon stone as long as daylight permitted. *This is a place of God encounters. This is holy ground,* I confessed in admiration.

Deep in this hidden mountain valley between Jericho and Jerusalem, there was a secret place, a portal from time to eternity. I easily could have missed it and never known of its existence. *I would love to come back here and spend a few months in the monastery,* I thought. *What a privilege that would be.*

Looking Across the Chasm

Just as I turned to head back to the bus, my eyes fell upon a lonely figure sitting on the edge of the cliff and gazing down at the monastery. His head was wrapped in a white turban. A linen garment was draped loosely over his shoulders and hung in white folds over his slender frame. I couldn't see his face. He sat with his legs crossed Indian-style in quietness and solitude, not moving, just staring in deep contemplation toward the monastery. I froze in my tracks as the image of this lone individual struck me.

He is so like me, Lord, I realized. *He's just sitting there, looking across the chasm. I wonder if he is thinking what I am: "If I could just get there; if somehow I could find a way to bridge the valley…." But the closest I can get is where this man is sitting right now, Lord.*

Then the full force of what God wanted to teach me struck home. *There is a way to get to the monastery. There is a way to encounter God. We don't have to travel to a place hidden deep in the wilderness. But we do have to become like this singular figure and sit at the edge of eternity, alone in the secret place, listening for God's voice.*

I slowly lifted my camera and framed the picture. *I must capture this scene,* I thought, *the lonely desert pilgrim sitting on the cliff, staring down at the distant monastery, so close, and yet so hard to reach. This faceless pilgrim waits for a door to open before him, a passageway into the presence of God. How long will he sit and wait? As long as it takes!*

This is another world, I finally concluded. *It's a world so foreign to our modern, bustling society and constant electronic connectedness that not many ever come here.*

Jesus' words from Matthew 7:13–14 came to mind:

> Enter by the narrow gate; for wide is the gate and broad is the way that leads to destruction, and there are many who go in by it. Because narrow is the gate and difficult is the way which leads to life, and there are few who find it.

I turned and boarded the bus. The next few weeks were a blur of archeological digs, ancient ruins, bustling cities, hotels, and holy places. But what remained constantly in my thoughts was the image of the solitary man in the wilderness, longing for a God encounter, waiting to move into the God-dimension and touch the hem of eternity.

The Other World That Now Is

We Christian mystics are not at home in this world. Yet we are not escapists. Our feet are solidly planted on *terra firma*. Instead, we are explorers, spiritual "pneumanauts." We are going "not in search of the *New* World, like Columbus and his adventurers, nor yet an *Other* World that is to come, but in search of the Other World that *now is*, and ever has been, though undreamt of by the many, and by the greater part even of the Few."[1]

Our goal is not to flee society but to obtain a wisdom that transcends it and thereby change it. That wisdom is Jesus Himself. In His light, we see light. He invades our world and invites us to experience union with Him. In the place of intimate communion, we are in this world but not of it.

Jesus said, *"My kingdom is not of this world"* (John 18:36). Simeon, the priest who tended the lampstand, understood this experientially and lived in this "otherworld" dimension while he tended the lamps within the Holy Place. Jacob the patriarch discovered a portal into the other world where time stands still. In the "know zone," the sons of Issachar obtained wisdom, revelation, and understanding of their times and how they should live. They were all spiritual timekeepers who understood history from God's perspective and became history shapers.

"Somewhere on the other side of what seems—right in front of us, if we would only look—there exists something more: an 'Other World that now is,' infused with Divine presence and power, and shimmering through our most cherished moments of beauty and love."[2] The vestibule into this other world is the secret place. Call it a monastery, a closet, a cave, a hermitage, or a cathedral, if you will. It may be on the back side of the desert or in the front seat of your car, but it exists. It is real, and it is available to you.

Foolish Wisdom

For it is written: "I will destroy the wisdom of the wise, and bring to nothing the understanding of the prudent." Where is the wise? Where is the scribe? Where is the disputer of this age? Has not God made foolish the wisdom of this world? For since, in the wisdom of God, the world through wisdom did not know God, it pleased God through the foolishness of the message preached to save those who believe. (1 Corinthians 1:19–21)

When you have read all of the books about the secrets of living and all of the chronicles of history, when you have exhausted all of the resources from the wisest of men and women and all of the success theories, you will finally discover that what Jesus says is true! The "tested and tried" solutions of man don't work. The advice of your counselors and the understanding of your professors aren't sufficient. When you have come to the end of it all and you are at the point of giving up, you have arrived at the door to the secret place. As Louis L'Amour put it, "There will come a time when you believe everything is finished. Yet that will be the beginning." We are driven by desperation into His presence.

Meet the Light Giver

"Among times there is a time that turns a corner and everything this side of it is new."³ That's what happened to me on that incredible day when I first entered the secret place in absolute desperation and God showed up. After twenty-four years of education, fifty years of ministry, and countless times of reading through the Bible, I finally had an audience with the Author. In the light of His glorious presence, uncommon wisdom, revelation, and understanding poured forth. *I discovered the secret of the golden fire…it is found in the secret place!*

Jesus is the Fire and Light of the entire universe! He is the Source of life and the Provider of uncommon wisdom! But only the desperate seek Him with enough determination and passion to succeed in finding Him. Are you desperate enough? If you are, then don't procrastinate another day.

This book is about light. Not just any light, but the only Light that can resolve the confusion and disorientation of mankind. Paul said it best:

For we do not preach ourselves, but Christ Jesus the Lord, and ourselves your bondservants for Jesus' sake. For it is the God who commanded light to shine out of darkness, who has shone in our hearts to give the light of the knowledge of the glory of God in the face of Jesus Christ. But we have this treasure in earthen vessels, that the excellence of the power may be of God and not of us.
(2 Corinthians 4:5–7)

This is the revelation that coursed through Paul's veins and led him to preach it everywhere he traveled. God has commanded His light to shine out of darkness. In the presence of Jesus Christ, the Golden Fire, we are encompassed in God's divine enlightenment. The Holy Spirit is the Illuminator. In His light, we know Him and become seers and prophets. Supernatural, Holy-Spirit-inspired revelation is the portion of the light keepers.

The crisis of this evil age urgently demands that we seek the Light Giver. You are His vessel, His lampstand. The world is waiting for His light to shine through you. Sons and daughters of Issachar, arise! The light of the knowledge and glory of God is available. The Light Giver is waiting for you in the secret place!

ENDNOTES

Introduction

1. From the *Proslogion* by Saint Anselm of Canterbury.

Chapter One

1. See Dale Fife, *The Hidden Kingdom: Journey into the Heart of God* (New Kensington, PA: Whitaker House, 2003), 53–65; see also Proverbs 20:27.

2. Ibid.

3. See Dale Fife, *The Secret Place: Passionately Pursuing His Presence* (New Kensington, PA: Whitaker House, 2001), 115.

Chapter Two

1. See Fife, *Hidden Kingdom*, 53–65.

2. The word *calyx* is translated as "bowl" or "cup." It is a botanical term in use today, and it signifies a cup-shaped organ or cavity; the outer covering or leaflike envelope of a flower. According to C. W. Slemming, *Made According to Pattern* (Fort Washington, PA: CLC, 1978), 99, "The principal function of the calyx is to enclose and protect the other parts of the flower while in bud. The calyx frequently plays a part in connection with fruit dispersal. From this we conclude that the calyxes of the almond were included in the design of the lampstand."

3. The wick trimmers and trays for the lamps were made of pure gold. (See Exodus 2:38–39; 40:4.)

Chapter Three

1. A survey of Scripture reveals some wonderful insights regarding *light*. There are over 200 occurrences of the word "light" in the Scriptures. The Bible begins and ends with "light" (see Genesis 1:3–4; Revelation 22:5); light was the first event of creation; there is an ongoing conflict between light and darkness, with light always proving more powerful; and light is shrouded in mystery (see Job 38:19, 24). Light is also used symbolically in the Bible, to represent (1) goodness and holiness (see John 3:20; Romans 13:12; Ephesians 5:8; Philippians 2:15); (2) God's favor (see Esther 8:16; Proverbs 4:18); (3) life (see Job 33:28; Psalm 49:19); (4) truth (see Psalm 119:105, 130; Daniel 5:14; 2 Peter 1:19); (5) revelation (see Job 28:11; 2 Corinthians 4:6); (6) God (see 1 John 1:5; 1 Timothy 6:16; Colossians 1:12); and (7) Jesus (see Isaiah 9:2; Luke 2:32; John 1:4–9; 8:12; 12:46).

2. Note the correlation between "breath" and "Spirit" in Genesis 1:2 and Genesis 2:7.

Chapter Four

1. Leland Ryken, James C. Wilhoit, and Tremper Longman III, gen. eds., *The Dictionary of Biblical Imagery* (Downers Grove, IL: InterVarsity Press, 1998), 509.

2. Ibid.

3. *Vine's Complete Expository Dictionary of Old and New Testament Words* (Nashville, TN: Thomas Nelson Publishers, 1985), 369.

4. Ibid.

5. Joel Achenbach, "Power of Light," *National Geographic* (October 2001): 28.

6. *Dictionary of Biblical Imagery*, 512.

Chapter Five

1. See Fife, *Hidden Kingdom*, 59.

2. The early Christians needed to be refilled with the Holy Spirit not many days after Pentecost. (See Acts 2:4; 4:13.) As they prayed for boldness, the place where they were assembled shook, and they were filled again with the Holy Spirit.

3. *"A bruised reed He will not break, and smoking flax He will not quench"* (Matthew 12:20).

Chapter Nine

1. C. W. Slemming, *These Are the Garments* (Fort Washington, PA: Christian Literature Crusade, 1995), 27.

Chapter Ten

1. Slemming, *Made According to Pattern*, 108.

2. For a more detailed description of the function and purpose of the showbread, see Fife, *Hidden Kingdom*, 53.

Chapter Eleven

1. Merrill C. Tenney, gen. ed., *Zondervan's Pictorial Bible Dictionary* (Grand Rapids, MI: Zondervan, 1963), 395.

2. Chaim Herzog and Mordechai Gichon, *Battles of the Bible: A Modern Military Evaluation of the Old Testament* (New York, NY: Random House, 1978), 48.

3. *Zondervan's Pictorial Bible Dictionary*, 395. See also Judges 5:15.

Chapter Twelve

1. Vilhelm Møller-Christenson and Kai Eduard Jordt Jørgenson, *Encyclopedia of Bible Creatures* (Philadelphia, PA: Fortress Press, 1965), 9–10.

2. William Wilson, *Wilson's Old Testament Word Studies* (McLean, VA: MacDonald Publishing Co., 1900), 461.

3. *The Word in Life Study Bible* (Nashville, TN: Thomas Nelson Publishers, 1996), 708.

4. *Adam Clarke's Commentary on the Bible.*

Chapter Thirteen

1. Daniel J. Boorstin, *The Discoverers: A History of Man's Search to Know His World and Himself* (New York, NY: Random House, 1983), 36.

2. See David Steindl-Rast and Sharon Lebell, *The Music of Silence: Entering the Sacred Space of the Monastic Experience* (San Francisco, CA: HarperSanFrancisco, 1995).

Chapter Fourteen

1. Boorstin, *Discoverers*, 1.

2. Walter Isaacson, *Einstein: His Life and Universe* (New York, NY: Simon and Schuster, 2007), 131.

3. "A Walk Through Time: The Evolution of Time Measurement through the Ages," National Institute of Standards and Technology (NIST) Physical Measurement Laboratory Presentation, http://www.nist.gov/pml/general/time/index.cfm.

4. See Boorstin, *Discoverers*, 71.

5. Isaacson, *Einstein*, 124.

6. Ibid., 138.

7. See David Filkin, *Stephen Hawking's Universe: The Cosmos Explained* (New York, NY: HarperCollins Publishers, Inc., 1997).

Chapter Fifteen

1. Robert Daniels, *Studying History: How and Why* (Englewood Cliffs, NJ: Prentice-Hall, Inc., 1966), 4.

2. E. H. Carr, *What Is History?* (New York, NY: Penguin Books, 1990), 22.

3. David A. Noebel, *Understanding the Times: The Religious Worldviews of Our Day and the Search for Truth* (Eugene, OR: Harvest House, 1994), 720–723.

Chapter Sixteen

1. Stephen Covey, *First Things First* (New York, NY: Fireside [a division of Simon & Schuster, Inc.], 1995), 27.

2. Rabbi Daniel Lapin, *Thou Shall Prosper: Ten Commandments for Making Money* (Hoboken, NJ: John Wiley & Sons, Inc., 2002), 248–250.

3. Babylonian Talmud.

4. Alvin Toffler coauthored his books with his wife, Heidi. A few of their well-known works include *Future Shock* (New York, NY: Bantam Books, 1970), *The Eco-Spasm Report* (New York, NY: Bantam Books, 1975), *The Third Wave* (New York: William Morrow and Company, Inc., 1980), *Previews & Premises* (New York, NY: William Morrow and Company, Inc., 1983), *The Adaptive Corporation* (New York, NY: McGraw-Hill, 1985), *Powershift: Knowledge, Wealth, and Violence at the Edge of the 21ˢᵗ Century* (New York, NY: Bantam Books, 1990), *War and Anti-War: Making Sense of Today's Global Chaos* (New York, NY: Warner Books [now called Grand Central Publishing], 1995), and *Revolutionary Wealth* (New York, NY: Knopf Publishing Group, 2006).

5. See Malcolm Gladwell, *The Tipping Point* (New York, NY: Little, Brown and Company, 2000).

6. http://thinkexist.com/quotes/john_naisbitt/

Chapter Seventeen

1. See Dale Fife, *Spirit Wind: The Ultimate Adventure* (Travelers Rest, SC: MileStones International Publishers, 2006).

2. See Fife, *Secret Place*, 115–130.

3. For an excellent resource on this subject, see Earl Jabay, *The Kingdom of Self* (Plainfield, NJ: Logos International, 1974).

4. E. Stanley Jones, *The Unshakable Kingdom and the Unchanging Person* (Nashville, TN: Abingdon Press, 1972), 9.

5. Two excellent resources that deal with the restoration of the church, both of them written by Dr. Bill Hamon, are *The Eternal Church* (Shippensburg, PA: Destiny Image Publishers, 2003) and *Apostles, Prophets, and the Coming Moves of God: God's End-Time Plans for His Church and Planet Earth* (Shippensburg, PA: Destiny Image Publishers, 1997).

Chapter Nineteen

1. Ed Vallowe, *Biblical Mathematics* (Columbia, SC: The Olive Press, 1998), 80.

2. For further study, see Lapin, *Thou Shall Prosper.*

3. See Jamie Buckingham, *Daughter of Destiny: Kathryn Kuhlman* (Plainfield, NJ: Logos International, 1976).

Chapter Twenty

1. Slemming, *These Are the Garments*, 149.

Chapter Twenty-one

1. Roger Green and Walter Hooper, *C. S. Lewis: A Biography* (New York, NY: Harcourt Brace Jovanovich, 1974), 169.

2. C. S. Lewis, *Letters to Malcolm, Chiefly on Prayer* (New York, NY: Harcourt, Inc., 1963), 64.

Chapter Twenty-two

1. *Atkinson & Hilgard's Introduction to Psychology*, Fourth Edition (New York, NY: Harcourt, Brace, and Co., 1967), 4–5, 237–240.

2. Covey, *First Things First*, slipcover.

3. Laurie Beth Jones, *Jesus, Life Coach: Learn from the Best* (Nashville, TN: Thomas Nelson Publishers, 2004), 10.

4. Joyce Meyer, *Battlefield of the Mind* (New York, NY: Warner Books, 1995), 15.

Chapter Twenty-three

1. Morton Kelsey, *Transcend: A Guide to the Spiritual Quest* (New York, NY: Crossroad Publishing, 1981), 132.

2. Lewis, *Letters to Malcolm*, 65.

Chapter Twenty-four

1. James Cutsinger, *Not of This World: A Treasury of Christian Mysticism* (Bloomington, IN: World Wisdom, Inc., 2003), 162.

2. R. T. Kendall, *The Sensitivity of the Spirit: Learning to Stay in the Flow of God's Direction* (Lake Mary, FL: Charisma House, 2002), 15–16.

3. Stephen Covey, *The Seven Habits of Highly Effective People* (New York, NY: Free Press [a division of Simon & Schuster, Inc., 1989), 237.

Chapter Twenty-five

1. Samuel Taylor Coleridge, quoted in Cutsinger, *Not of This World*, xii.

2. Cutsinger, *Not of This World*, xiii.

3. C. S. Lewis, *Perelandra* (New York, NY: Scribner, 1944, 1996), 40.

ABOUT THE AUTHOR

Dr. Dale Arthur Fife is a gifted pastor, author, teacher, and musician with an insatiable passion for intimacy with God. His zeal for the Lord has led him on an incredible journey from his first pastorate of a small rural church in a coal-mining town outside of Johnstown, Pennsylvania, to the cofounding of a large multiracial inner-city church in Pittsburgh. After five decades of ministry experience and increasing requests from others for mentoring and ministry relationships, Dale and his wife, Eunice, founded Mountain Top Global Ministries, a network of pastors, ministries, businesses, and leaders with local, regional, and international impact.

From leading worship in the mid-seventies at the first outdoor Jesus Festivals, which numbered over 50,000, to serving in his present ministry, speaking at churches, conferences, colleges, and gatherings for leaders and intercessors, Dale has an enthusiastic hunger for God that has been contagious. His wisdom, maturity, and genuine spiritual concern for others have caused many to regard him as a "spiritual father" in the Lord. His insightful teaching has inspired and blessed believers and leaders in many nations.

"Doctor D," as he is affectionately called, graduated summa cum laude from the University of Pittsburgh. He completed seminary studies at Boston

University School of Theology and did graduate study at Pittsburgh Theological Seminary. The Doctor of Divinity degree was conferred upon him by New Life College in Bangalore, India.

His best-selling books, *The Secret Place: Passionately Pursuing God's Presence*, *The Hidden Kingdom: Journey into the Heart of God*, and *Spirit Wind: The Ultimate Adventure*, continue to bless and encourage thousands of people around the world to seek a closer walk with Jesus.

Dale and Eunice were married in 1963, and they have two sons and six grandchildren. They now live in Florida, where Dale serves as the apostolic pastor of SonPointe Church, a growing congregation in Bradenton. The Fifes travel throughout the world proclaiming the good news of God's kingdom and encouraging the body of Christ to passionately pursue God's presence.

Dr. Fife is available for speaking engagements upon request. He can be contacted at MnTopMin@aol.com. For more information regarding available resources and itinerary, or to schedule Dr. Fife for ministry at your church or event, log on to www.SonPointeChurch.org.